AKIM ALIU
DREAMER

WRITTEN WITH
GREG ANDERSON ELYSÉE

ILLUSTRATED BY
KAREN DE LA VEGA
AND
MARCUS WILLIAMS

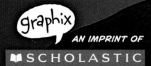
graphix
AN IMPRINT OF
SCHOLASTIC

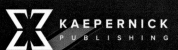
KAEPERNICK
PUBLISHING

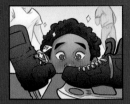

This book is dedicated to my beautiful parents: I wouldn't be here without you and your relentless pursuit of your children's happiness through the countless obstacles you faced in your lifetimes. Thank you, and I love you with all of my heart.

—Akim "Dreamer" Aliu

To all of my parents (Rose, Daniel, Marie, Kethy, John) who stood behind and beside me in support through all my dreams and endeavors, and to the ones who refuse to quit their dreams . . . we persevere. Go get them.

—Greg Anderson Elysée

To my loving parents and friends, who always encouraged me to keep going and celebrated my art, and now I can illustrate inspiring stories like this one. Thank you for supporting my unconventional lifestyle.

—Karen De la Vega

Library of Congress Control Number: Available

ISBN 978-1-338-78761-0

10 9 8 7 6 5 4 3 2 1   23 24 25 26 27

Printed in China 62
First edition, May 2023
Edited by Michael Petranek
Lettering by Micah Myers
Book design by Jeff Shake
Color by Warnia Sahadewa

CHAPTER
ONE

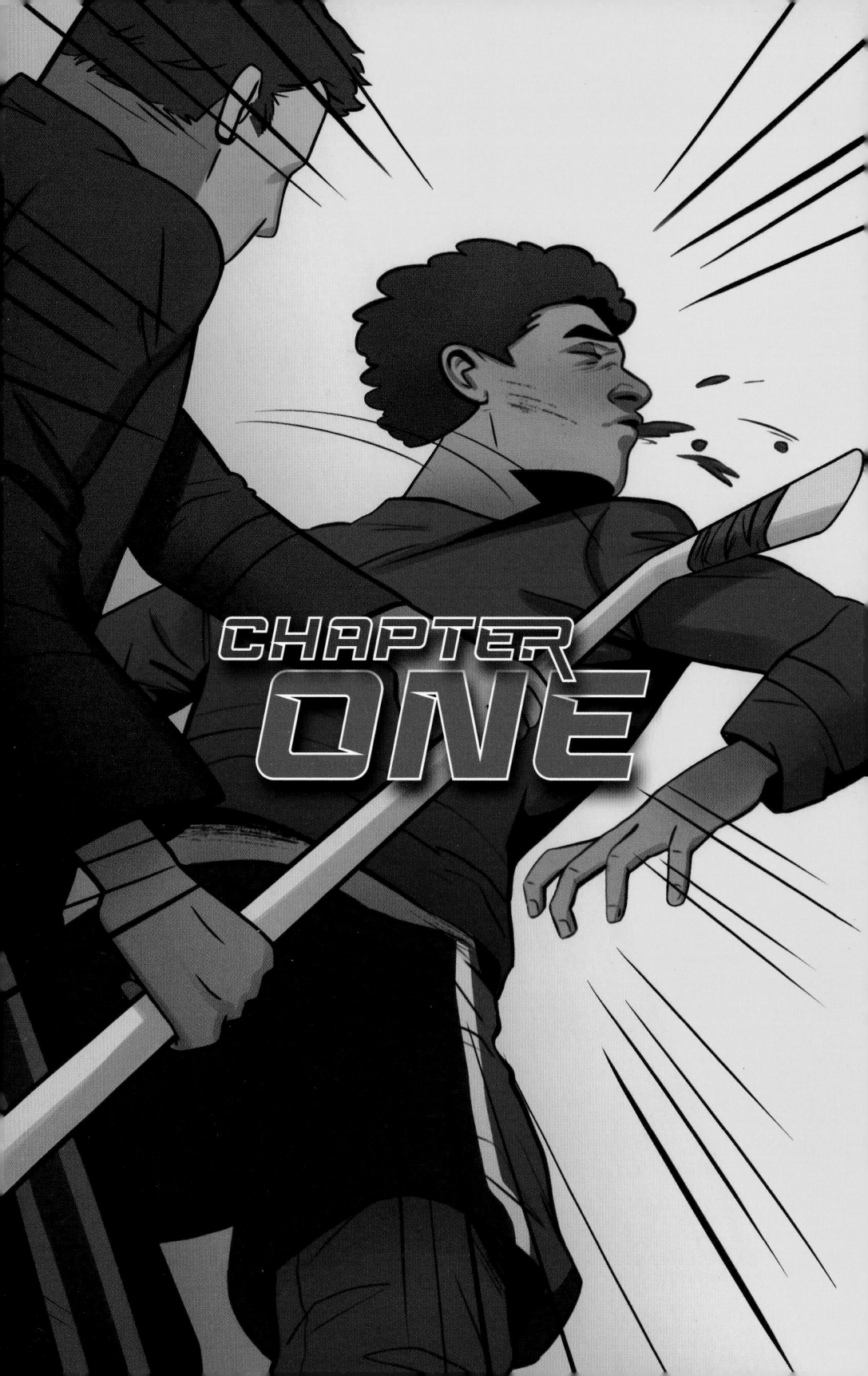

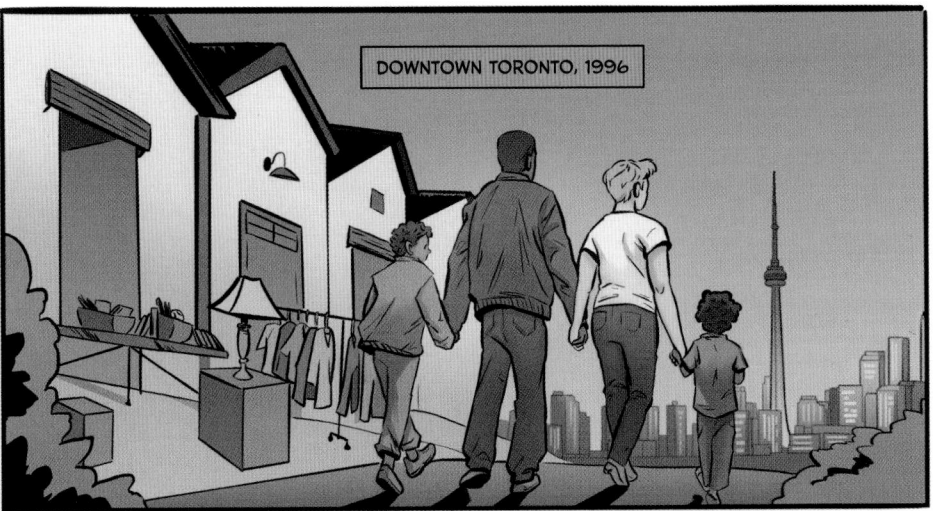

DOWNTOWN TORONTO, 1996

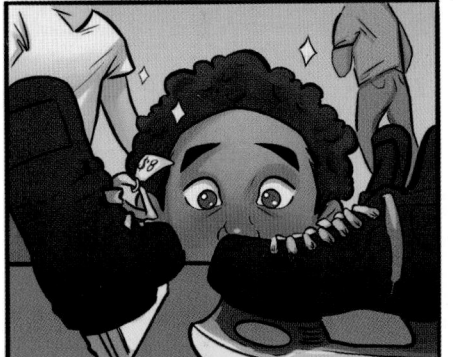

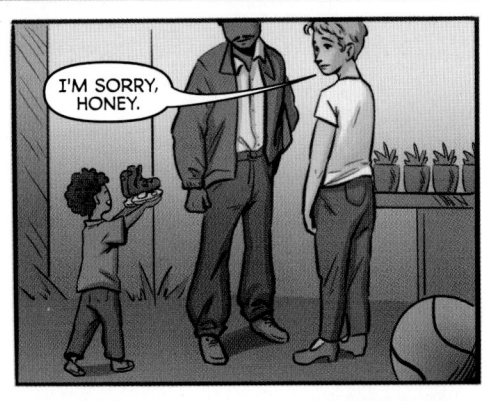

I'M SORRY, HONEY.

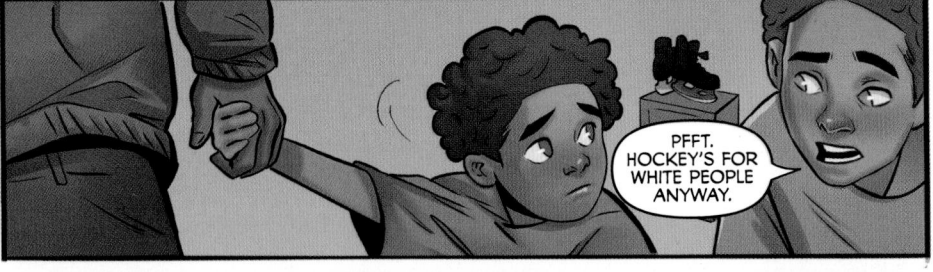

PFFT. HOCKEY'S FOR WHITE PEOPLE ANYWAY.

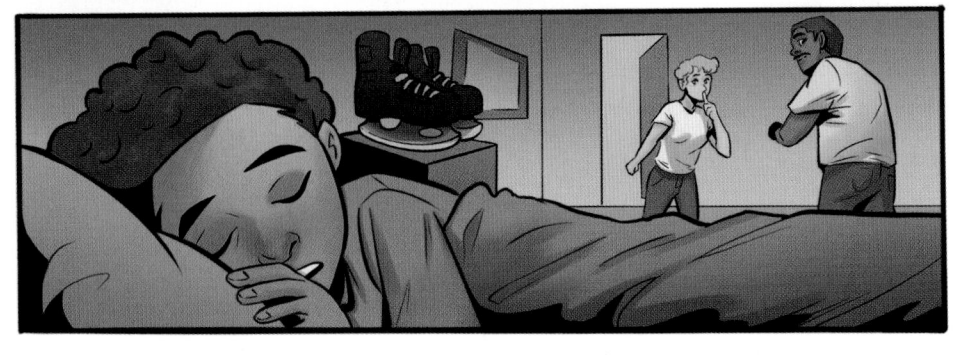

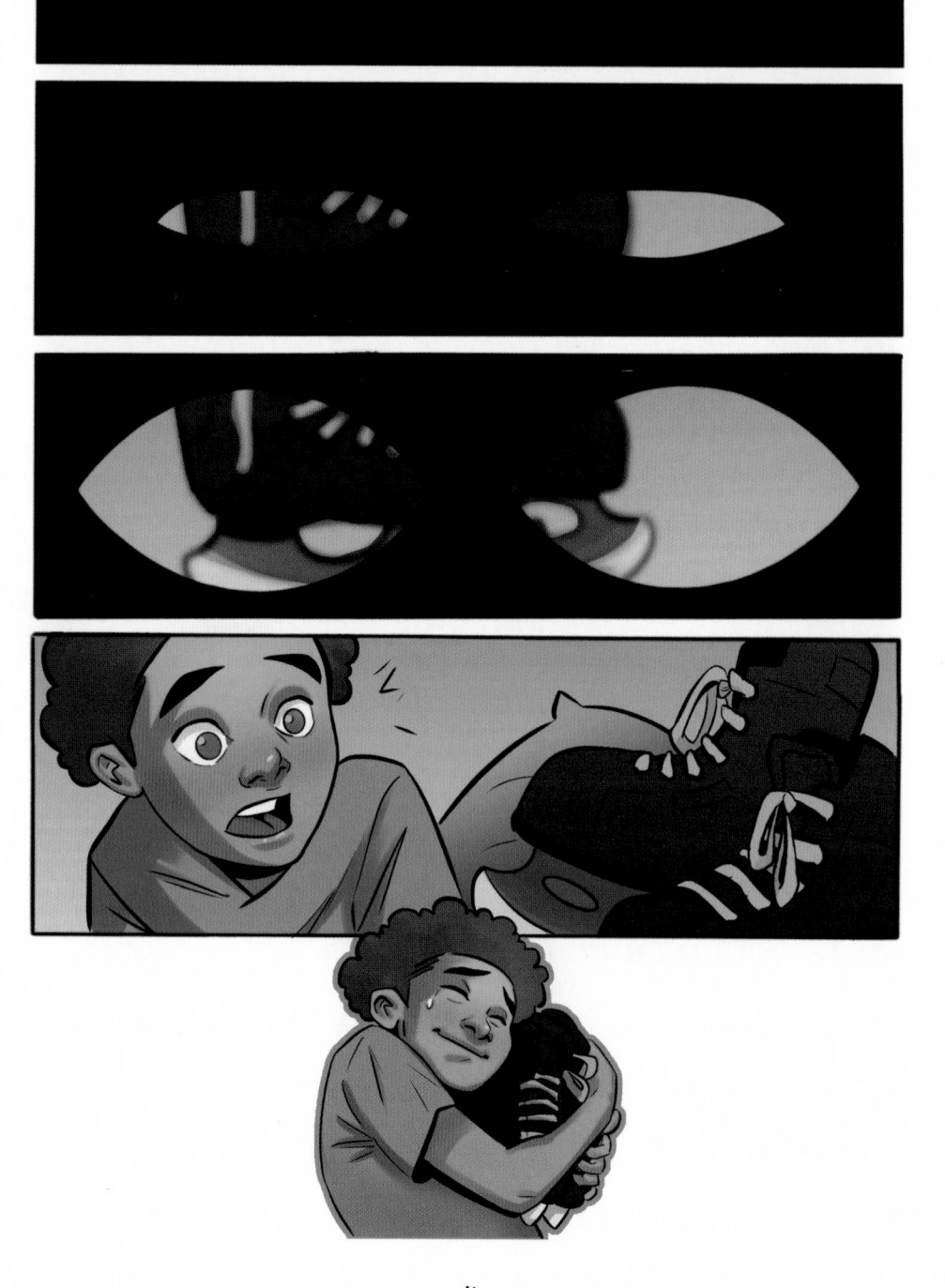

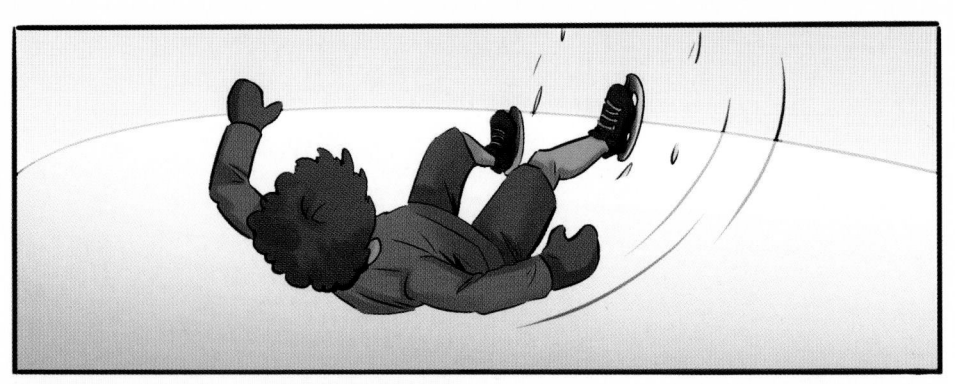

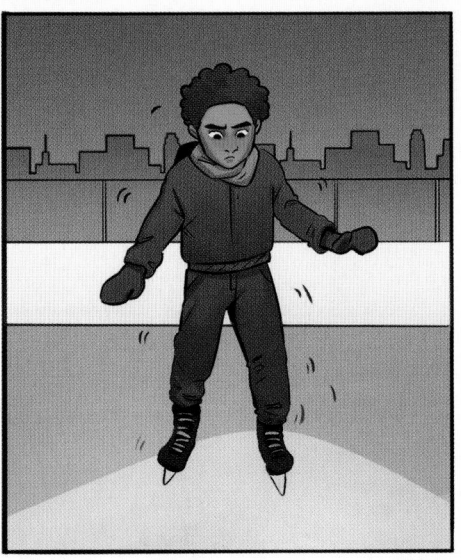

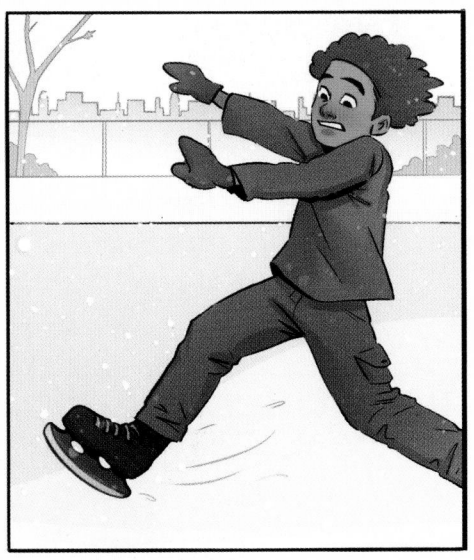

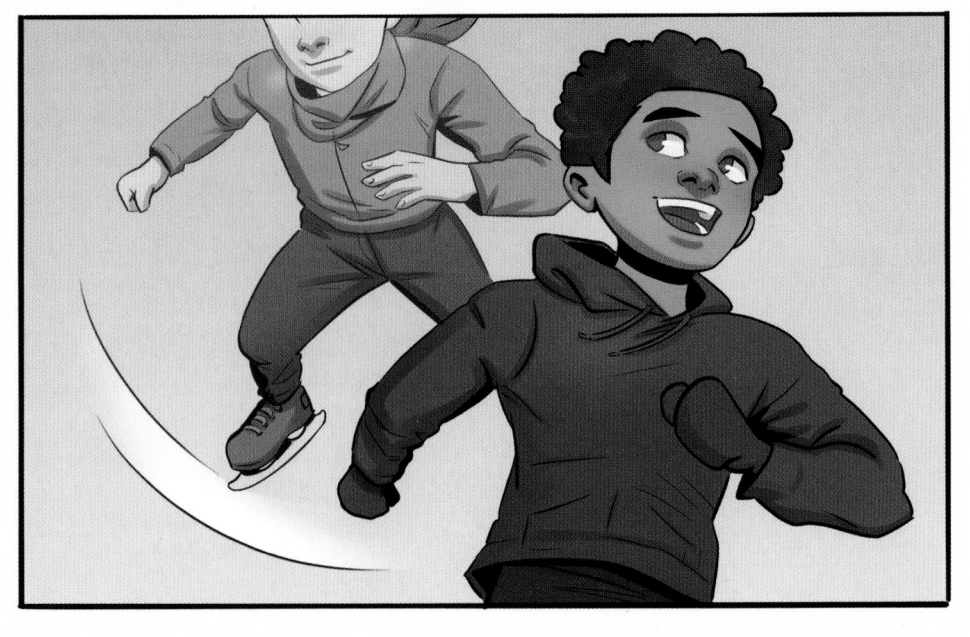

SKATING...
THIS... IS *IT.*
THERE'S REALLY NOTHING LIKE IT.

THE SPEED, THE AGILITY, THE COLD AIR ON YOUR FACE.
?

WINDSOR, ONTARIO, 2005
WHACK
...THE COLD AIR ON YOUR FACE...
...LIKE THE FEELING OF FACING REALITY FOR THE FIRST TIME.
LIKE FACING THE FACT THAT YOU WERE AN OUTSIDER WITHIN A WORLD OR COMMUNITY YOU LOVED SO DANG MUCH.
SO DANG MUCH THAT YOU HAD TO FIGHT AGAINST, AND ENDURE, HATE AND BIGOTRY–***YEARS*** OF RACISM–JUST TO KEEP ON FOLLOWING YOUR DREAMS, JUST TO BE HAPPY...OR TO MAKE A BETTER PLACE FOR THE NEXT ONES FOLLOWING IN YOUR FOOTSTEPS...
...THIS IS THAT STORY... ABOUT PERSEVERANCE AND FOLLOWING YOUR DREAM AGAINST ALL ODDS...

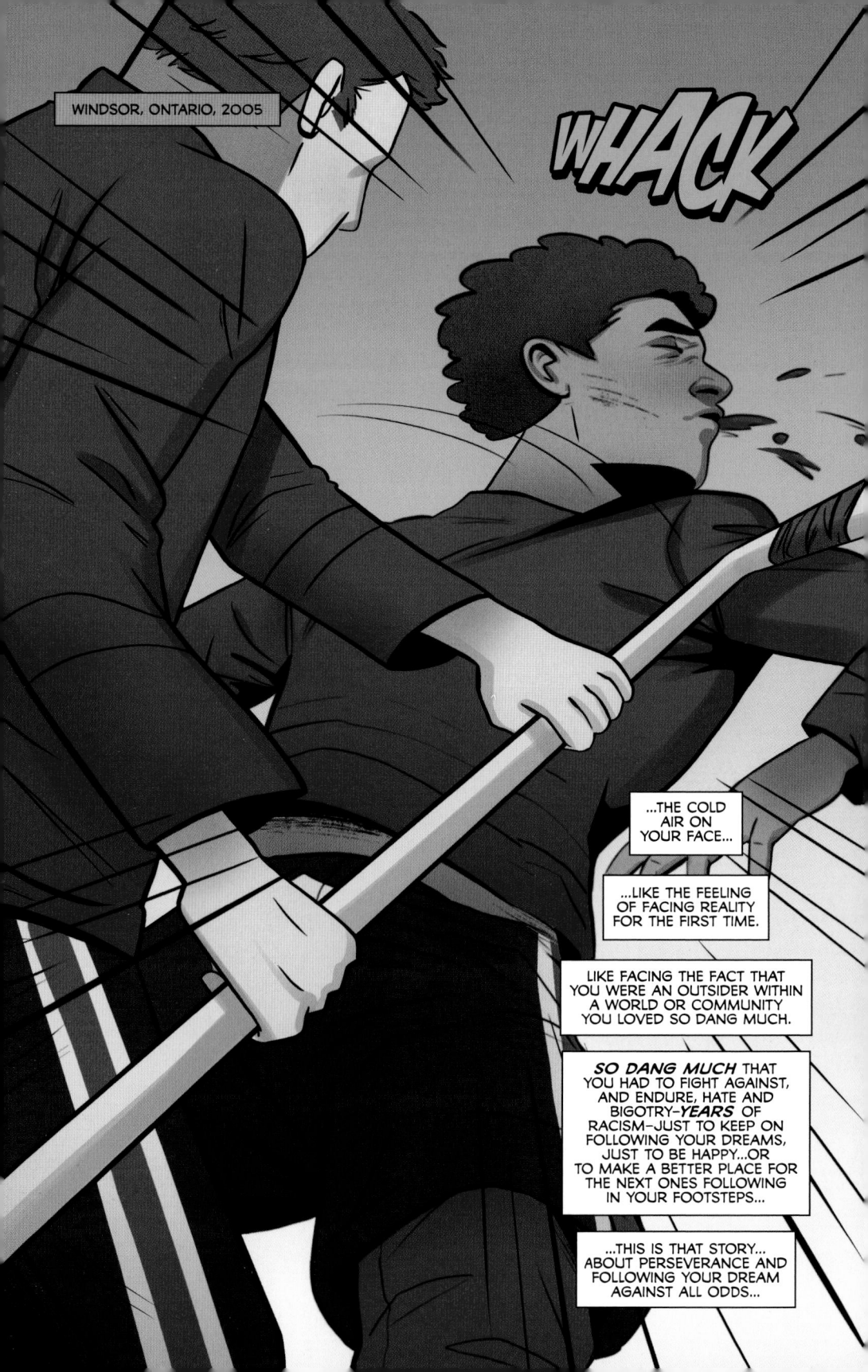

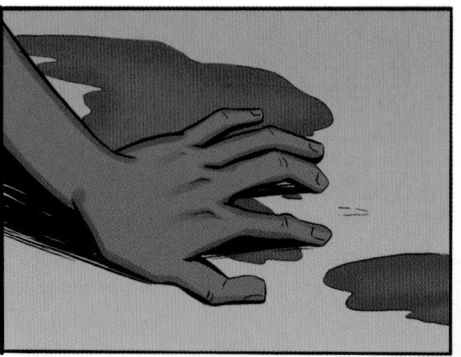

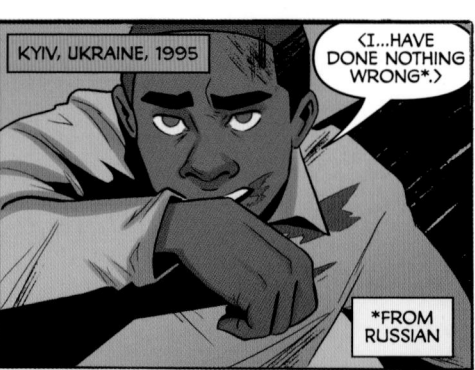

KYIV, UKRAINE, 1995

<I...HAVE DONE NOTHING WRONG*.>

*FROM RUSSIAN

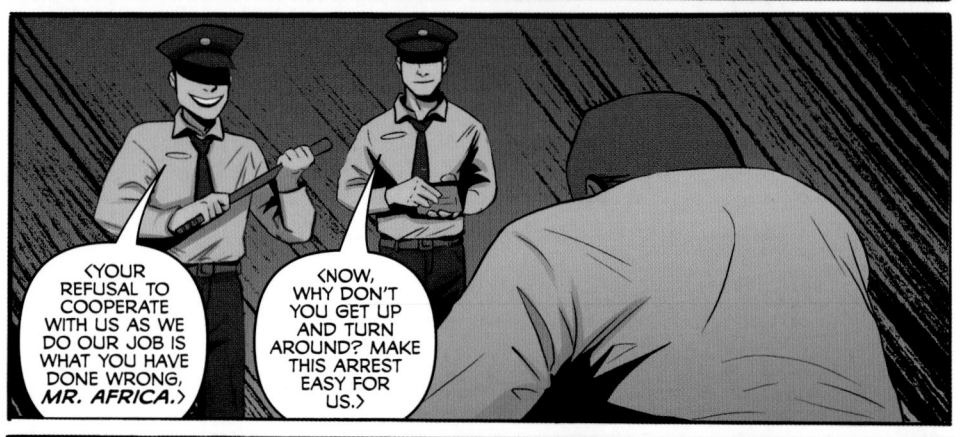

<YOUR REFUSAL TO COOPERATE WITH US AS WE DO OUR JOB IS WHAT YOU HAVE DONE WRONG, **MR. AFRICA.**>

<NOW, WHY DON'T YOU GET UP AND TURN AROUND? MAKE THIS ARREST EASY FOR US.>

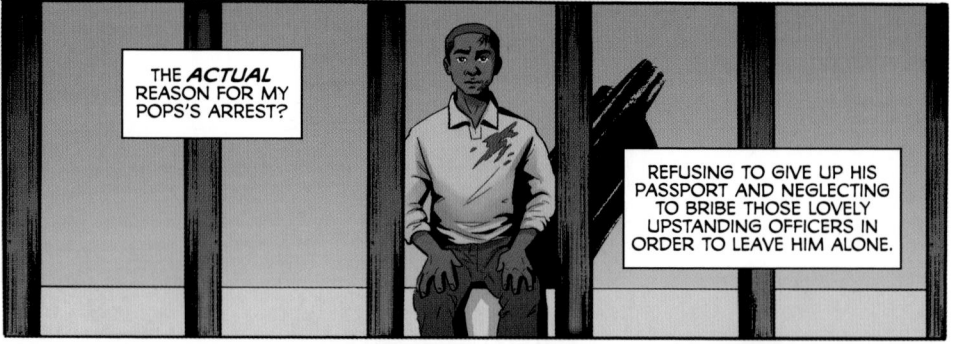

THE *ACTUAL* REASON FOR MY POPS'S ARREST?

REFUSING TO GIVE UP HIS PASSPORT AND NEGLECTING TO BRIBE THOSE LOVELY UPSTANDING OFFICERS IN ORDER TO LEAVE HIM ALONE.

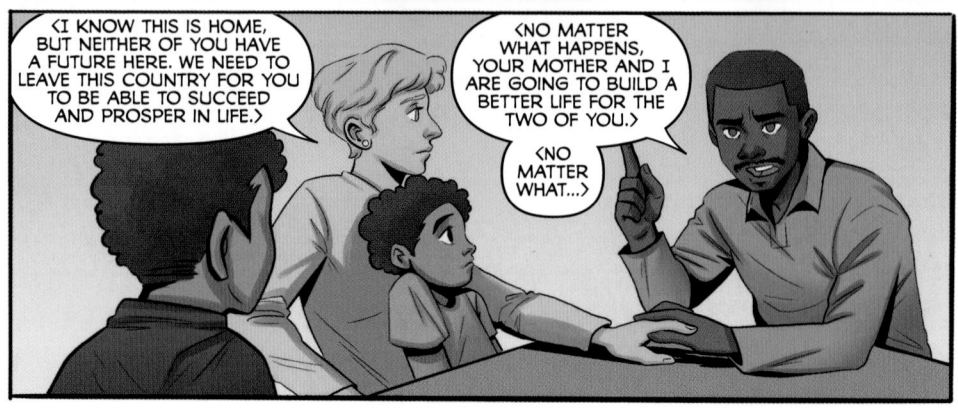

<I KNOW THIS IS HOME, BUT NEITHER OF YOU HAVE A FUTURE HERE. WE NEED TO LEAVE THIS COUNTRY FOR YOU TO BE ABLE TO SUCCEED AND PROSPER IN LIFE.>

<NO MATTER WHAT HAPPENS, YOUR MOTHER AND I ARE GOING TO BUILD A BETTER LIFE FOR THE TWO OF YOU.>

<NO MATTER WHAT...>

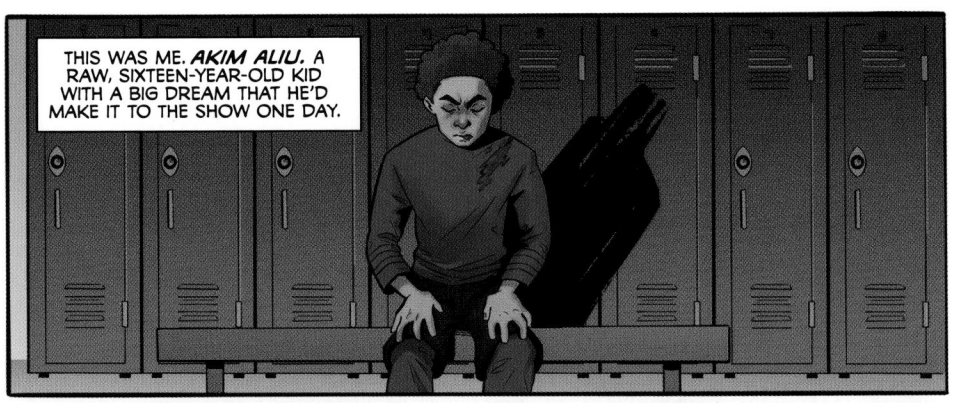

THIS WAS ME. *AKIM ALIU.* A RAW, SIXTEEN-YEAR-OLD KID WITH A BIG DREAM THAT HE'D MAKE IT TO THE SHOW ONE DAY.

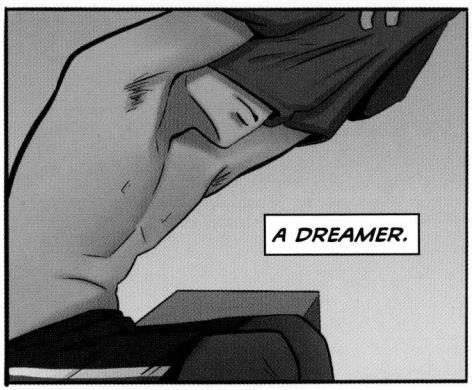

A DREAMER.

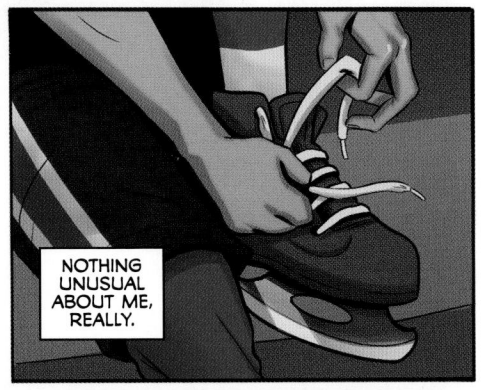

NOTHING UNUSUAL ABOUT ME, REALLY.

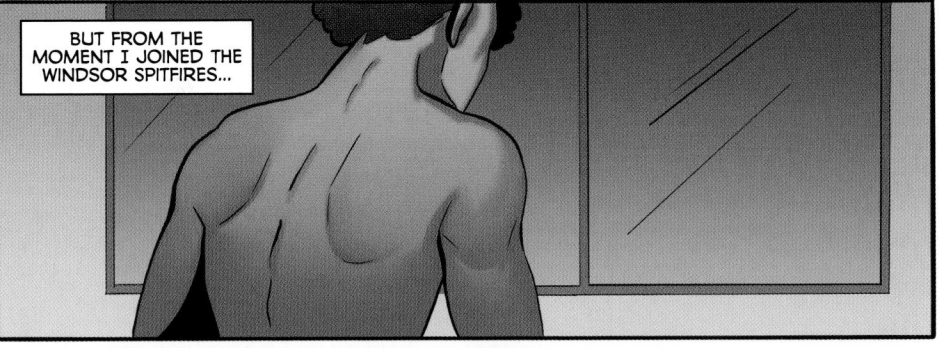

BUT FROM THE MOMENT I JOINED THE WINDSOR SPITFIRES...

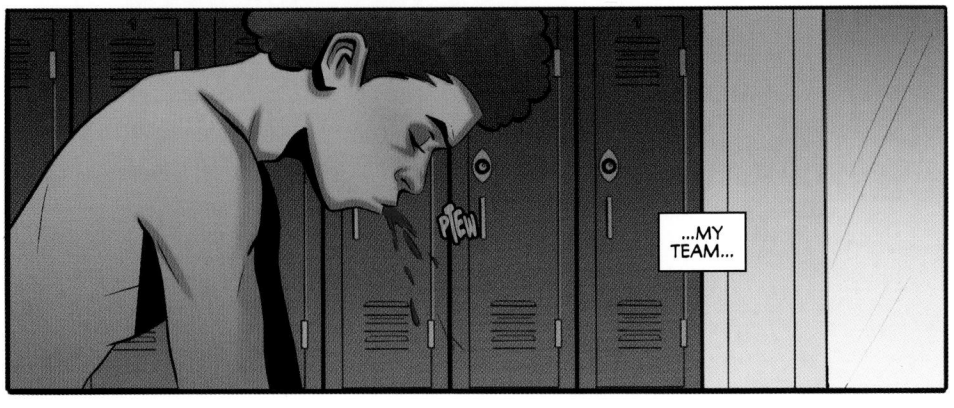

...MY TEAM...

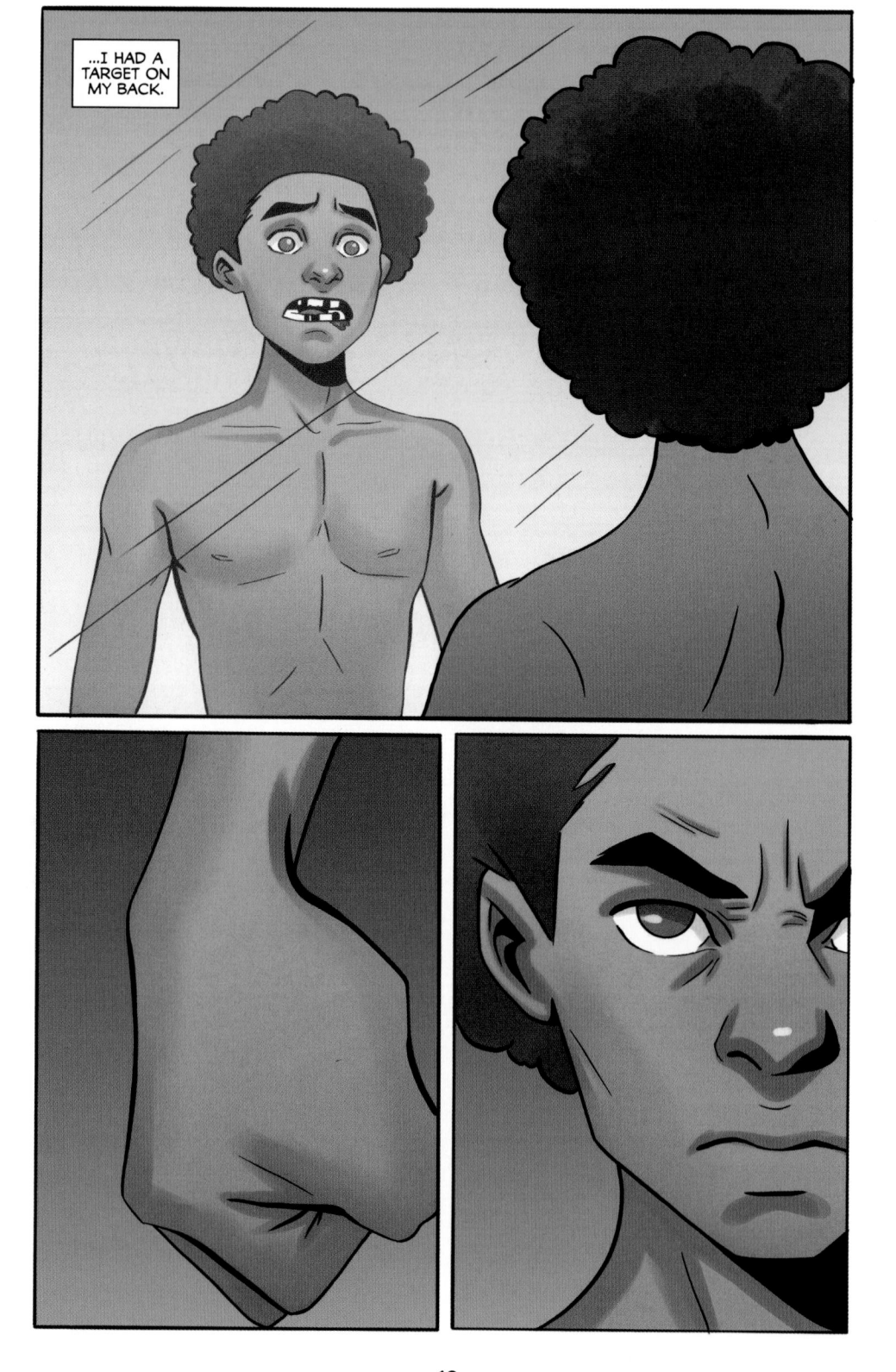

...I HAD A TARGET ON MY BACK.

10

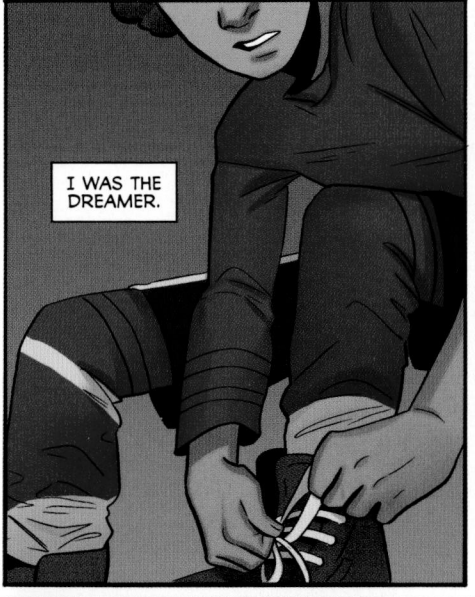

I WAS THE DREAMER.

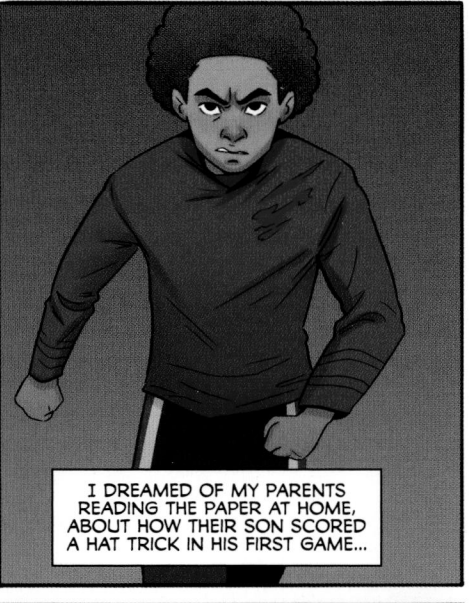

I DREAMED OF MY PARENTS READING THE PAPER AT HOME, ABOUT HOW THEIR SON SCORED A HAT TRICK IN HIS FIRST GAME...

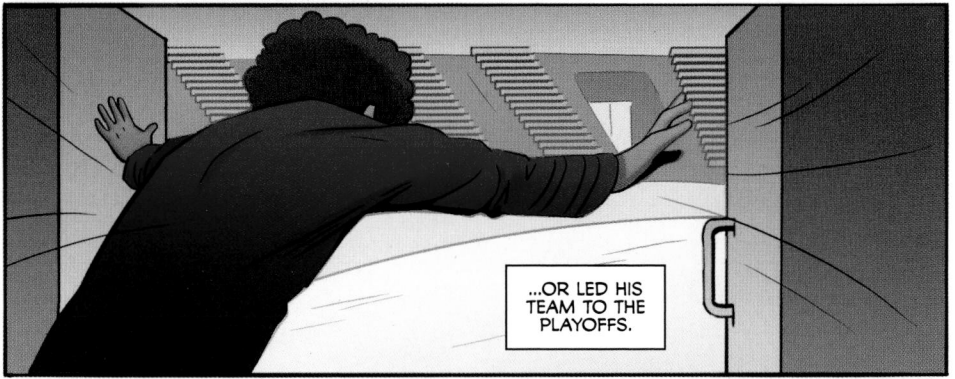

...OR LED HIS TEAM TO THE PLAYOFFS.

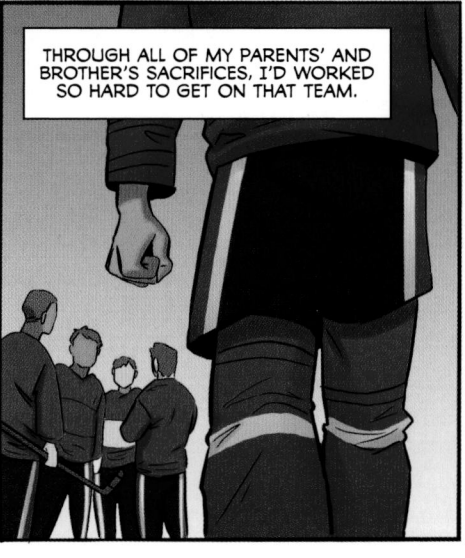

THROUGH ALL OF MY PARENTS' AND BROTHER'S SACRIFICES, I'D WORKED SO HARD TO GET ON THAT TEAM.

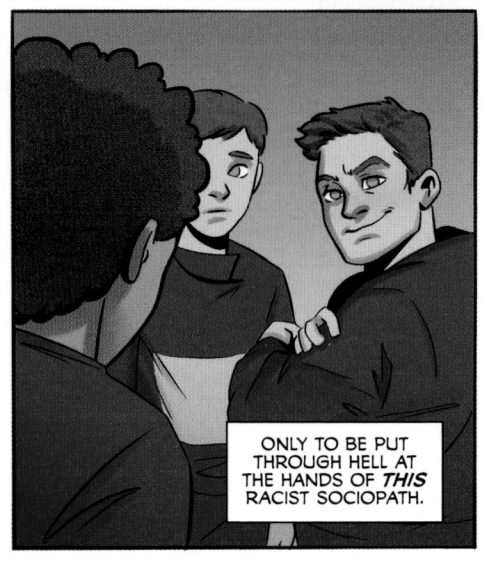

ONLY TO BE PUT THROUGH HELL AT THE HANDS OF *THIS* RACIST SOCIOPATH.

OUT OF EVERYTHING I FELT THAT DAY IN WINDSOR–THE RAGE, THE CRIPPLING PAIN, THE SADNESS–THE WORST PART WAS THE FEELING I HAD WHEN I GOT A LOOK AT MY TEAMMATES, ***MY PEERS,*** STANDING IN A CIRCLE, WATCHING THIS GO ON.
THAT'S WHAT HOCKEY IS ALL ABOUT: BROTHERHOOD. TOGETHERNESS. TEAMWORK.

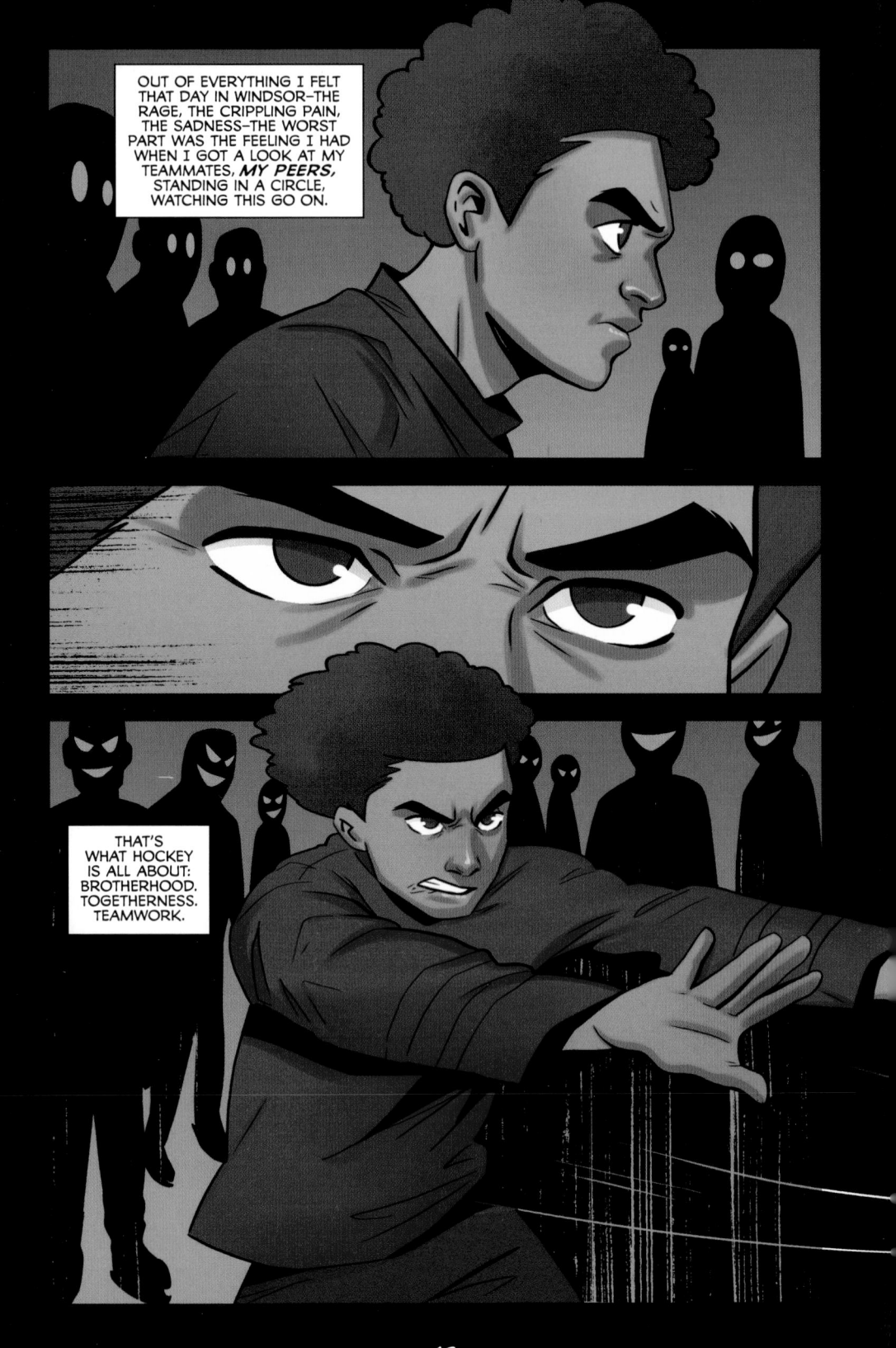

IT FELT...TRIBAL. OR LIKE I WAS AN ANIMAL IN THE CIRCUS. I WAS WITH ALL THESE PEOPLE WHO WERE SUPPOSED TO BE MY BROTHERS, RIGHT?
AND THEY JUST STOOD THERE. I WAS SURROUNDED BY THE TYPES OF PLAYERS I HAD DREAMED OF PLAYING WITH...

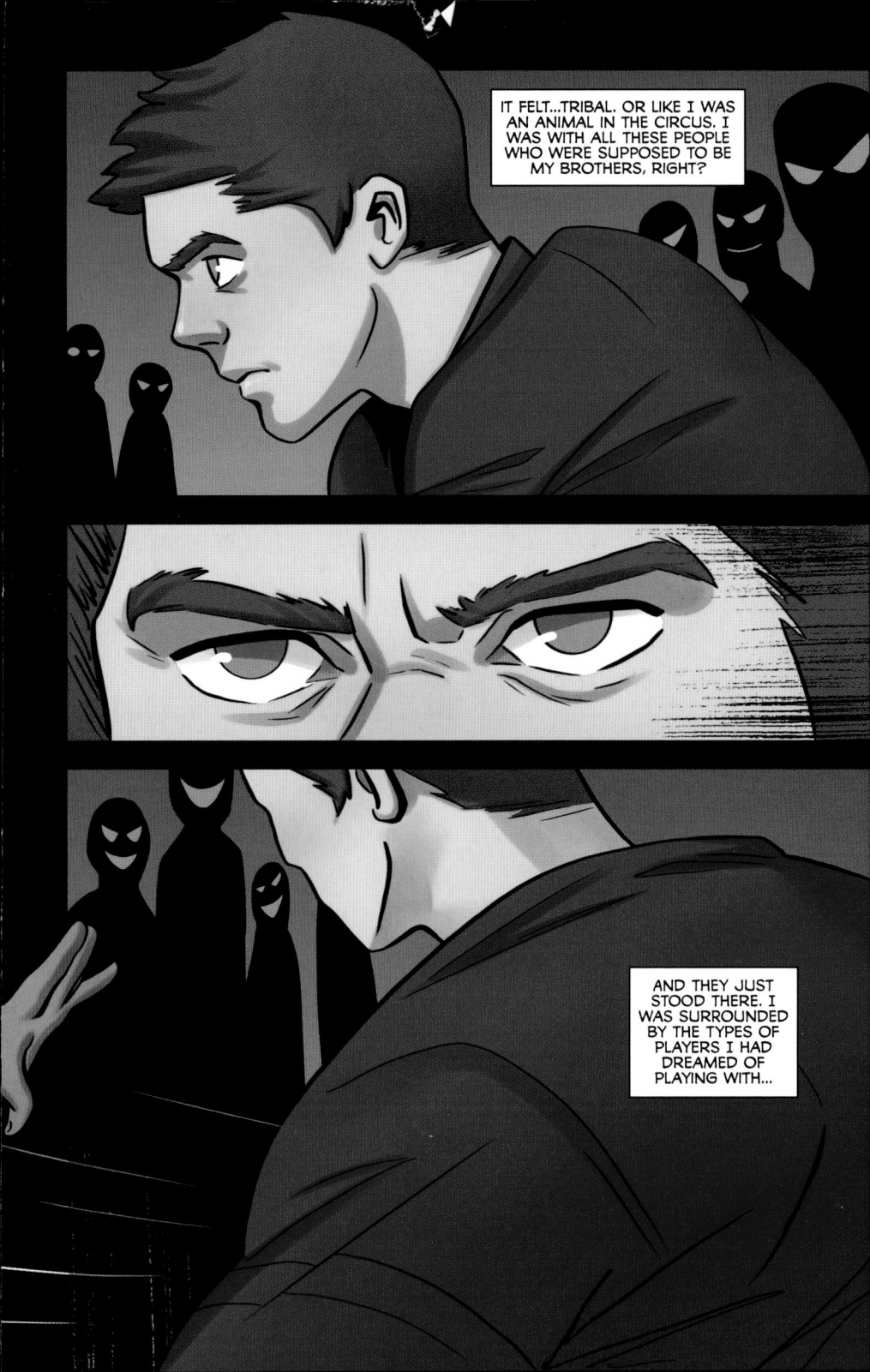

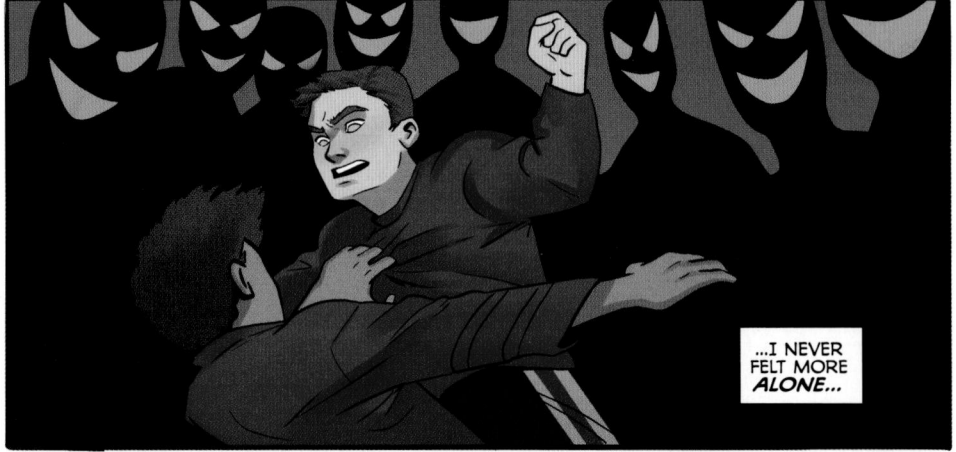

...I NEVER FELT MORE *ALONE*...

IN CANADA, SKATING IS THE LANGUAGE EVERYONE CAN SPEAK.

YOU DO A CROSSOVER...

...OR SCORE A GOAL...
...ALL OF A SUDDEN, YOU'RE APPROACHABLE.
YOU'RE *ONE OF THEM.*
I FELT THAT.
AND IT FELT NICE.

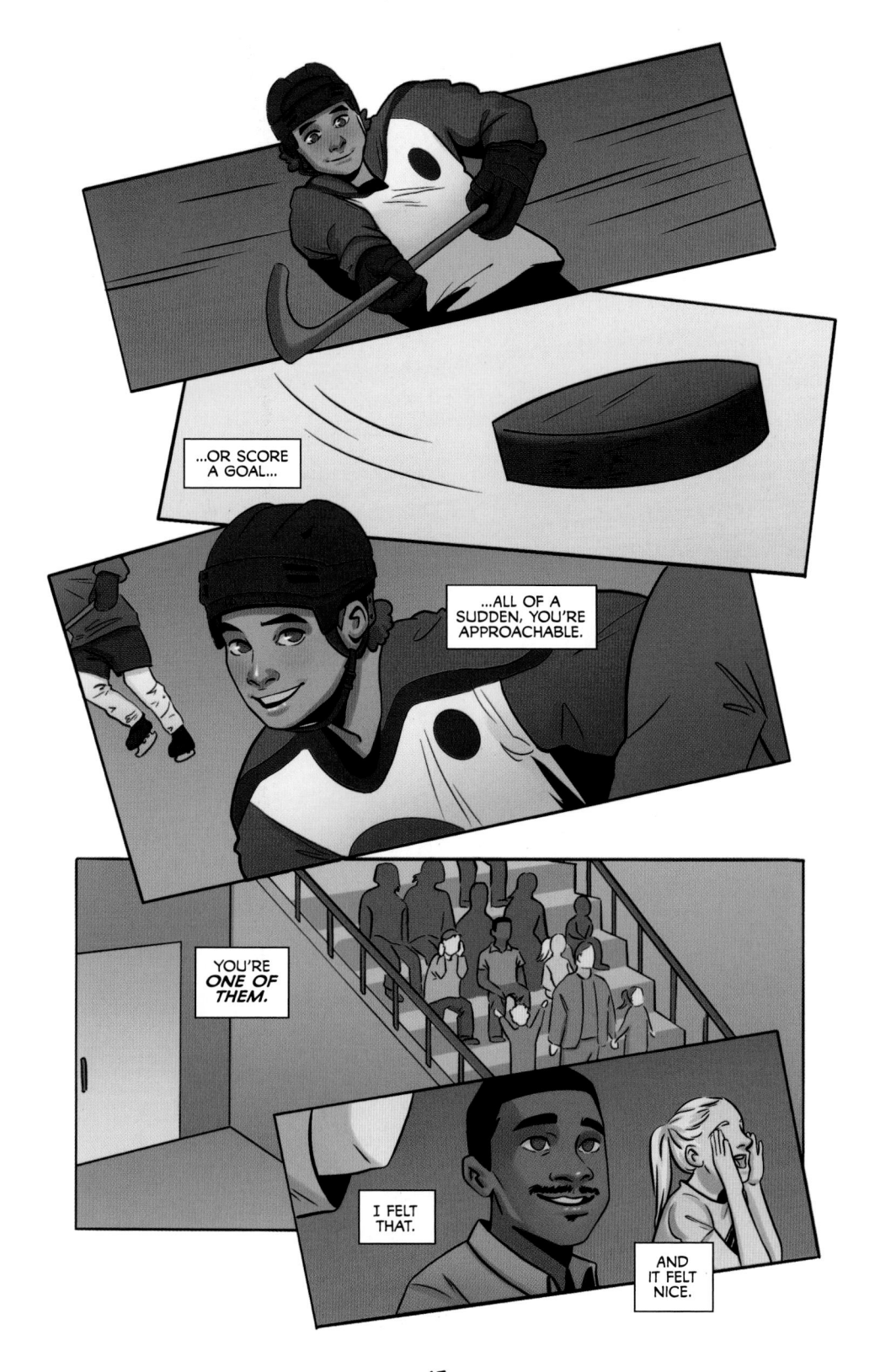

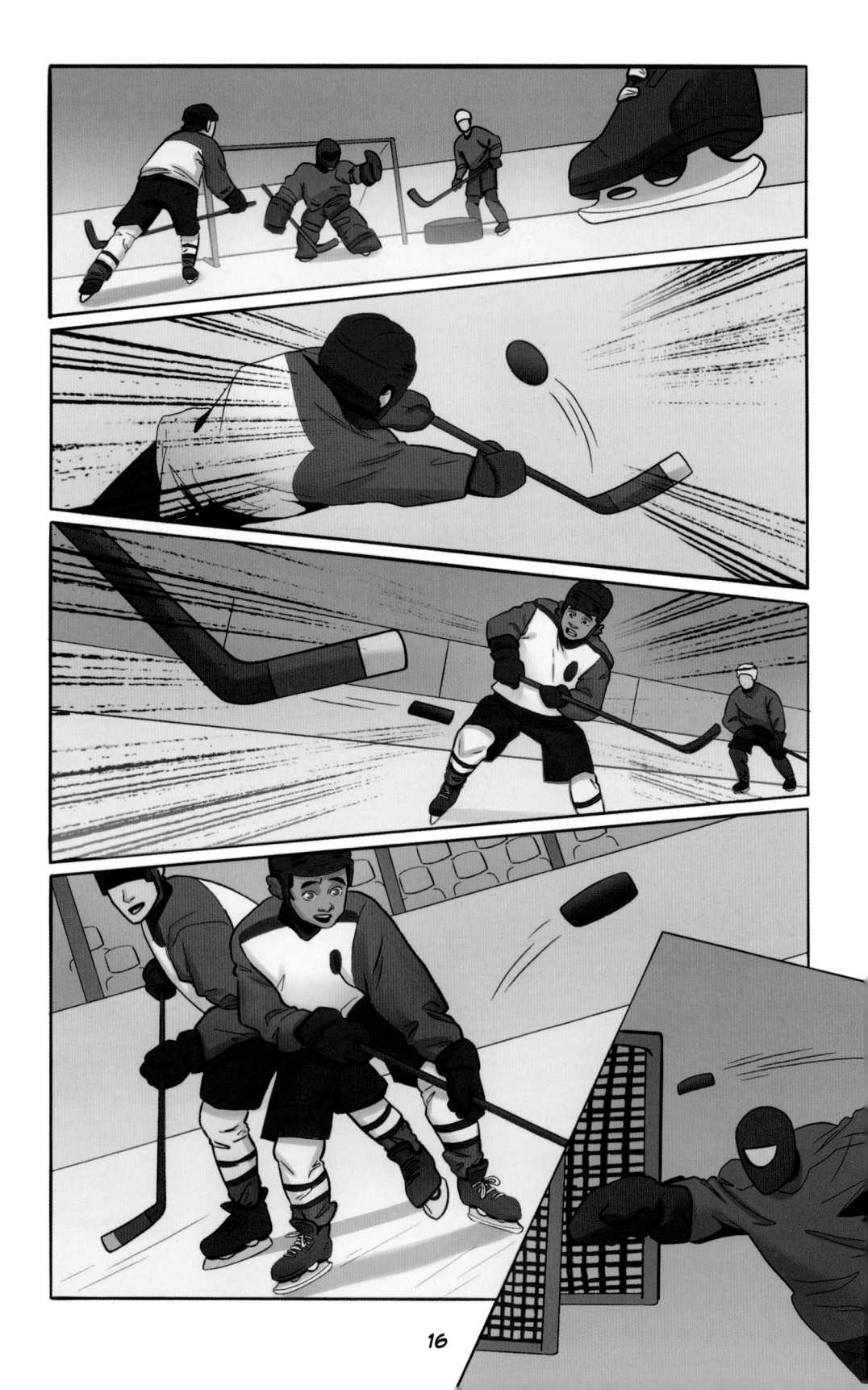

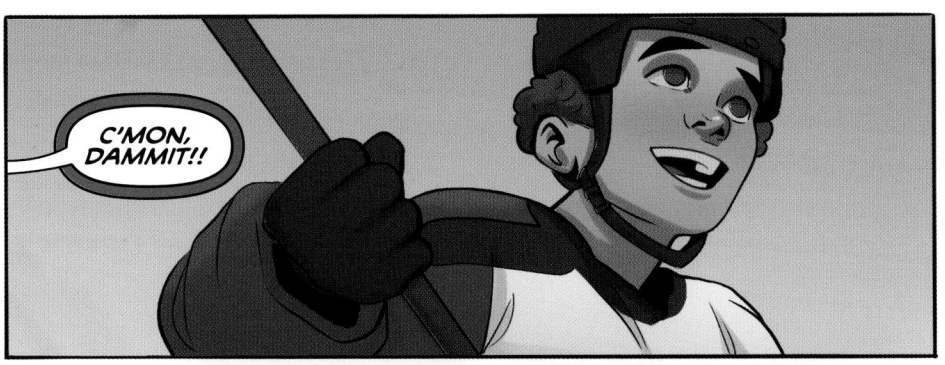

HOW MANY TIMES ARE WE GOING TO LET THIS N̶̶̶̶R SCORE?!

AND THERE IT WAS...

...THE REALITY CHECK.

I HEARD HIM AS CLEAR AS DAY.

HIS VOICE JUST PUNCHED THROUGH THE AIR IN THE RINK.

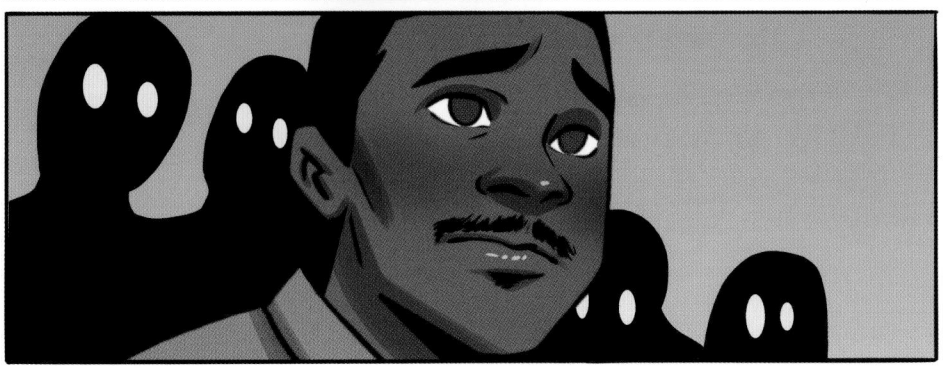

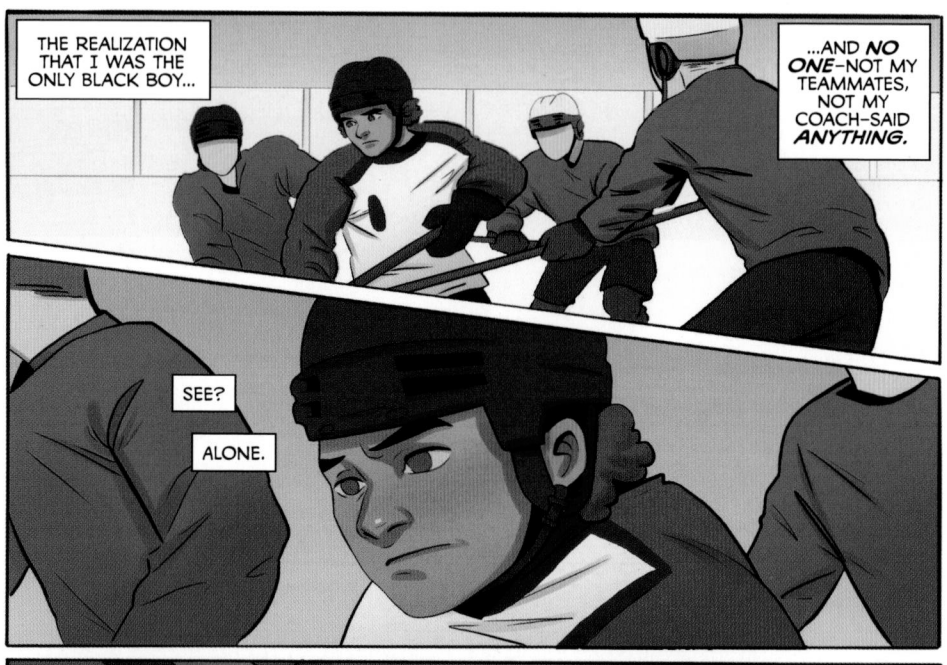

THE REALIZATION THAT I WAS THE ONLY BLACK BOY...

...AND *NO ONE*—NOT MY TEAMMATES, NOT MY COACH—SAID *ANYTHING.*

SEE?

ALONE.

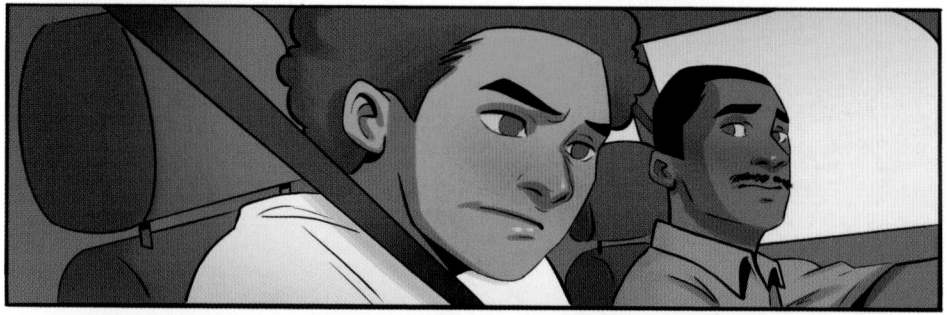

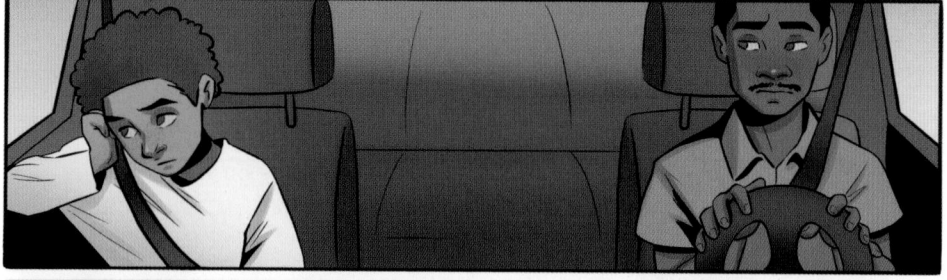

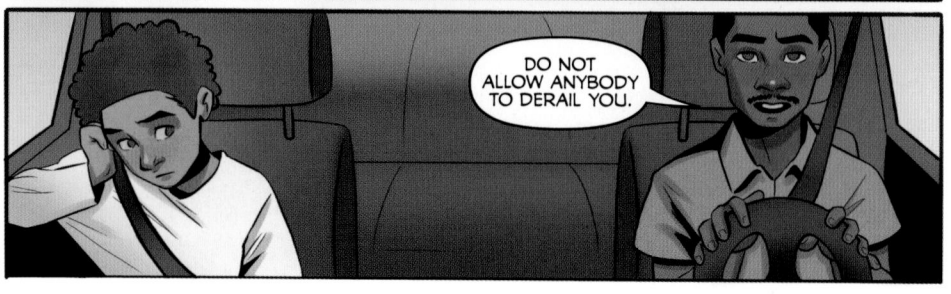

DO NOT ALLOW ANYBODY TO DERAIL YOU.

RACISM IS EVERYWHERE IN THE WORLD. ***EVERYWHERE.***
SO IF YOU FALL DOWN BECAUSE OF THEM, YOU ARE GOING TO REGRET IT. YOU HEAR IT, YOU LET IT PASS...
YOU LET IT GO INTO ANOTHER THING AND FOCUS ON WHATEVER YOU ARE DOING.
YOU KEEP FOCUS ON YOUR ***DREAM.***
MY POPS AND HIS LECTURES.
WHILE I HEARD HIM AND KNEW THAT HE AND MY FAMILY HAD MY BACK...

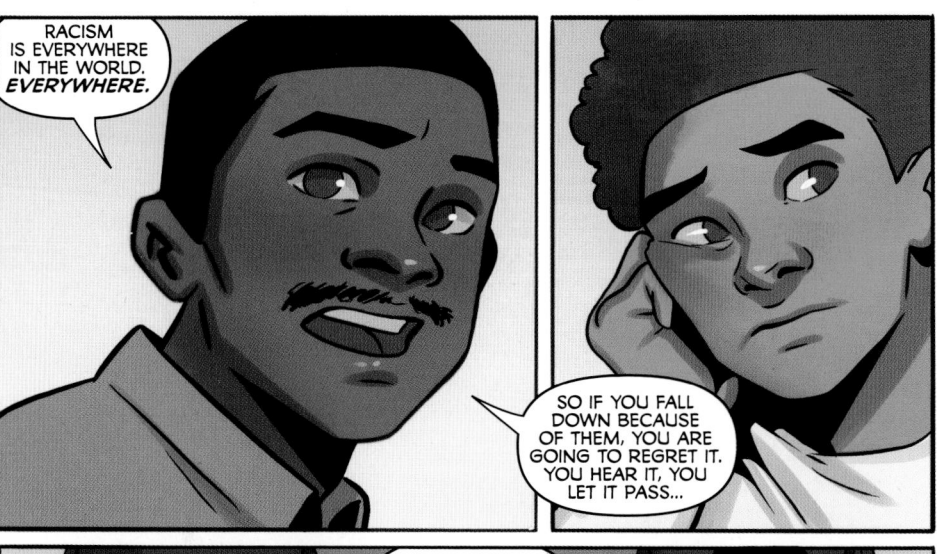

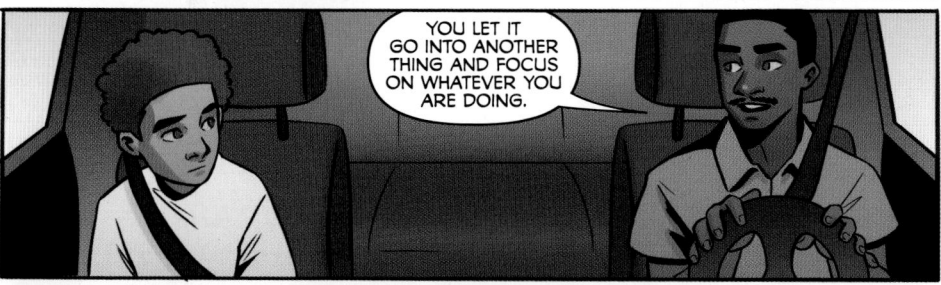

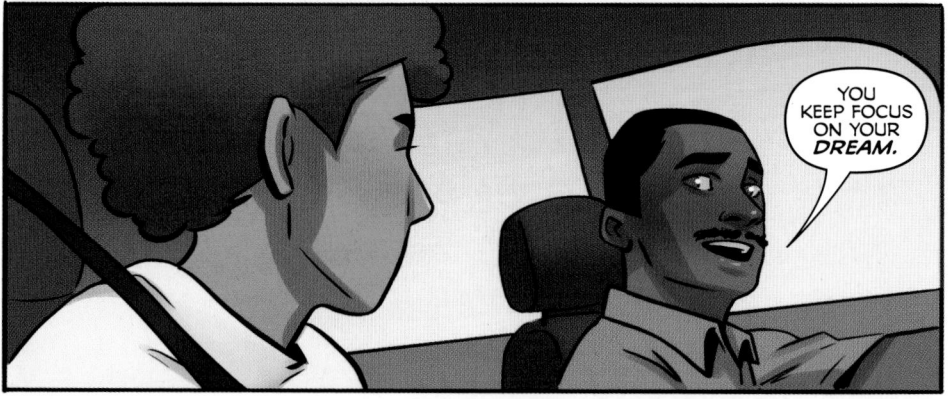

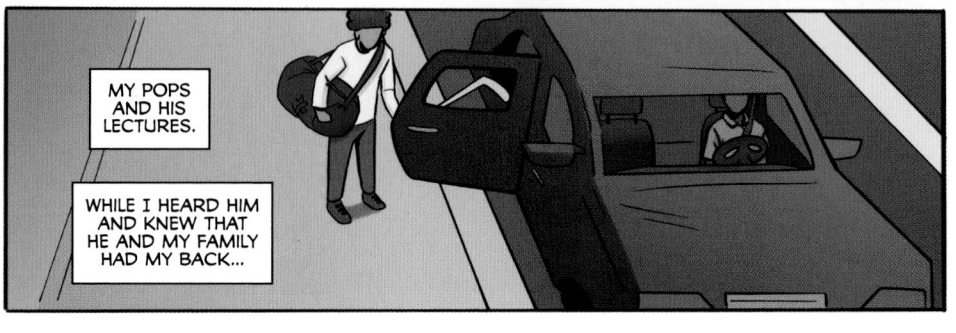

I STILL FELT SO ***ALONE...***

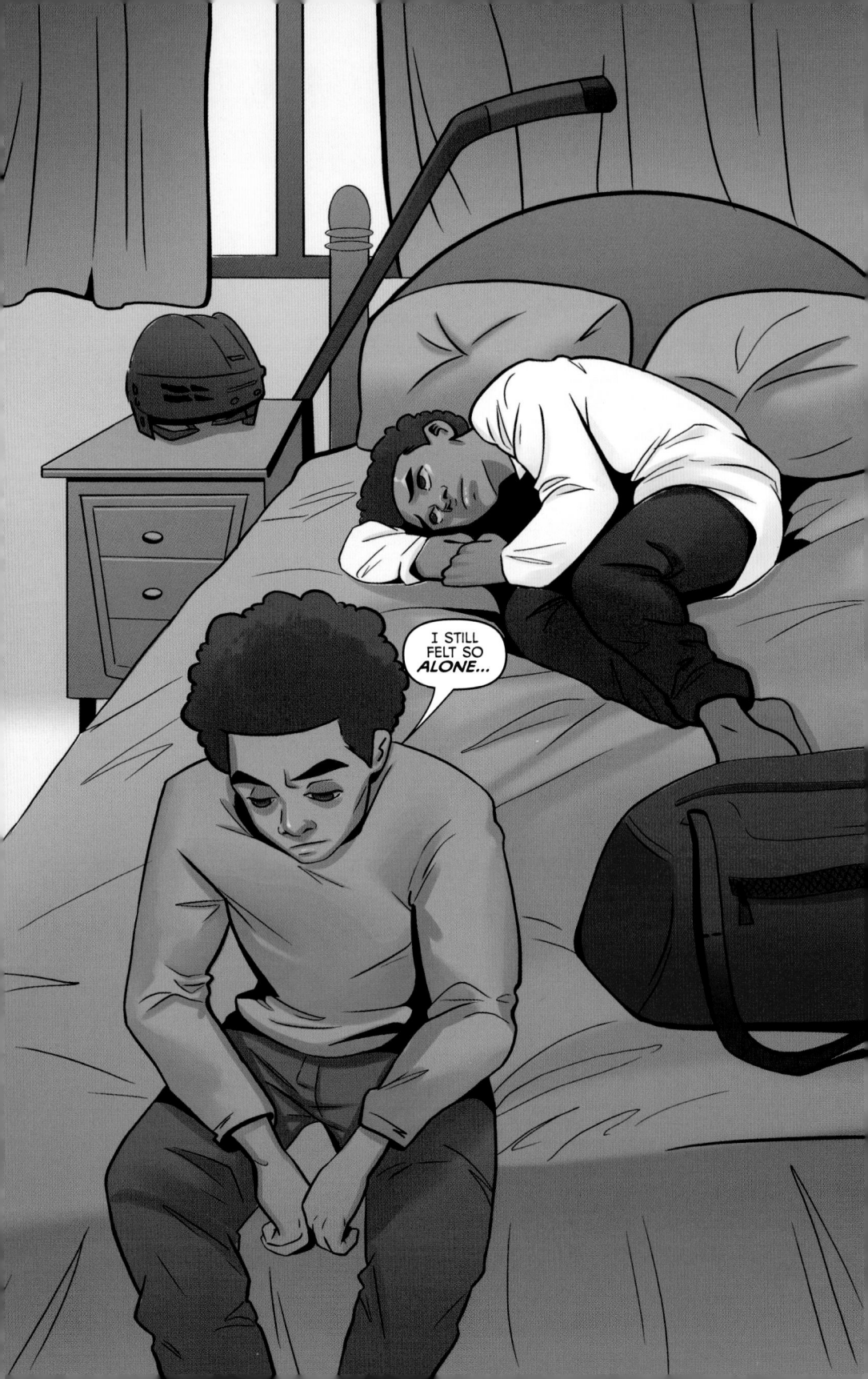

CHAPTER
TWO

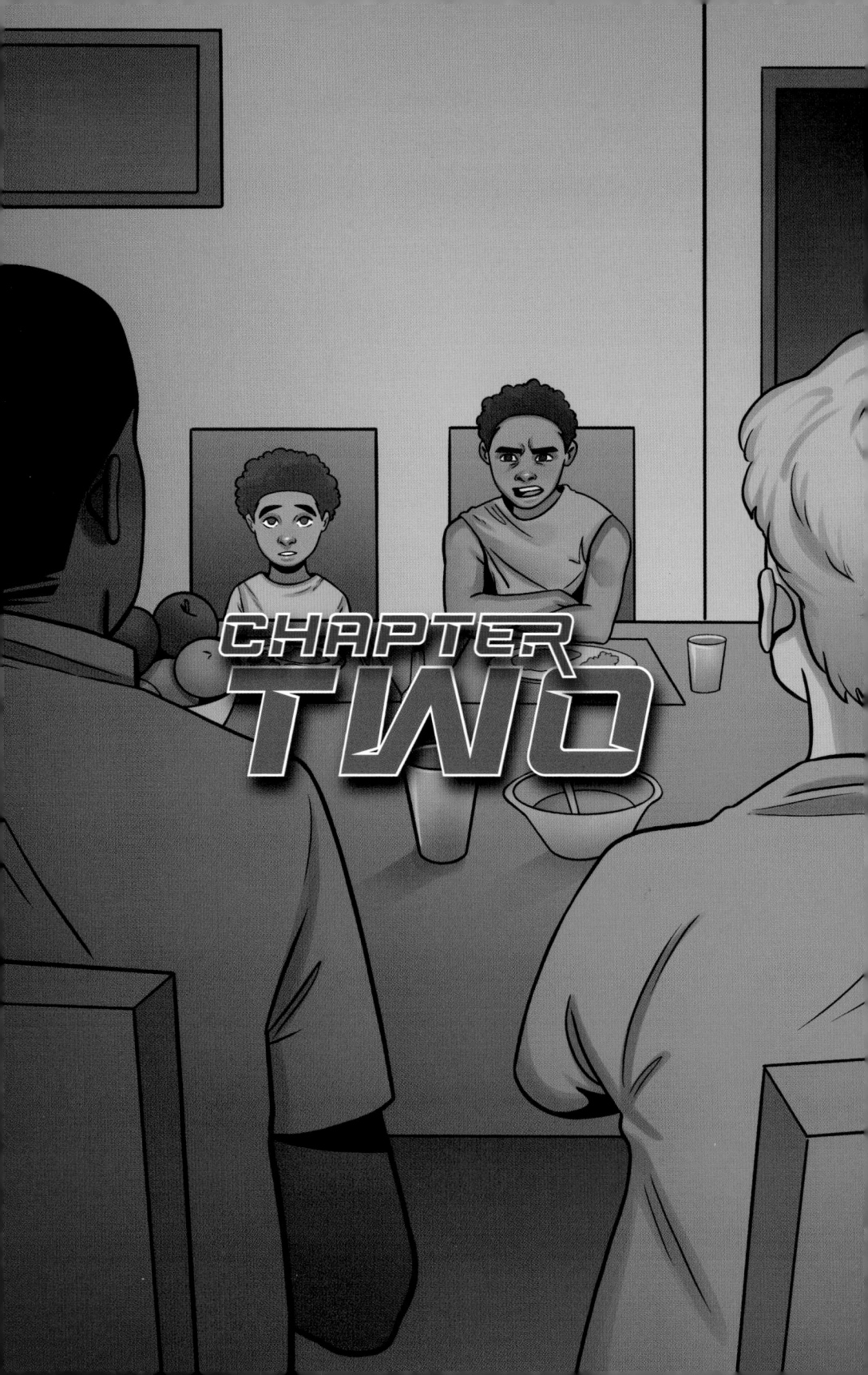

YOU WANNA MEET THE FOLKS WHO MADE AKIM ALIU?
THEY'RE ACTUALLY HERE RIGHT NOW.
COME WITH ME. THEY'RE REALLY COOL PARENTS.

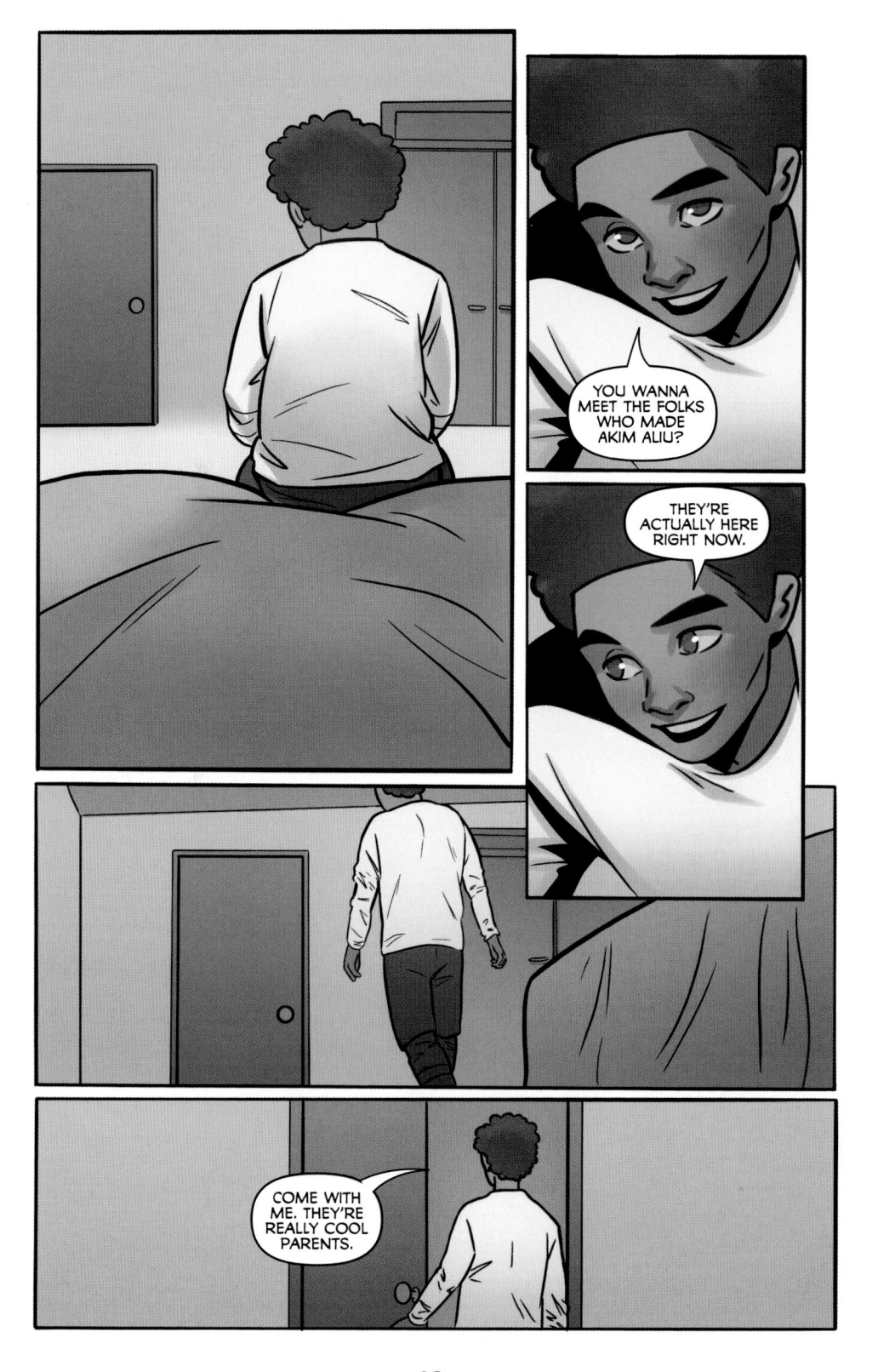

THESE ARE MY FOLKS. HE LOVES WATCHING TV SHOWS, AND SHE LOVES TO COOK, DAY AND NIGHT. OR AS SHE WOULD SAY, "I WAS PUSHED TO ENJOY IT!"
I WOULDN'T BE WHO I AM OR WHERE I AM TODAY WITHOUT ALL THEY'VE DONE FOR ME. I WOULDN'T TRADE THEM FOR THE WORLD.
KYIV, USSR, 1978
MY POPS, TAI ALIU, WAS COMING IN FROM AFRICA ON A SCHOLARSHIP THAT WAS FOR EQUAL PARTS TRACK AND ACADEMICS.
MY MOTHER, LARISSA KHREBET, WAS A PART-TIME STUDENT WHO WORKED AT THE SCHOOL LIBRARY.
HE WAS A BLACK BOY FROM NIGERIA WHO FELL IN LOVE WITH A WHITE GIRL FROM UKRAINE.
THEY MET AT UNIVERSITY IN KYIV.

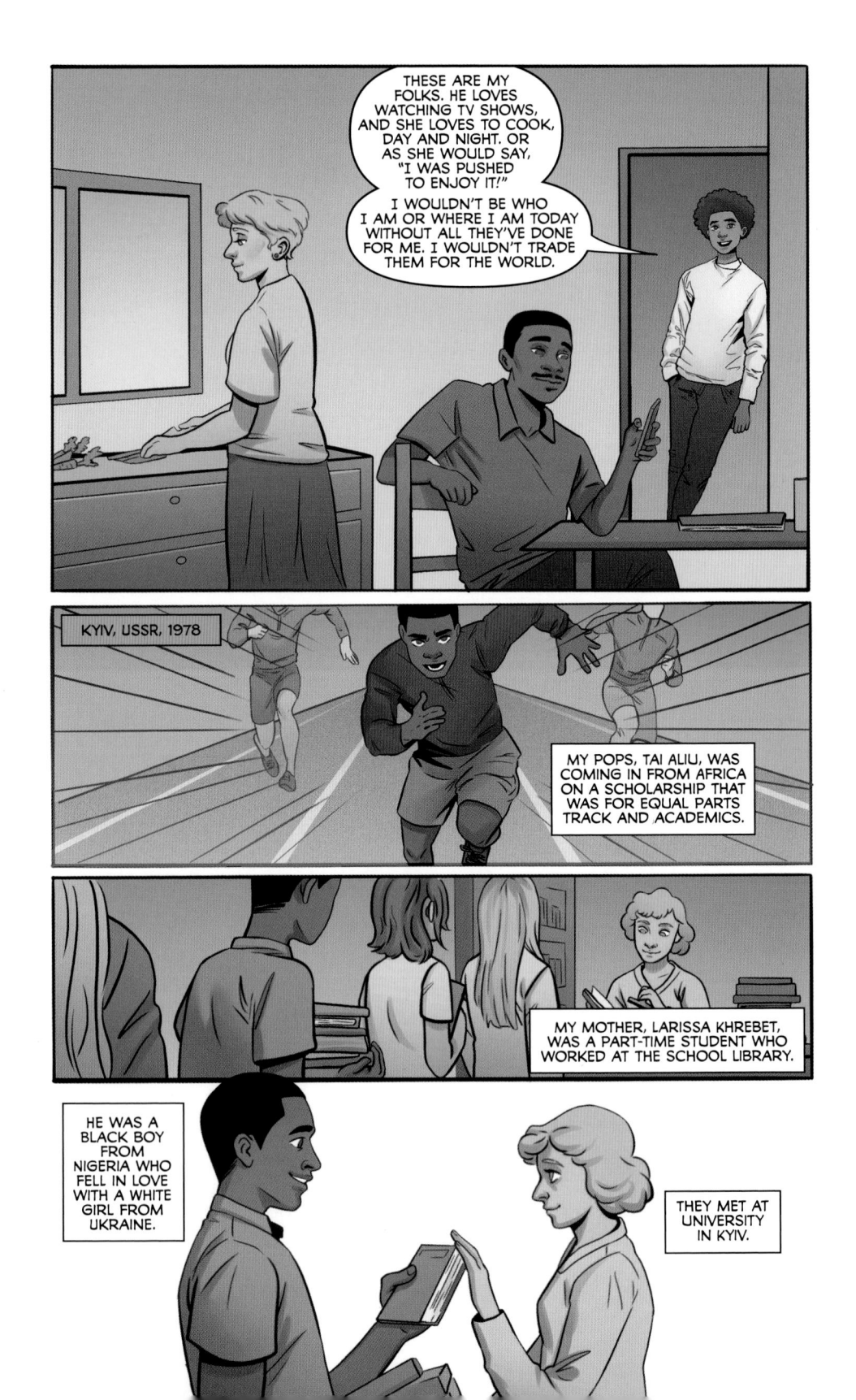

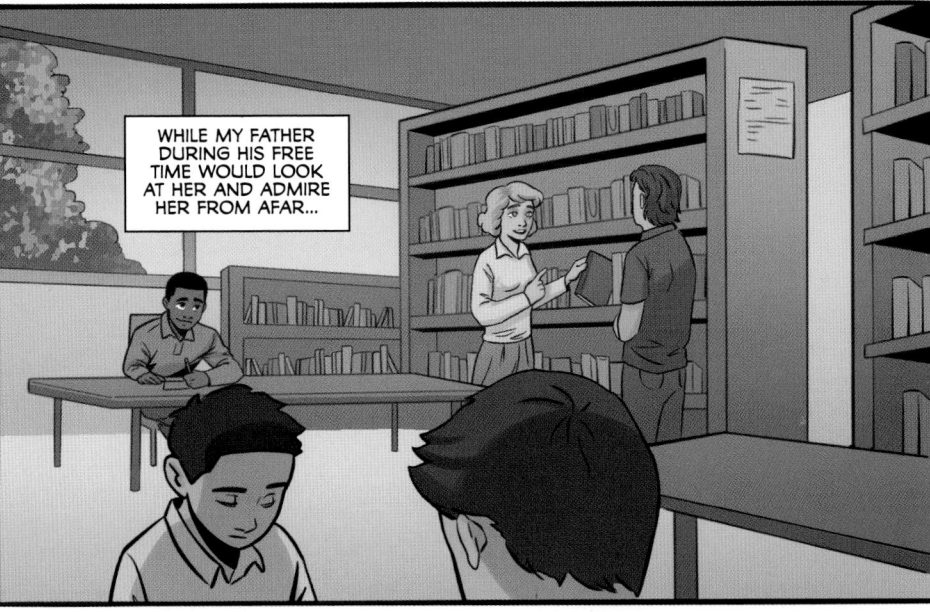

WHILE MY FATHER DURING HIS FREE TIME WOULD LOOK AT HER AND ADMIRE HER FROM AFAR...

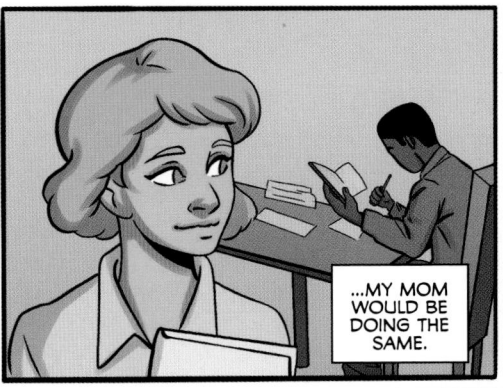

...MY MOM WOULD BE DOING THE SAME.

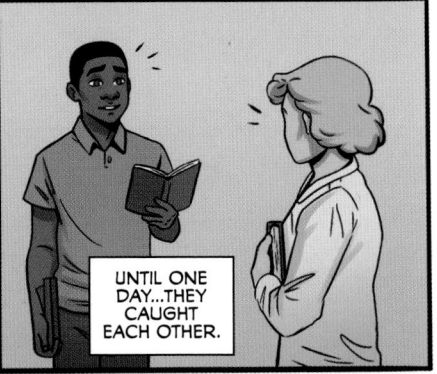

UNTIL ONE DAY...THEY CAUGHT EACH OTHER.

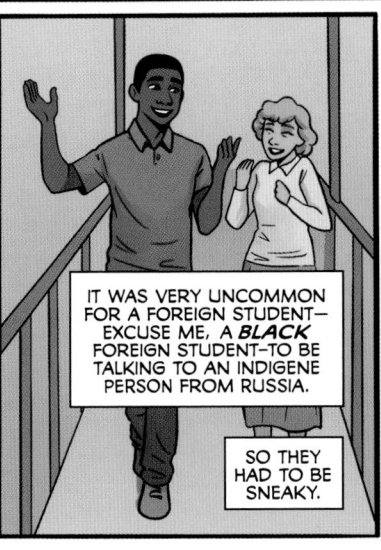

IT WAS VERY UNCOMMON FOR A FOREIGN STUDENT— EXCUSE ME, A *BLACK* FOREIGN STUDENT—TO BE TALKING TO AN INDIGENE PERSON FROM RUSSIA.

SO THEY HAD TO BE SNEAKY.

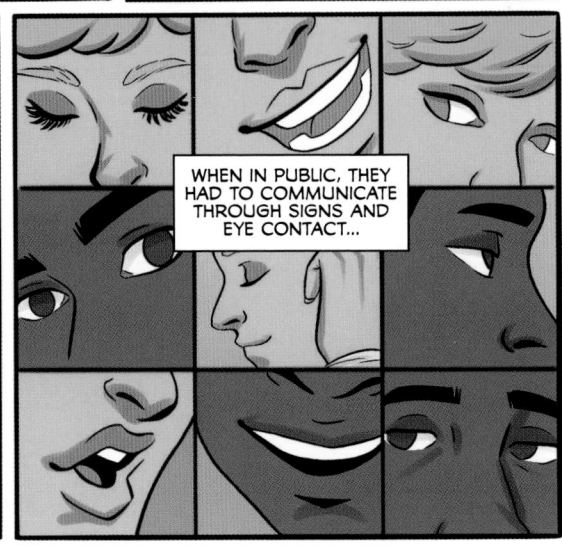

WHEN IN PUBLIC, THEY HAD TO COMMUNICATE THROUGH SIGNS AND EYE CONTACT...

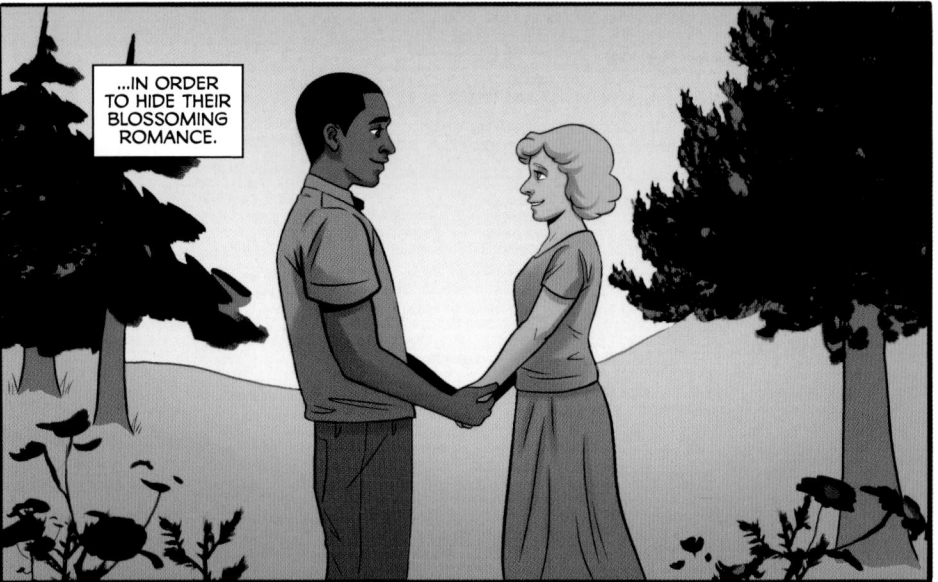

...IN ORDER TO HIDE THEIR BLOSSOMING ROMANCE.

FOR ABOUT TWO TO THREE YEARS, THEY SECRETLY DATED, NOT EVEN MOM'S PARENTS KNOWING.

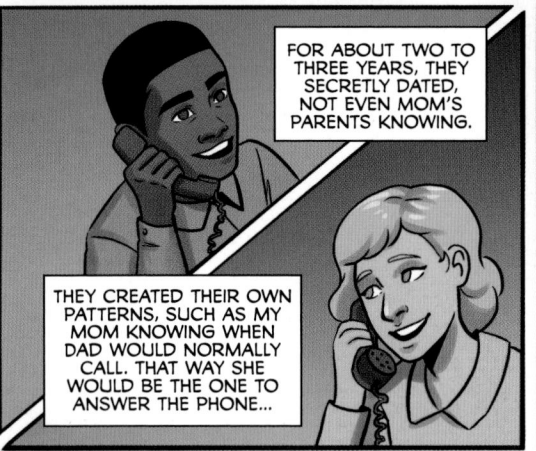

THEY CREATED THEIR OWN PATTERNS, SUCH AS MY MOM KNOWING WHEN DAD WOULD NORMALLY CALL. THAT WAY SHE WOULD BE THE ONE TO ANSWER THE PHONE...

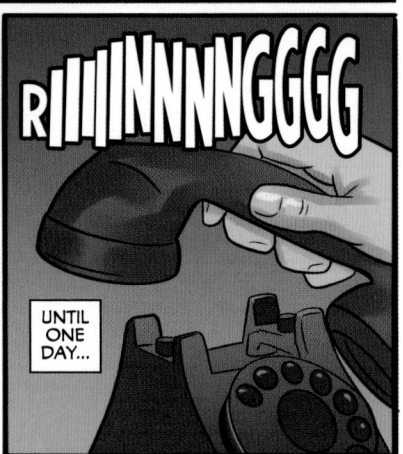

RIIIINNNNGGGG

UNTIL ONE DAY...

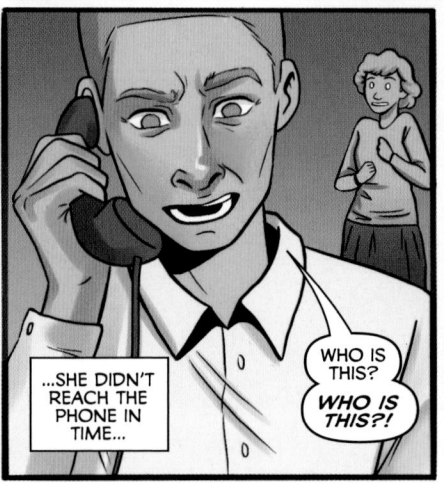

...SHE DIDN'T REACH THE PHONE IN TIME...

WHO IS THIS?

WHO IS THIS?!

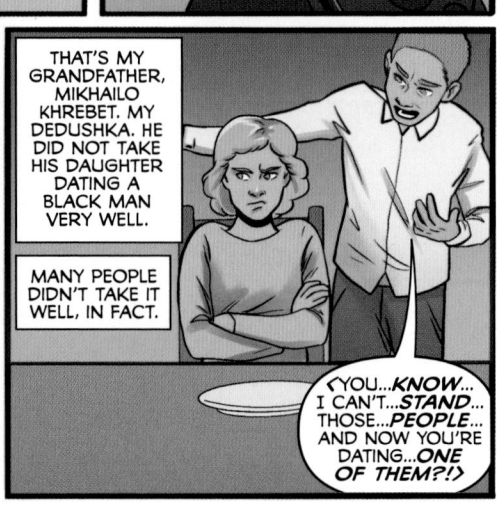

THAT'S MY GRANDFATHER, MIKHAILO KHREBET. MY DEDUSHKA. HE DID NOT TAKE HIS DAUGHTER DATING A BLACK MAN VERY WELL.

MANY PEOPLE DIDN'T TAKE IT WELL, IN FACT.

‹YOU...*KNOW*... I CAN'T...*STAND*... THOSE...*PEOPLE*... AND NOW YOU'RE DATING...*ONE OF THEM?!*›

26

THEY CONTINUED TO SEE EACH OTHER IN SECRET BEHIND HER PARENTS' BACKS.

AND THENNNN...

JUST TO MAKE MATTERS *EASIER*, THEY DECIDED IT WAS TIME TO GET MARRIED.

IN RUSSIA, IN ORDER TO GET MARRIED, YOU HAD TO REGISTER, SECURE A DATE, HAVE YOUR PASSPORT, AND THEN FINALLY GET YOUR PASSPORT STAMPED TO LEGALIZE SAID MARRIAGE.

GUESS WHO TOOK AND HID HER PASSPORT THE DAY OF THEIR WEDDING.

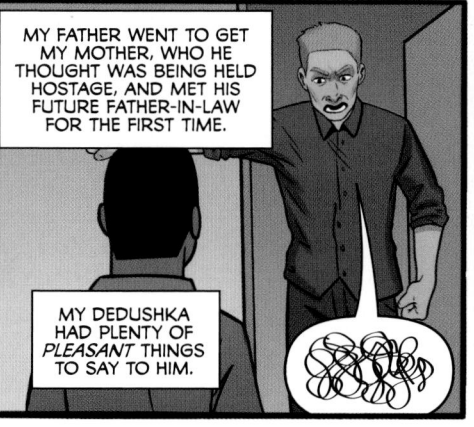

MY FATHER WENT TO GET MY MOTHER, WHO HE THOUGHT WAS BEING HELD HOSTAGE, AND MET HIS FUTURE FATHER-IN-LAW FOR THE FIRST TIME.

MY DEDUSHKA HAD PLENTY OF *PLEASANT* THINGS TO SAY TO HIM.

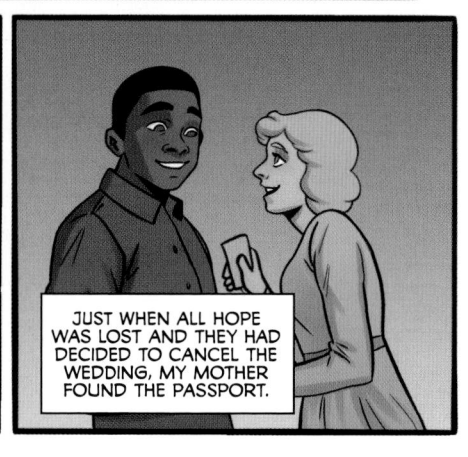

JUST WHEN ALL HOPE WAS LOST AND THEY HAD DECIDED TO CANCEL THE WEDDING, MY MOTHER FOUND THE PASSPORT.

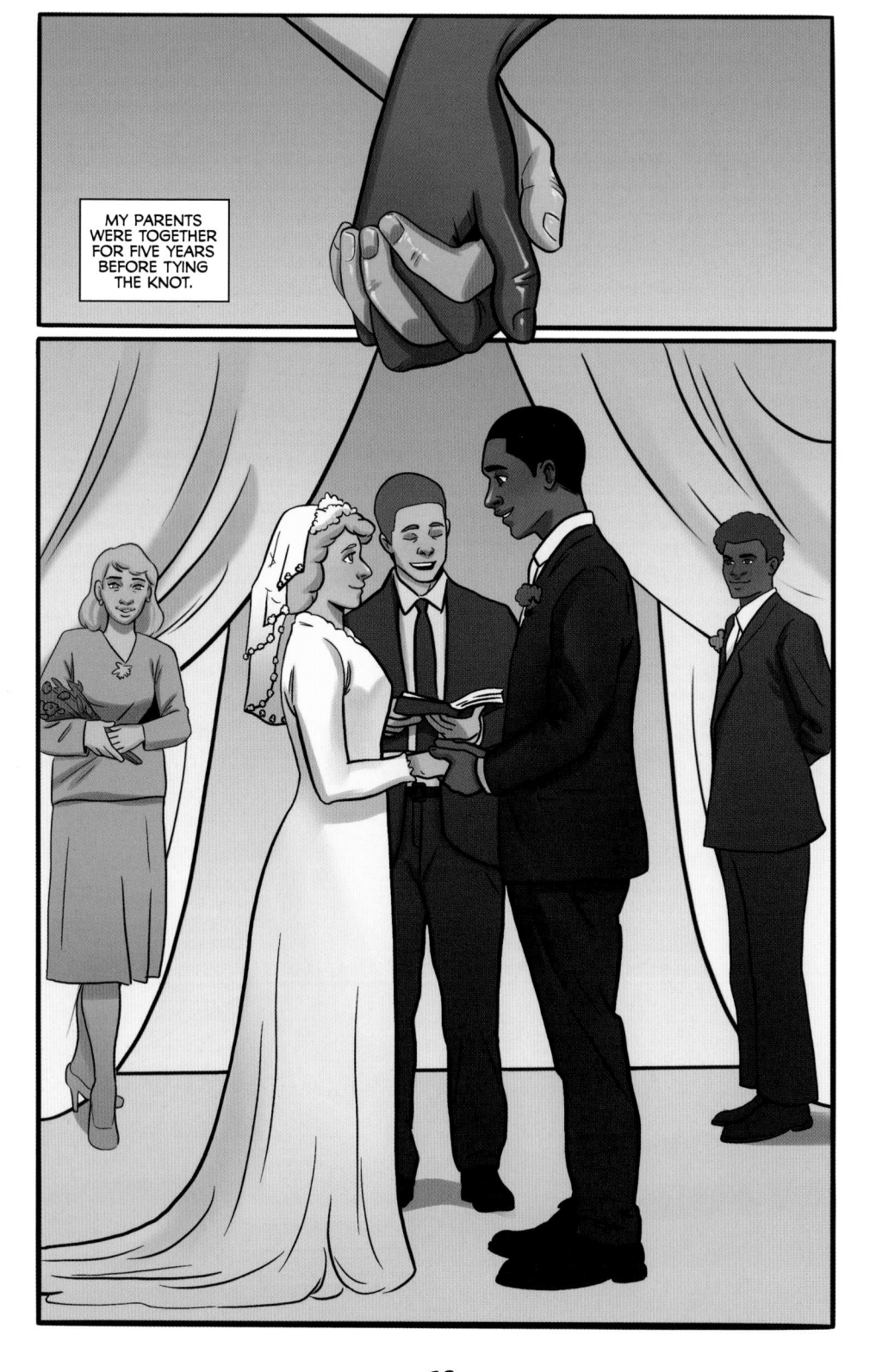

MY PARENTS WERE TOGETHER FOR FIVE YEARS BEFORE TYING THE KNOT.

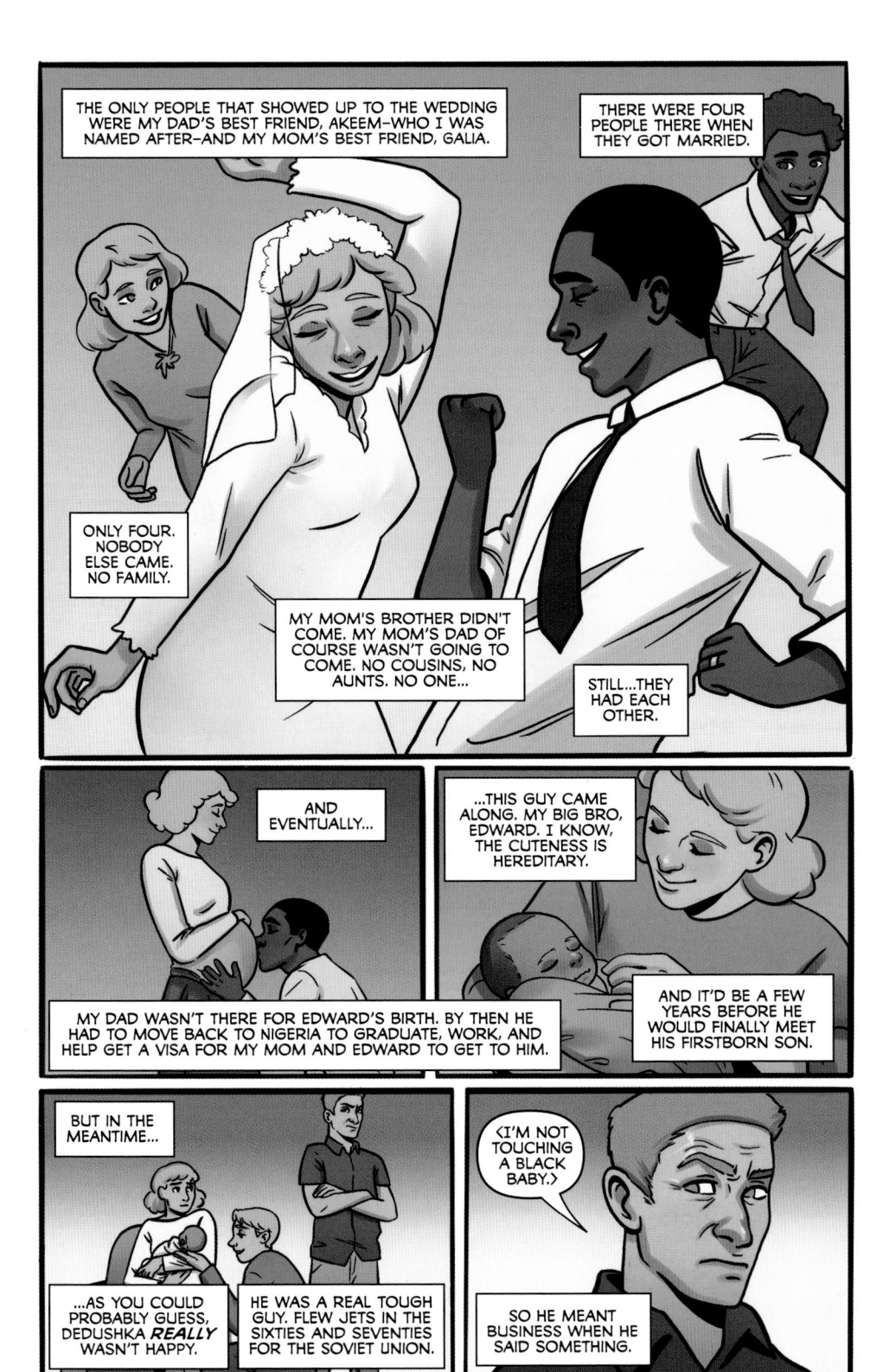

THE ONLY PEOPLE THAT SHOWED UP TO THE WEDDING WERE MY DAD'S BEST FRIEND, AKEEM—WHO I WAS NAMED AFTER—AND MY MOM'S BEST FRIEND, GALIA.

THERE WERE FOUR PEOPLE THERE WHEN THEY GOT MARRIED.

ONLY FOUR. NOBODY ELSE CAME. NO FAMILY.

MY MOM'S BROTHER DIDN'T COME. MY MOM'S DAD OF COURSE WASN'T GOING TO COME. NO COUSINS, NO AUNTS. NO ONE...

STILL...THEY HAD EACH OTHER.

AND EVENTUALLY...

...THIS GUY CAME ALONG. MY BIG BRO, EDWARD. I KNOW, THE CUTENESS IS HEREDITARY.

MY DAD WASN'T THERE FOR EDWARD'S BIRTH. BY THEN HE HAD TO MOVE BACK TO NIGERIA TO GRADUATE, WORK, AND HELP GET A VISA FOR MY MOM AND EDWARD TO GET TO HIM.

AND IT'D BE A FEW YEARS BEFORE HE WOULD FINALLY MEET HIS FIRSTBORN SON.

BUT IN THE MEANTIME...

...AS YOU COULD PROBABLY GUESS, DEDUSHKA *REALLY* WASN'T HAPPY.

HE WAS A REAL TOUGH GUY. FLEW JETS IN THE SIXTIES AND SEVENTIES FOR THE SOVIET UNION.

‹I'M NOT TOUCHING A BLACK BABY.›

SO HE MEANT BUSINESS WHEN HE SAID SOMETHING.

29

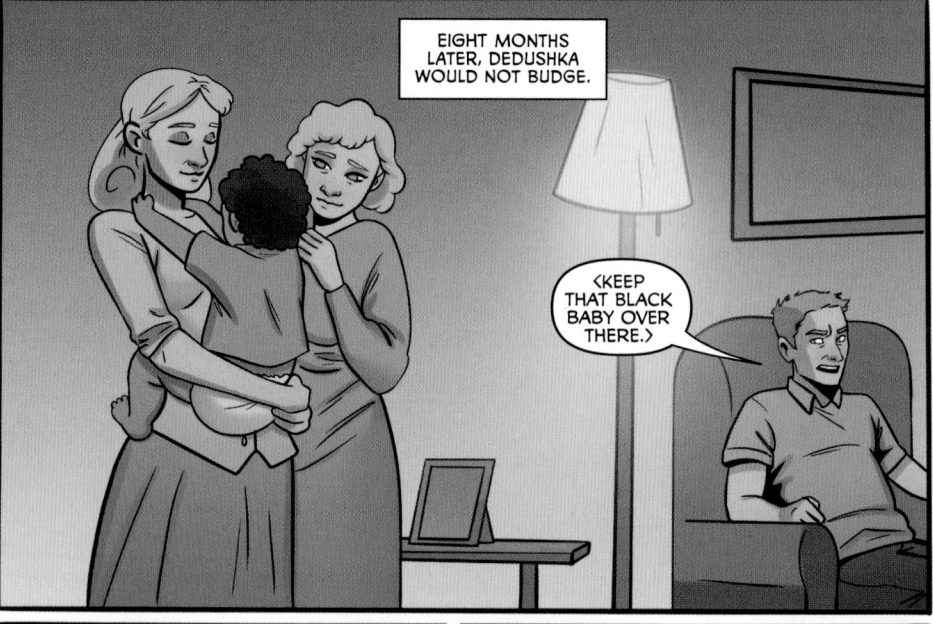

EIGHT MONTHS LATER, DEDUSHKA WOULD NOT BUDGE.

⟨KEEP THAT BLACK BABY OVER THERE.⟩

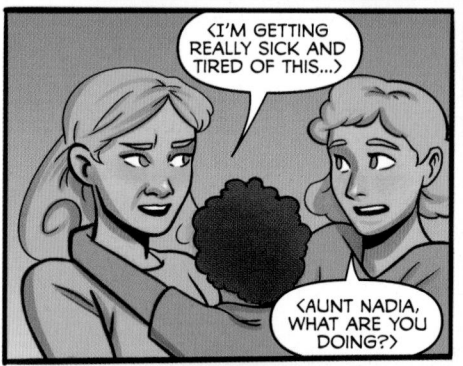

⟨I'M GETTING REALLY SICK AND TIRED OF THIS...⟩

⟨AUNT NADIA, WHAT ARE YOU DOING?⟩

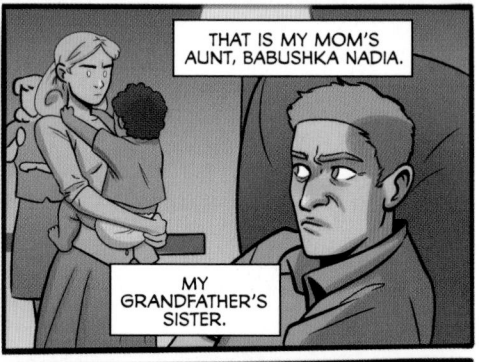

THAT IS MY MOM'S AUNT, BABUSHKA NADIA.

MY GRANDFATHER'S SISTER.

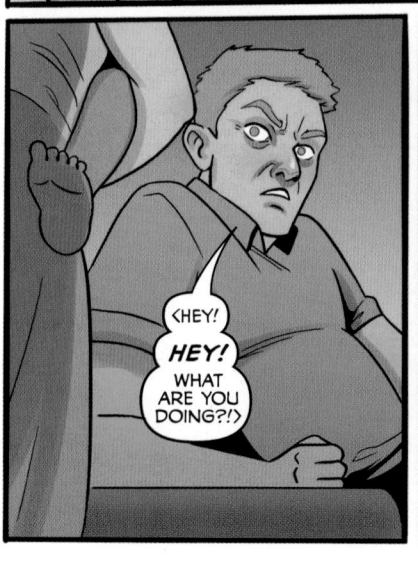

⟨HEY!

HEY!

WHAT ARE YOU DOING?!⟩

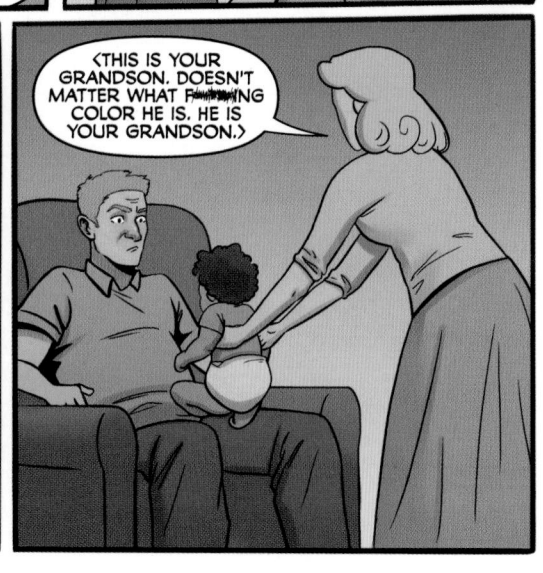

⟨THIS IS YOUR GRANDSON. DOESN'T MATTER WHAT F̶̶̶̶̶̶ING COLOR HE IS, HE IS YOUR GRANDSON.⟩

HEH!
HE NEVER PUT HIM DOWN AGAIN. DEDUSHKA FELL IN LOVE WITH HIM.

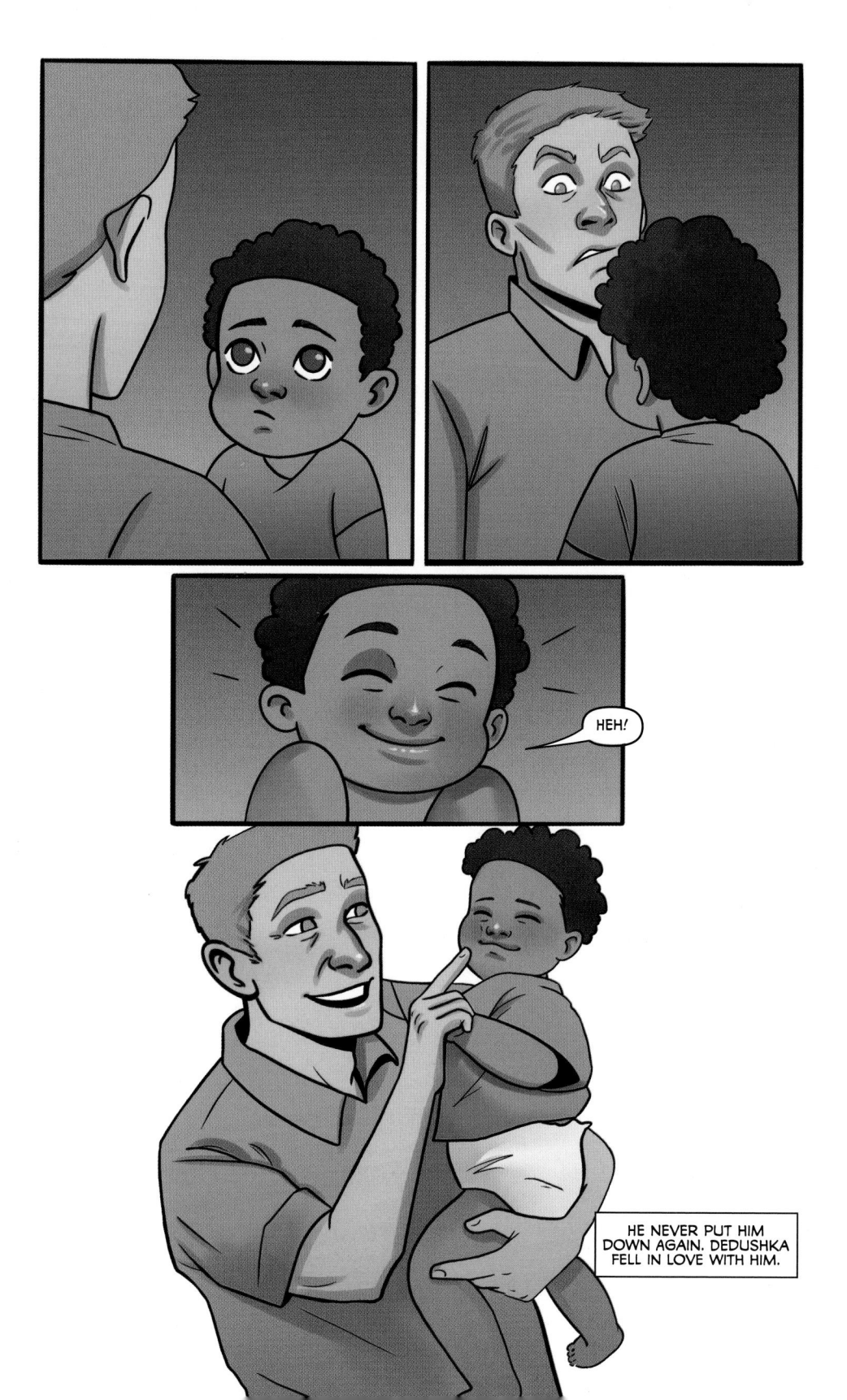

WHILE IT WASN'T OVERNIGHT, AS YEARS PASSED, MY GRANDFATHER EVENTUALLY GOT TO KNOW MY DAD, AND HIS GRANDCHILDREN.

SOMETHING IN HIS HEART CHANGED.

AND WHEN MY PARENTS NEEDED MONEY TO START A LIFE IN CANADA IN 1996, MY GRANDFATHER SOLD THE APARTMENT THAT HAD BEEN GIVEN TO HIM AFTER HIS MILITARY CAREER ENDED.

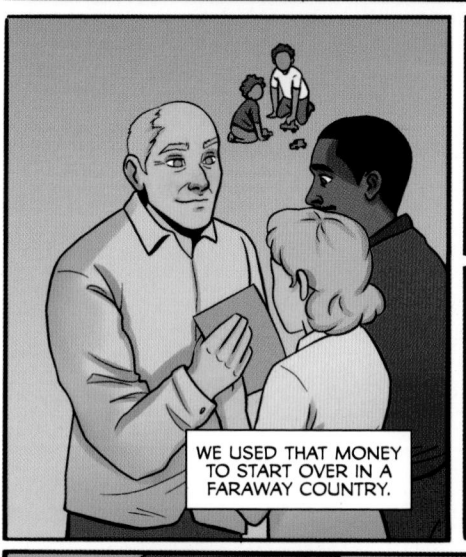

WE USED THAT MONEY TO START OVER IN A FARAWAY COUNTRY.

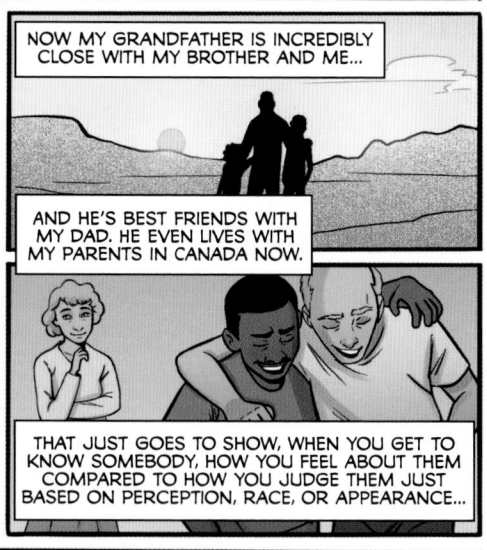

NOW MY GRANDFATHER IS INCREDIBLY CLOSE WITH MY BROTHER AND ME...

AND HE'S BEST FRIENDS WITH MY DAD. HE EVEN LIVES WITH MY PARENTS IN CANADA NOW.

THAT JUST GOES TO SHOW, WHEN YOU GET TO KNOW SOMEBODY, HOW YOU FEEL ABOUT THEM COMPARED TO HOW YOU JUDGE THEM JUST BASED ON PERCEPTION, RACE, OR APPEARANCE...

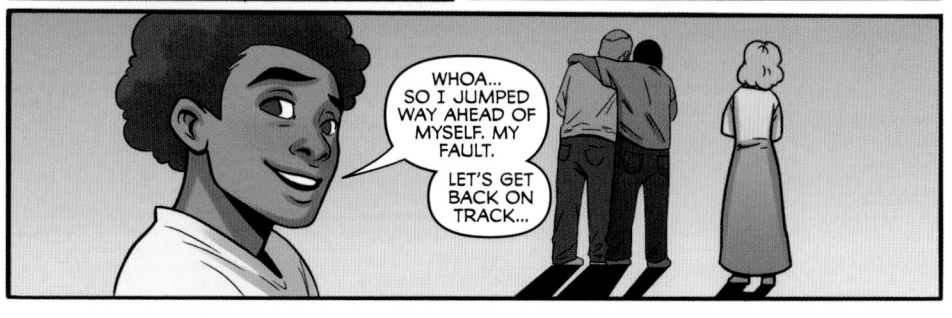

WHOA... SO I JUMPED WAY AHEAD OF MYSELF. MY FAULT.

LET'S GET BACK ON TRACK...

IN 1987, MY MOM AND EDWARD MOVED TO NIGERIA.
MY DAD'S HOMELAND.
WHEN THEY ARRIVED, MY DAD HAD BEEN WAITING ANXIOUSLY AT THE AIRPORT FOR TWO HOURS TO BE REUNITED WITH THE LOVE OF HIS LIFE AND TO MEET HIS SON FOR THE FIRST TIME.
TAI, THIS IS YOUR SON. EDWARD, MEET YOUR FATHER.
HELLO THERE, MY SON. IT'S SO GOOD TO FINALLY MEET YOU.

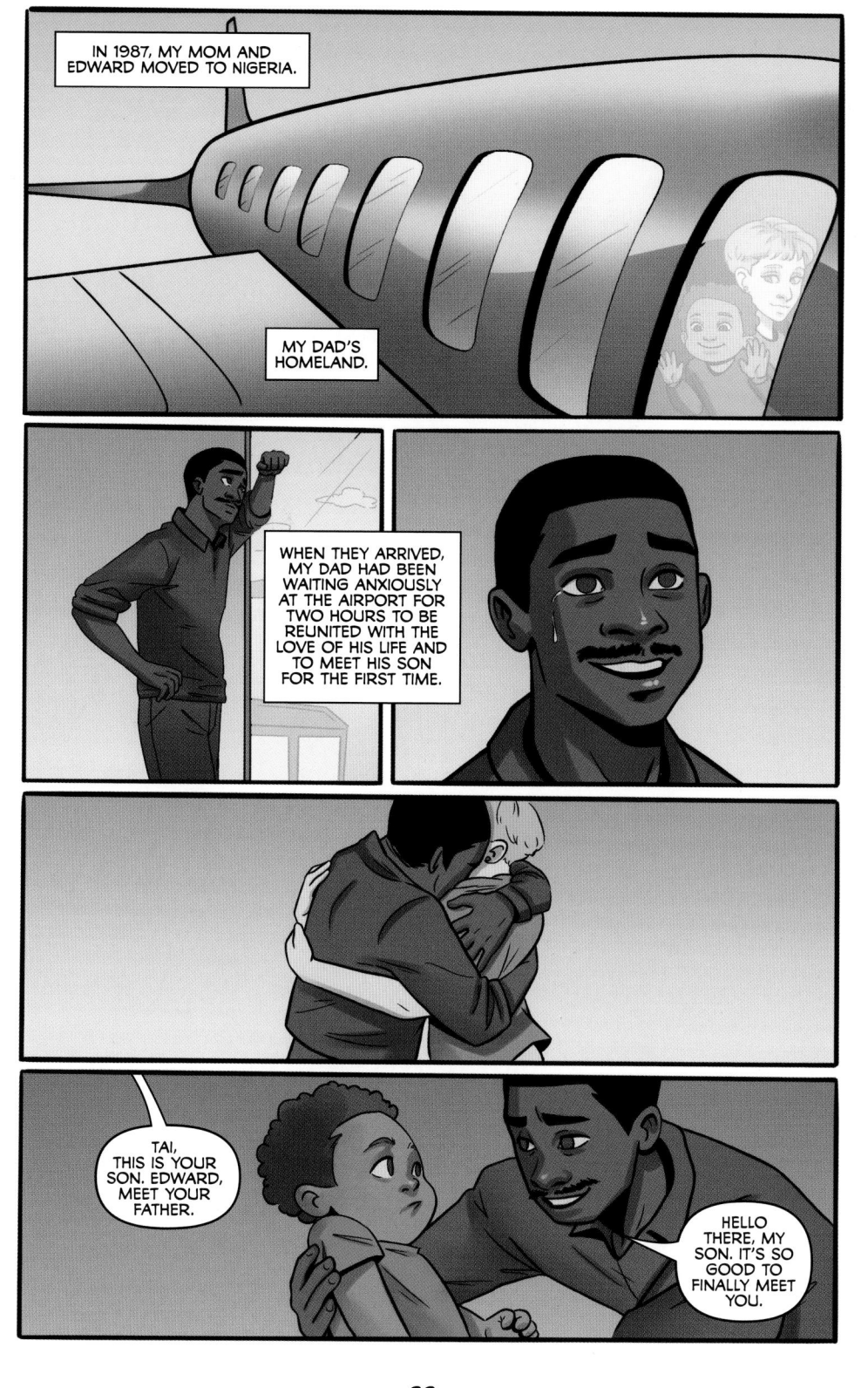

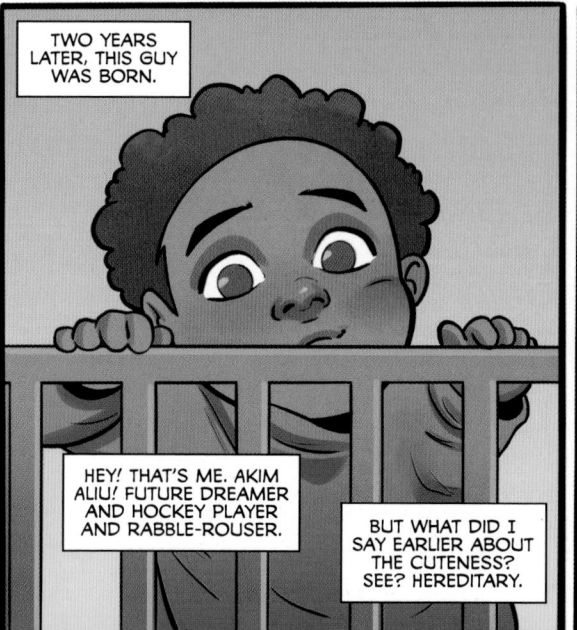

TWO YEARS LATER, THIS GUY WAS BORN.

HEY! THAT'S ME. AKIM ALIU! FUTURE DREAMER AND HOCKEY PLAYER AND RABBLE-ROUSER.

BUT WHAT DID I SAY EARLIER ABOUT THE CUTENESS? SEE? HEREDITARY.

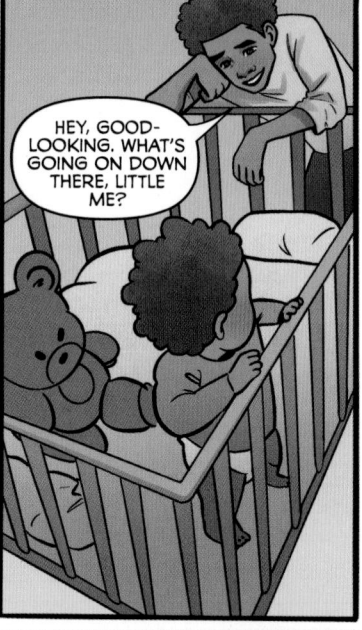

HEY, GOOD-LOOKING. WHAT'S GOING ON DOWN THERE, LITTLE ME?

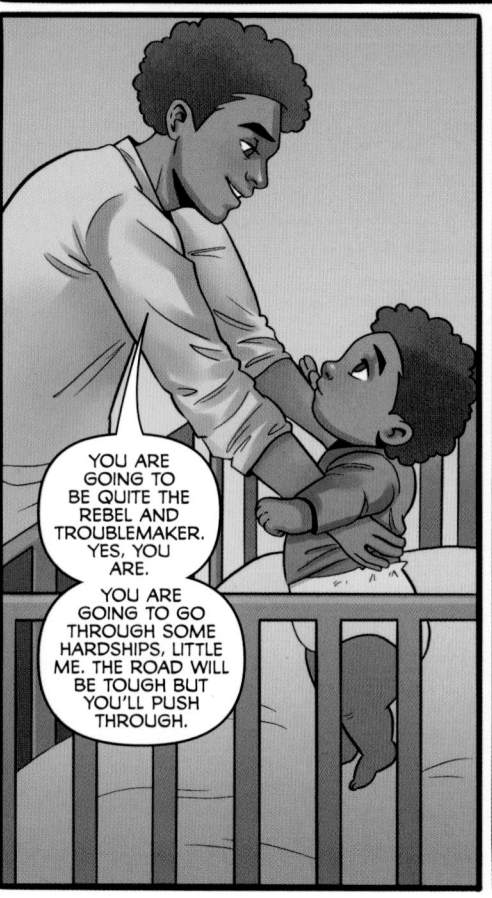

YOU ARE GOING TO BE QUITE THE REBEL AND TROUBLEMAKER. YES, YOU ARE.

YOU ARE GOING TO GO THROUGH SOME HARDSHIPS, LITTLE ME. THE ROAD WILL BE TOUGH BUT YOU'LL PUSH THROUGH.

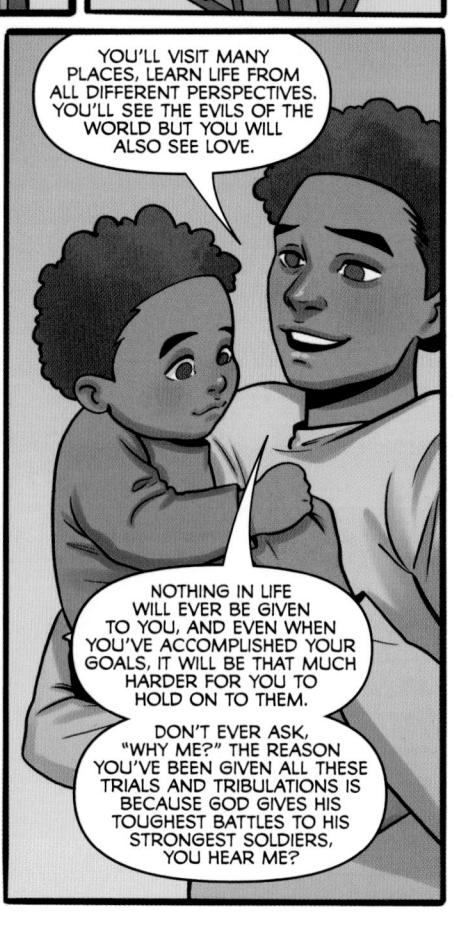

YOU'LL VISIT MANY PLACES, LEARN LIFE FROM ALL DIFFERENT PERSPECTIVES. YOU'LL SEE THE EVILS OF THE WORLD BUT YOU WILL ALSO SEE LOVE.

NOTHING IN LIFE WILL EVER BE GIVEN TO YOU, AND EVEN WHEN YOU'VE ACCOMPLISHED YOUR GOALS, IT WILL BE THAT MUCH HARDER FOR YOU TO HOLD ON TO THEM.

DON'T EVER ASK, "WHY ME?" THE REASON YOU'VE BEEN GIVEN ALL THESE TRIALS AND TRIBULATIONS IS BECAUSE GOD GIVES HIS TOUGHEST BATTLES TO HIS STRONGEST SOLDIERS, YOU HEAR ME?

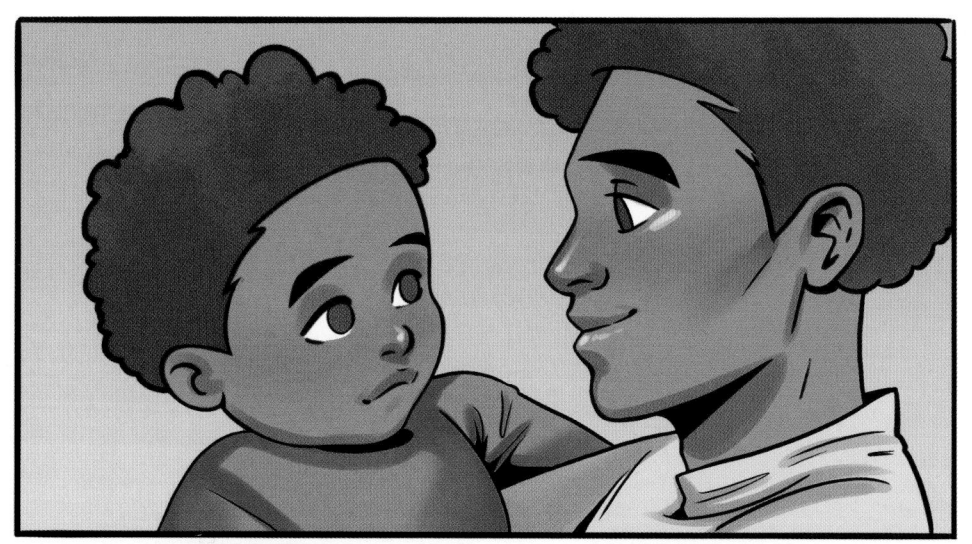

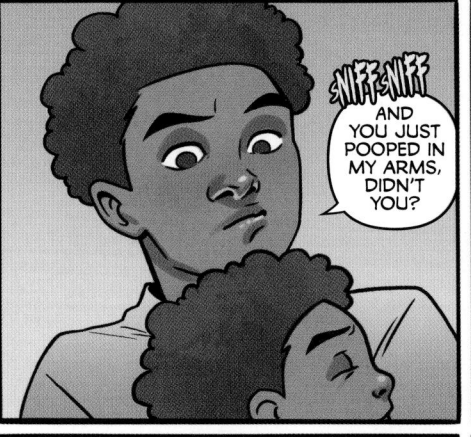

SNIFF SNIFF
AND YOU JUST POOPED IN MY ARMS, DIDN'T YOU?

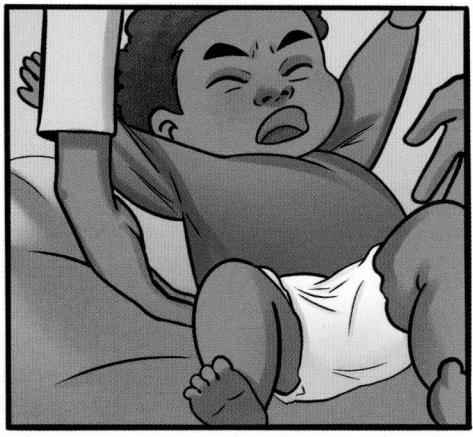

SHH SHH SHH! IT'S OKAY, AKIM! I'M HERE.

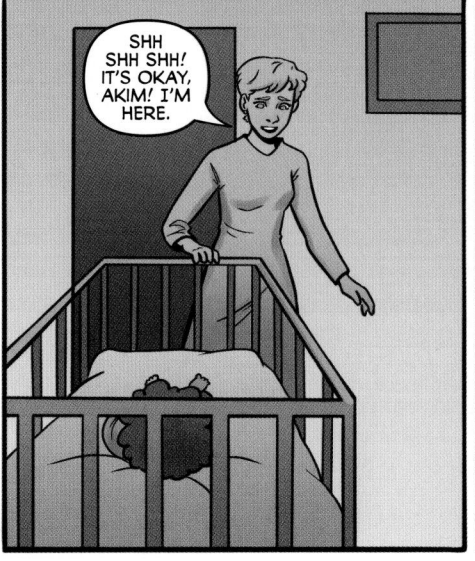

OH! YOU MADE QUITE THE STINK BOMB, DIDN'T YOU?

NOPE. YOUR FATHER IS DEALING WITH THIS ONE, NOT ME!

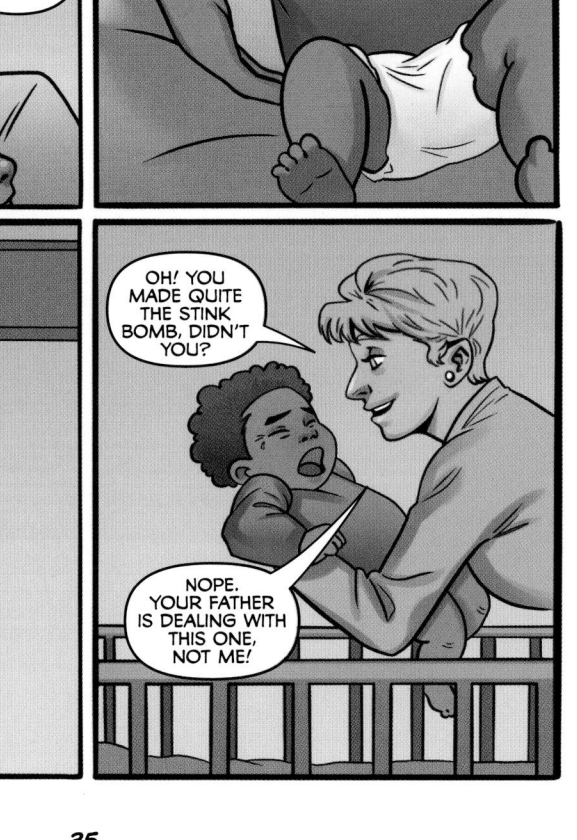

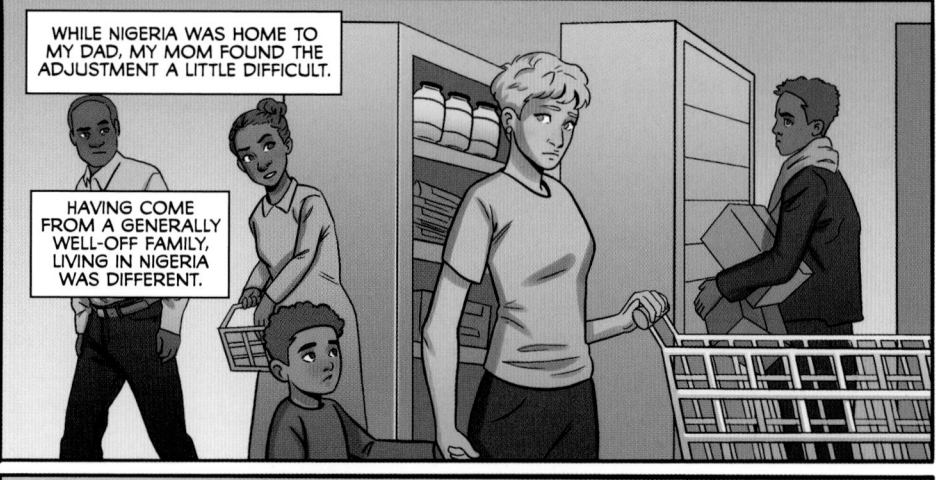

WHILE NIGERIA WAS HOME TO MY DAD, MY MOM FOUND THE ADJUSTMENT A LITTLE DIFFICULT.

HAVING COME FROM A GENERALLY WELL-OFF FAMILY, LIVING IN NIGERIA WAS DIFFERENT.

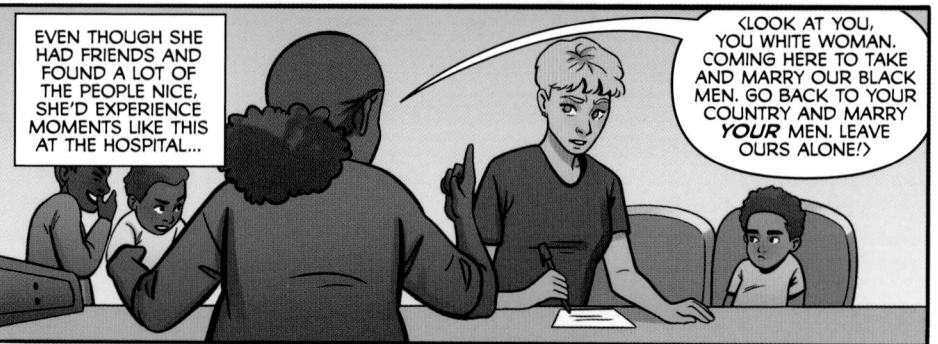

EVEN THOUGH SHE HAD FRIENDS AND FOUND A LOT OF THE PEOPLE NICE, SHE'D EXPERIENCE MOMENTS LIKE THIS AT THE HOSPITAL...

‹LOOK AT YOU, YOU WHITE WOMAN. COMING HERE TO TAKE AND MARRY OUR BLACK MEN. GO BACK TO YOUR COUNTRY AND MARRY *YOUR* MEN. LEAVE OURS ALONE!›

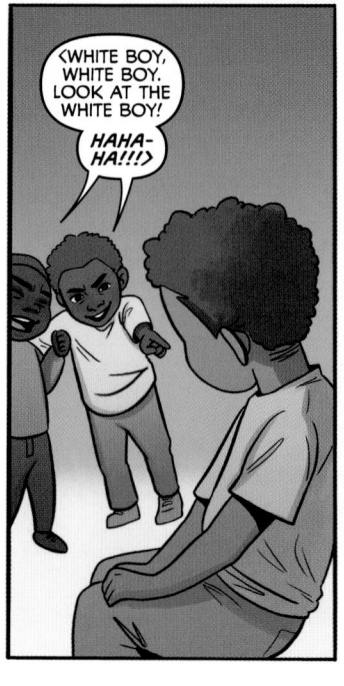

‹WHITE BOY, WHITE BOY. LOOK AT THE WHITE BOY!

HAHA-HA!!!›

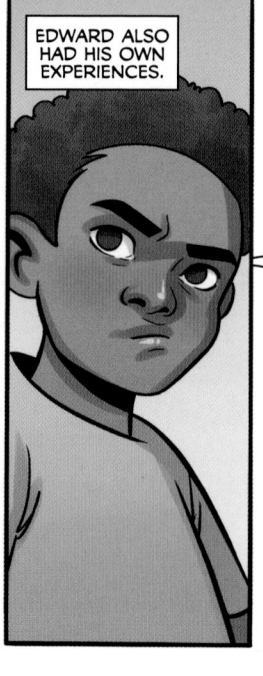

EDWARD ALSO HAD HIS OWN EXPERIENCES.

MOM HAD TO DEAL WITH SITUATIONS LIKE THIS...

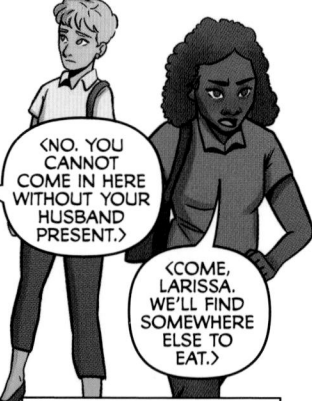

‹NO. YOU CANNOT COME IN HERE WITHOUT YOUR HUSBAND PRESENT.›

‹COME, LARISSA. WE'LL FIND SOMEWHERE ELSE TO EAT.›

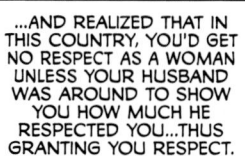

...AND REALIZED THAT IN THIS COUNTRY, YOU'D GET NO RESPECT AS A WOMAN UNLESS YOUR HUSBAND WAS AROUND TO SHOW YOU HOW MUCH HE RESPECTED YOU...THUS GRANTING YOU RESPECT.

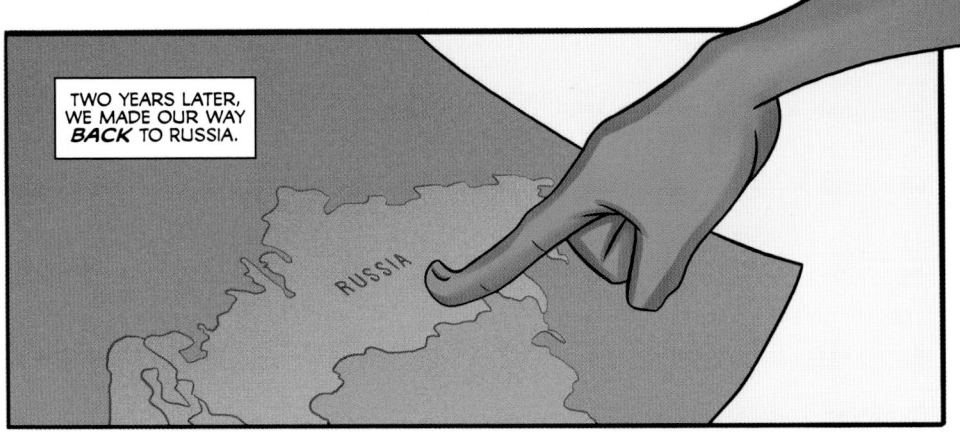

TWO YEARS LATER, WE MADE OUR WAY *BACK* TO RUSSIA.

RUSSIA

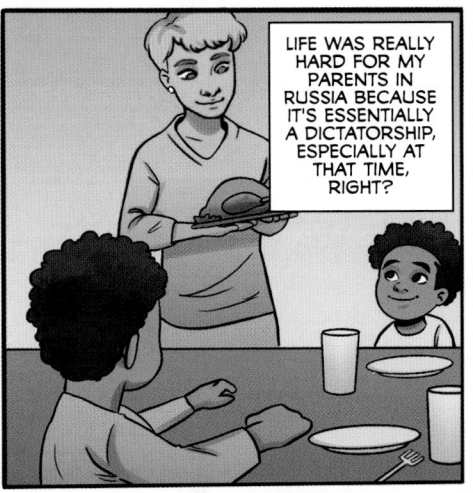

LIFE WAS REALLY HARD FOR MY PARENTS IN RUSSIA BECAUSE IT'S ESSENTIALLY A DICTATORSHIP, ESPECIALLY AT THAT TIME, RIGHT?

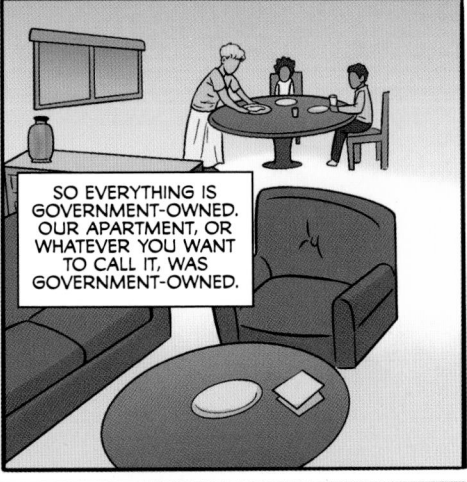

SO EVERYTHING IS GOVERNMENT-OWNED. OUR APARTMENT, OR WHATEVER YOU WANT TO CALL IT, WAS GOVERNMENT-OWNED.

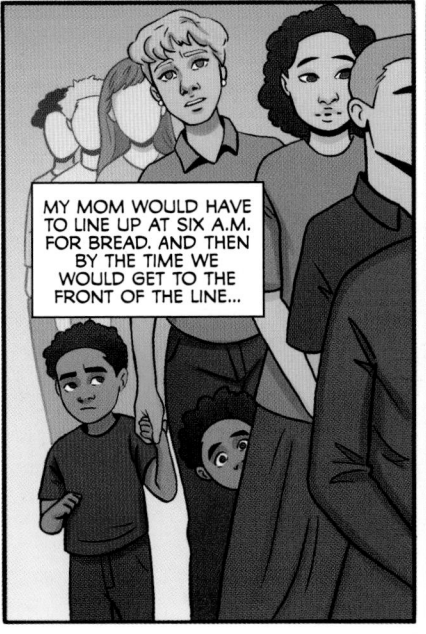

MY MOM WOULD HAVE TO LINE UP AT SIX A.M. FOR BREAD. AND THEN BY THE TIME WE WOULD GET TO THE FRONT OF THE LINE...

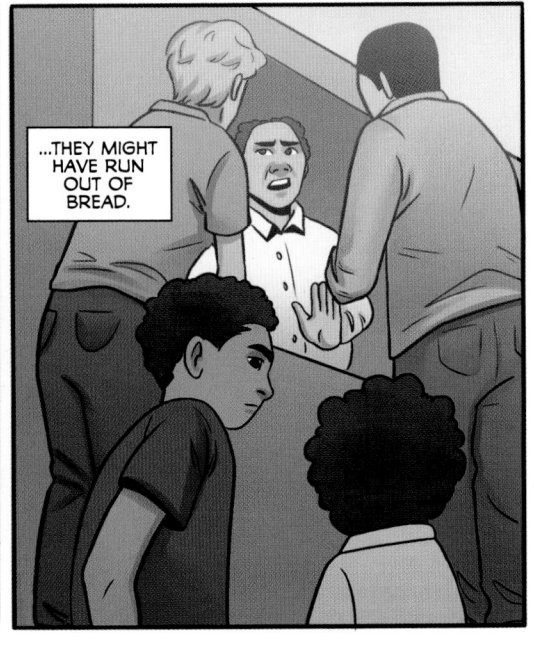

...THEY MIGHT HAVE RUN OUT OF BREAD.

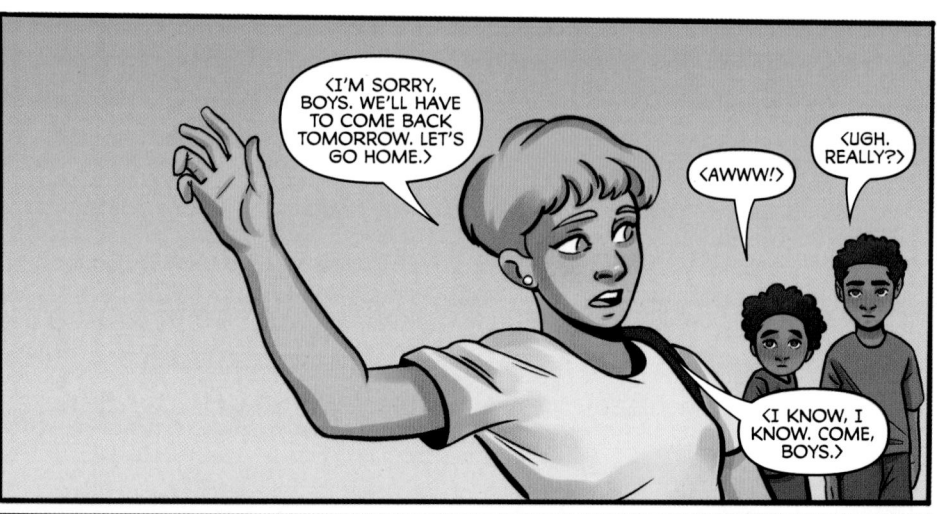

<I'M SORRY, BOYS. WE'LL HAVE TO COME BACK TOMORROW. LET'S GO HOME.>

<AWWW!>

<UGH. REALLY?>

<I KNOW, I KNOW. COME, BOYS.>

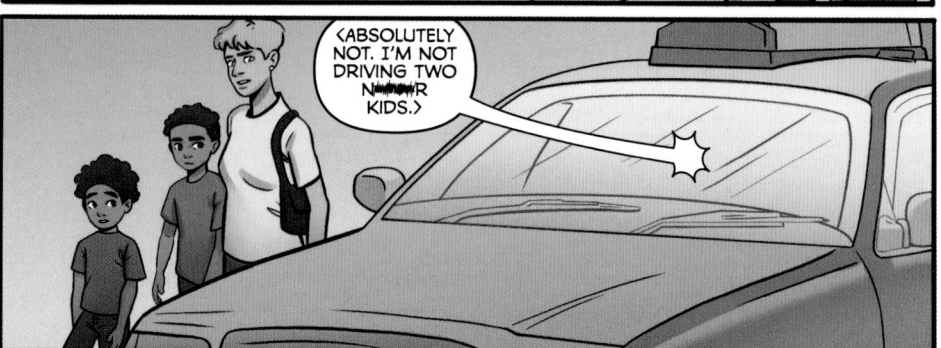

<ABSOLUTELY NOT. I'M NOT DRIVING TWO N▓▓▓R KIDS.>

<EXCUSE ME?! YOU PIECE OF→>

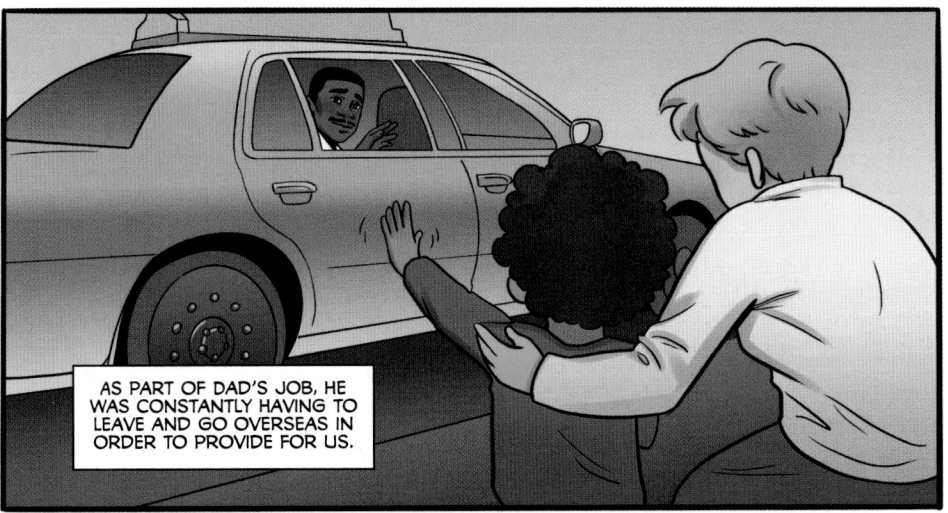

AS PART OF DAD'S JOB, HE WAS CONSTANTLY HAVING TO LEAVE AND GO OVERSEAS IN ORDER TO PROVIDE FOR US.

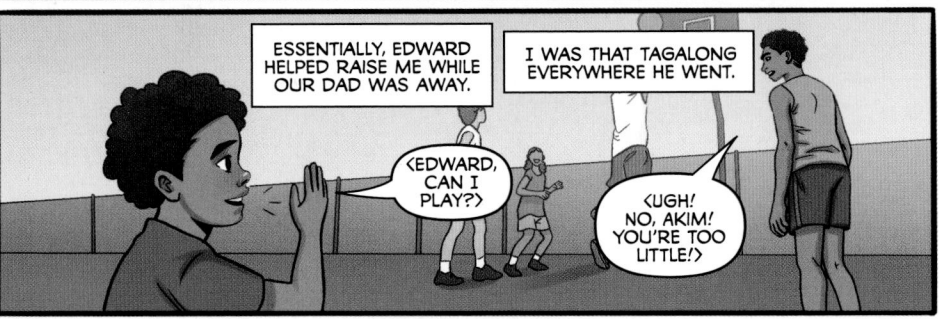

ESSENTIALLY, EDWARD HELPED RAISE ME WHILE OUR DAD WAS AWAY.

I WAS THAT TAGALONG EVERYWHERE HE WENT.

<EDWARD, CAN I PLAY?>

<UGH! NO, AKIM! YOU'RE TOO LITTLE!>

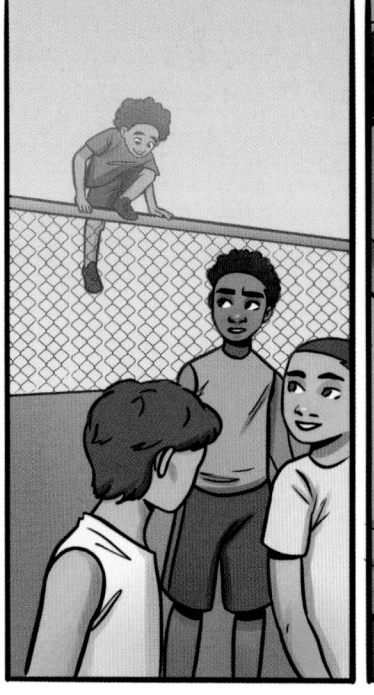

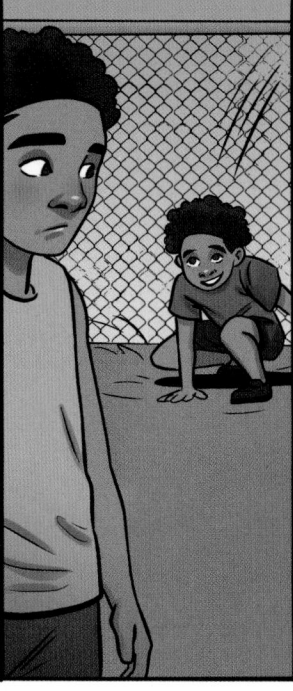

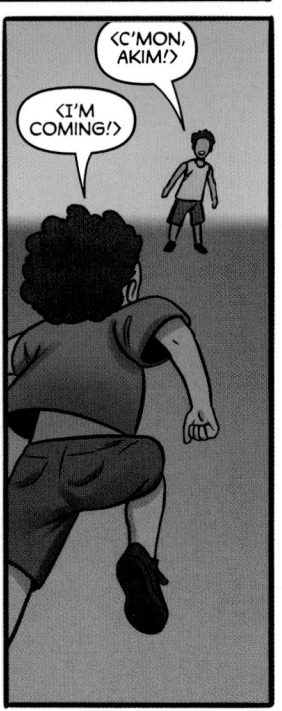

<C'MON, AKIM!>

<I'M COMING!>

<THEY JUST CAME UP FROM BEHIND ME. THEY TOOK THE MONEY. I'M SO SORRY. I TRIED TO FIGHT...>
<HUSH, HUSH. IT'S OKAY.>
<THIS JUST KEEPS HAPPENING, LARISSA. I DON'T KNOW HOW MUCH LONGER WE CAN TAKE THIS.>
WHILE SITUATIONS LIKE THAT WERE GOING ON, MY BROTHER DISTRACTED ME AND KEPT ME OCCUPIED.
WHOA! I FORGOT ALL ABOUT THIS.
AAA HAHA HA!!!
CAN YOU GUESS WHICH ONE IS ME?
THIS PICTURE SPEAKS A LOT OF WORDS, DOESN'T IT?

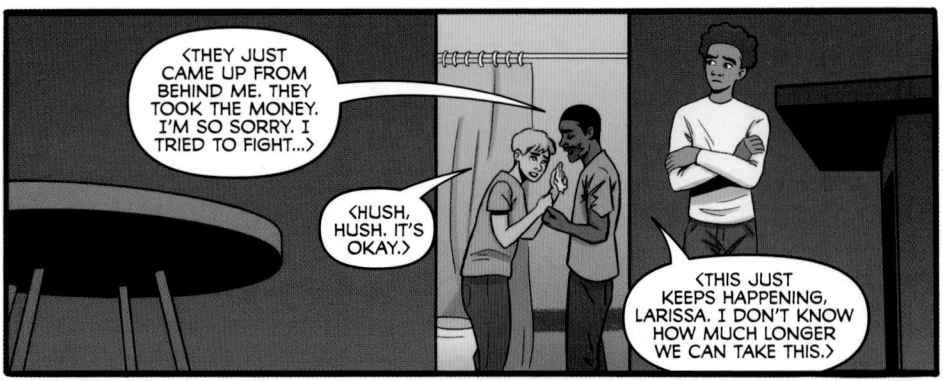

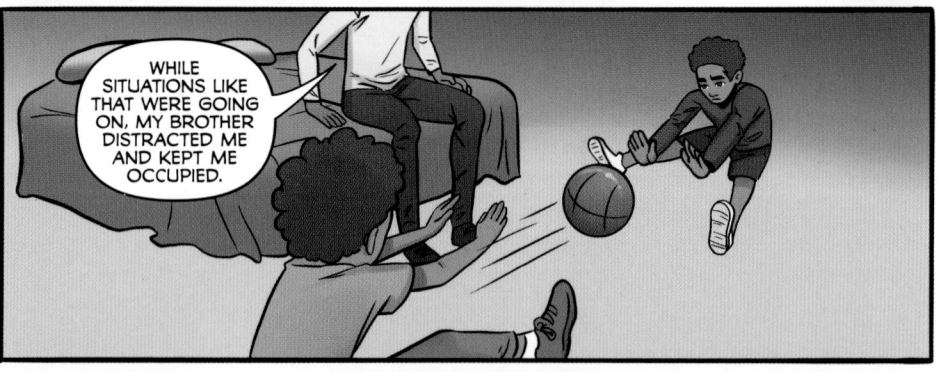

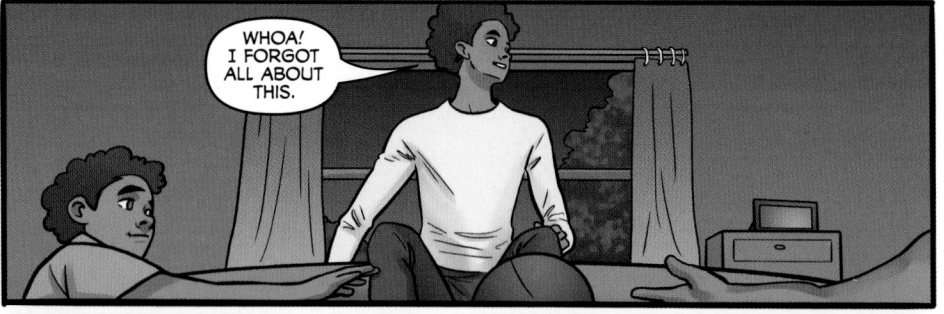

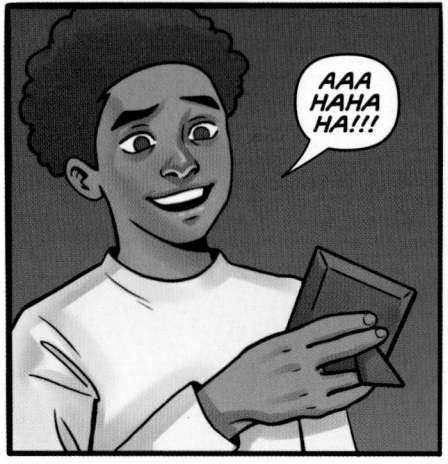

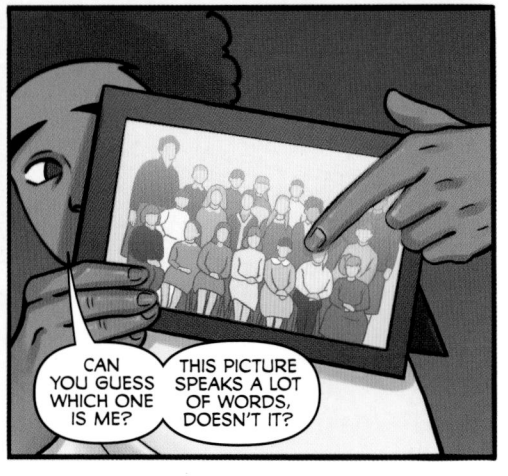

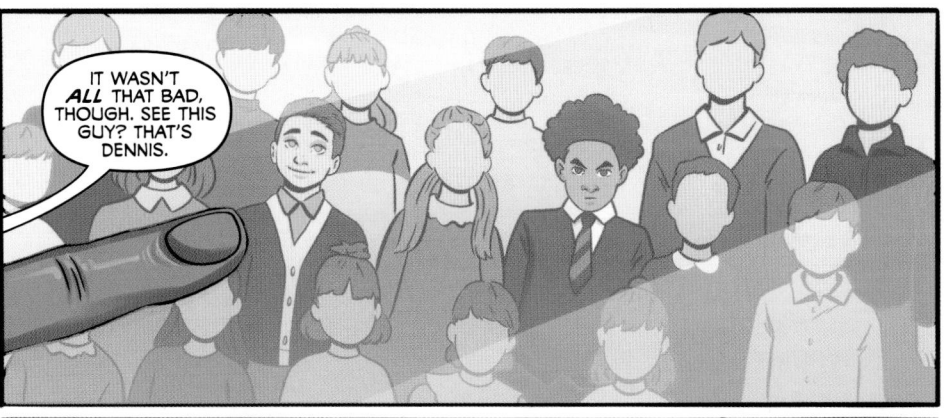

IT WASN'T *ALL* THAT BAD, THOUGH. SEE THIS GUY? THAT'S DENNIS.

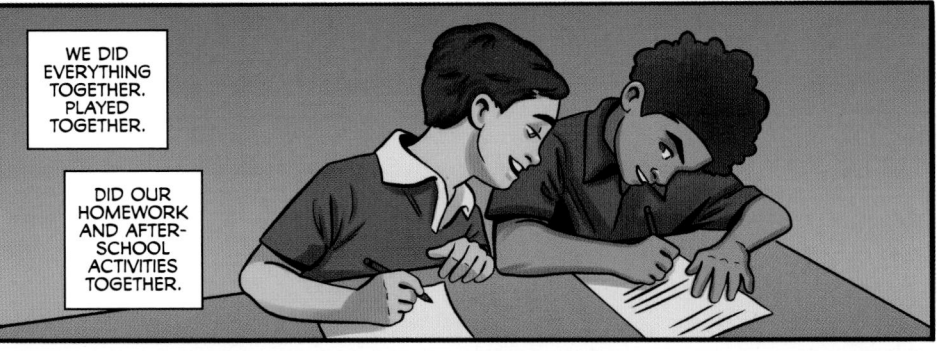

HE WAS MY BEST FRIEND.

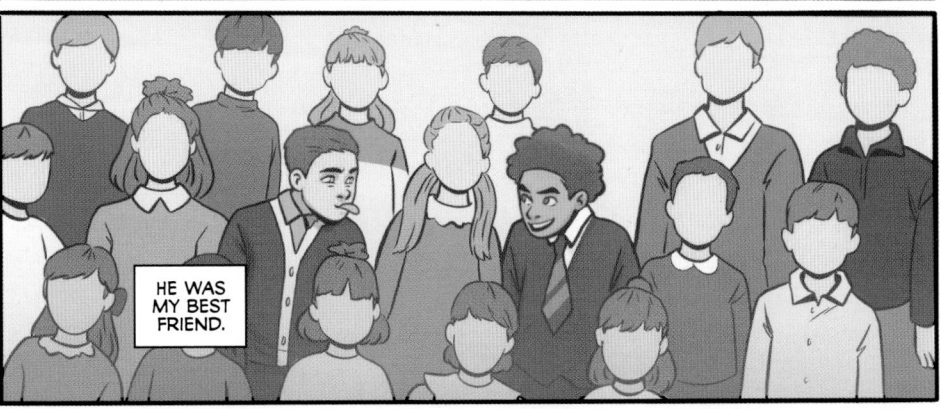

WE DID EVERYTHING TOGETHER. PLAYED TOGETHER.

DID OUR HOMEWORK AND AFTER-SCHOOL ACTIVITIES TOGETHER.

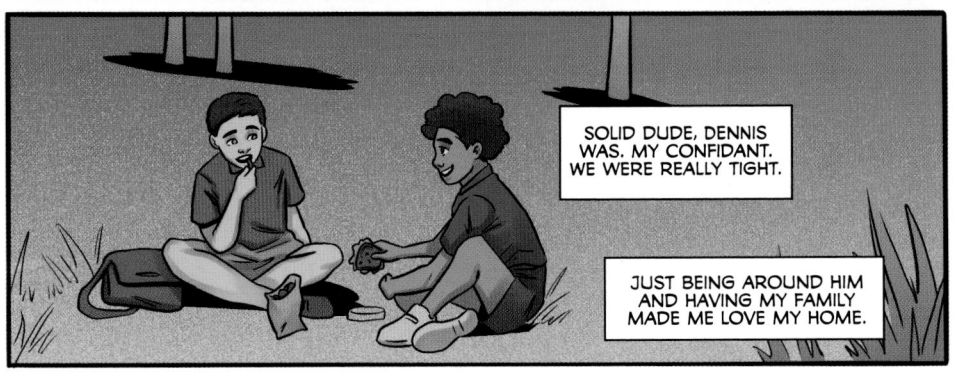

SOLID DUDE, DENNIS WAS. MY CONFIDANT. WE WERE REALLY TIGHT.

JUST BEING AROUND HIM AND HAVING MY FAMILY MADE ME LOVE MY HOME.

AS YOU SAW, EDWARD HAD HIS OWN SET OF FRIENDS AND INTERESTS.
BASKETBALL WAS HIS GO-TO, AND HE WAS DANG GREAT AT IT.
GAME, BABY! WHAT YOU THOUGHT WAS GOING TO HAPPEN?!
RUSSIA WAS ALL MY BROTHER AND I KNEW.
WE WERE GENERALLY HAPPY HERE...

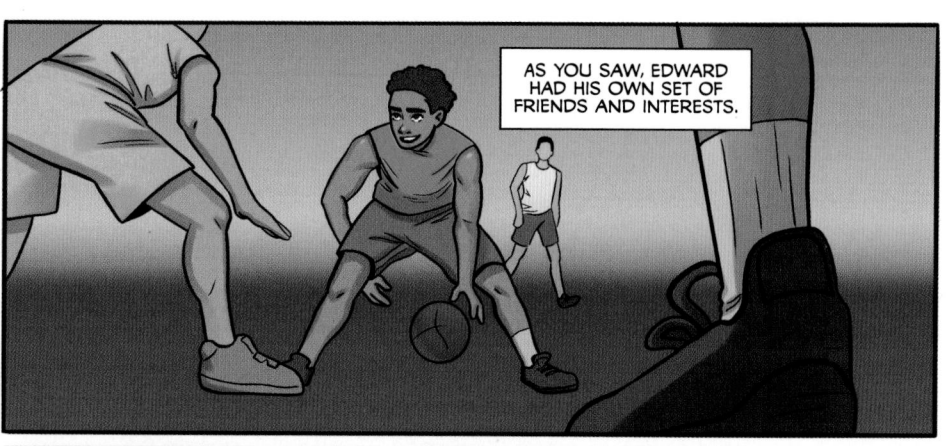

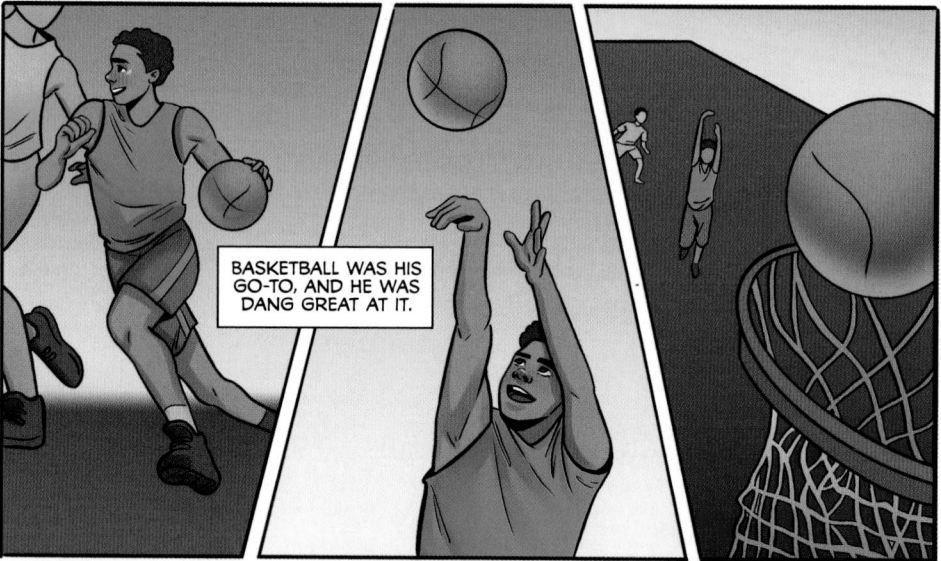

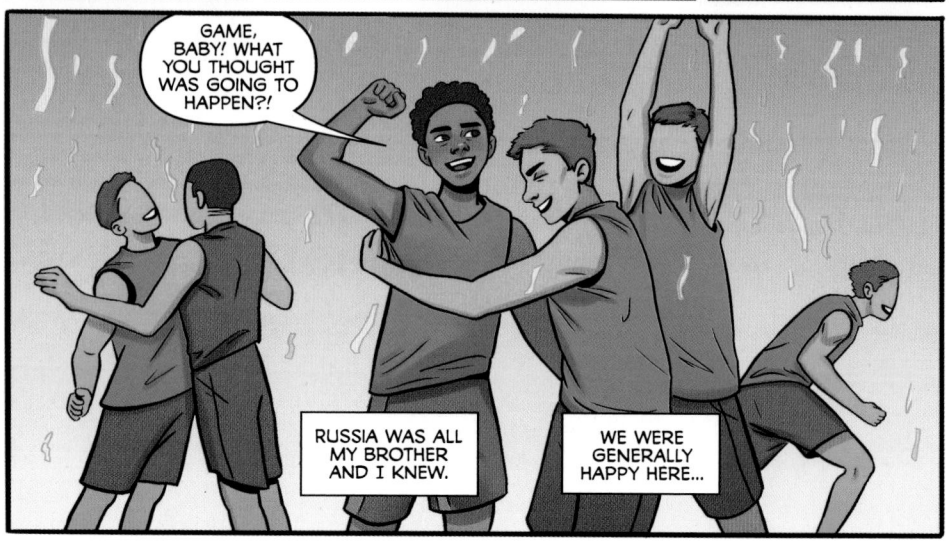

WE ARE MOVING TO CANADA.
YOU'VE GOT TO BE KIDDING ME...
?

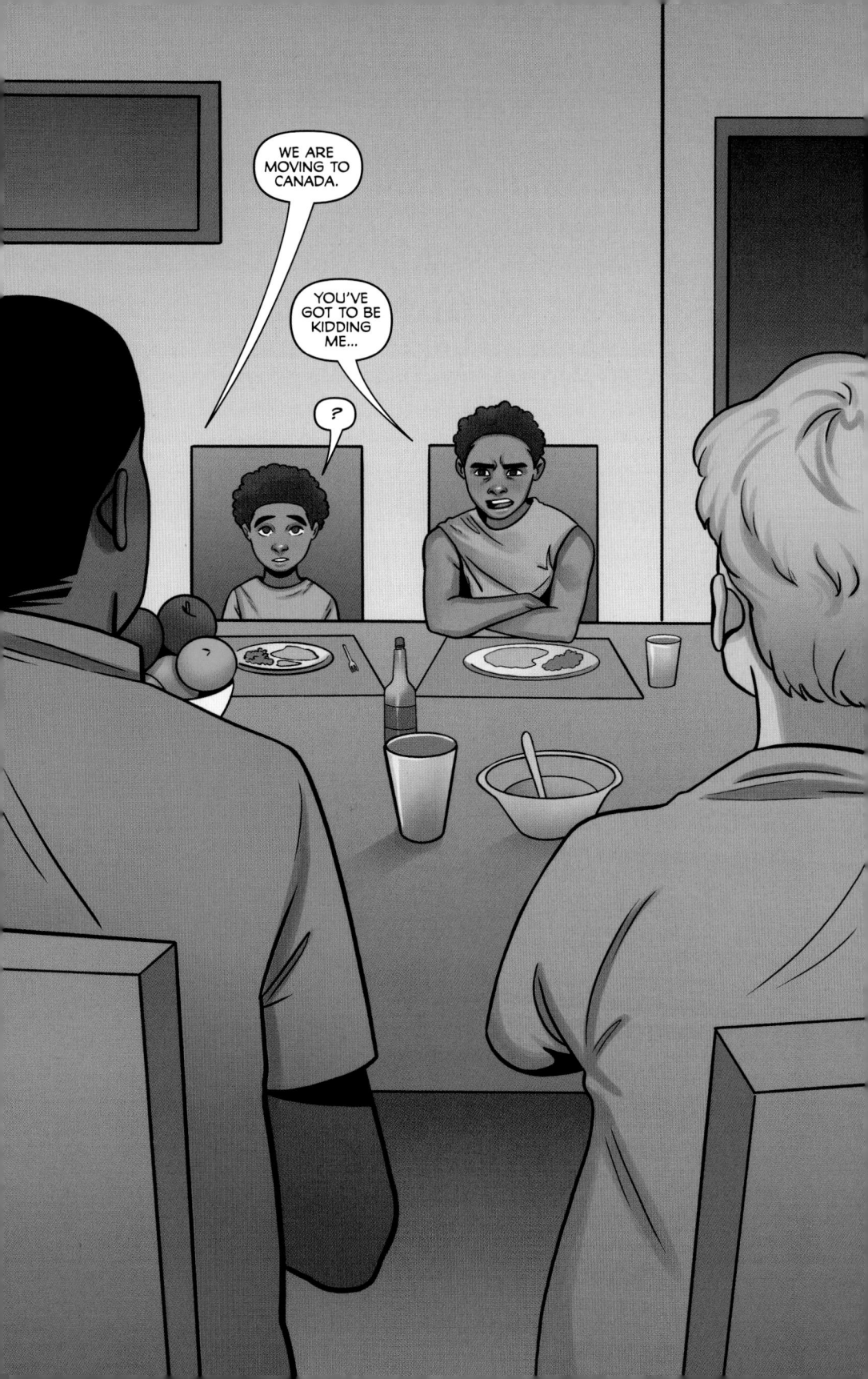

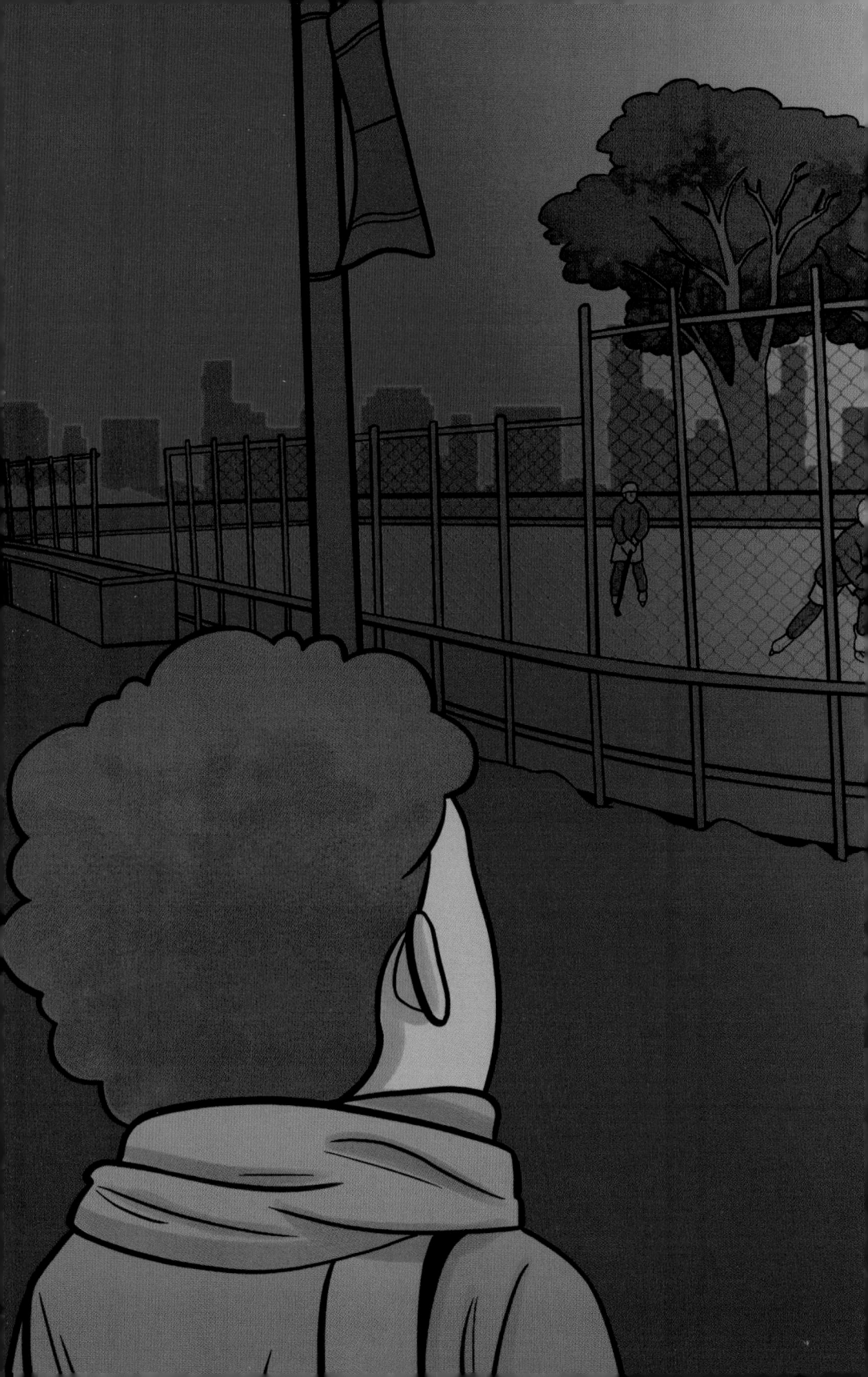

CHAPTER THREE

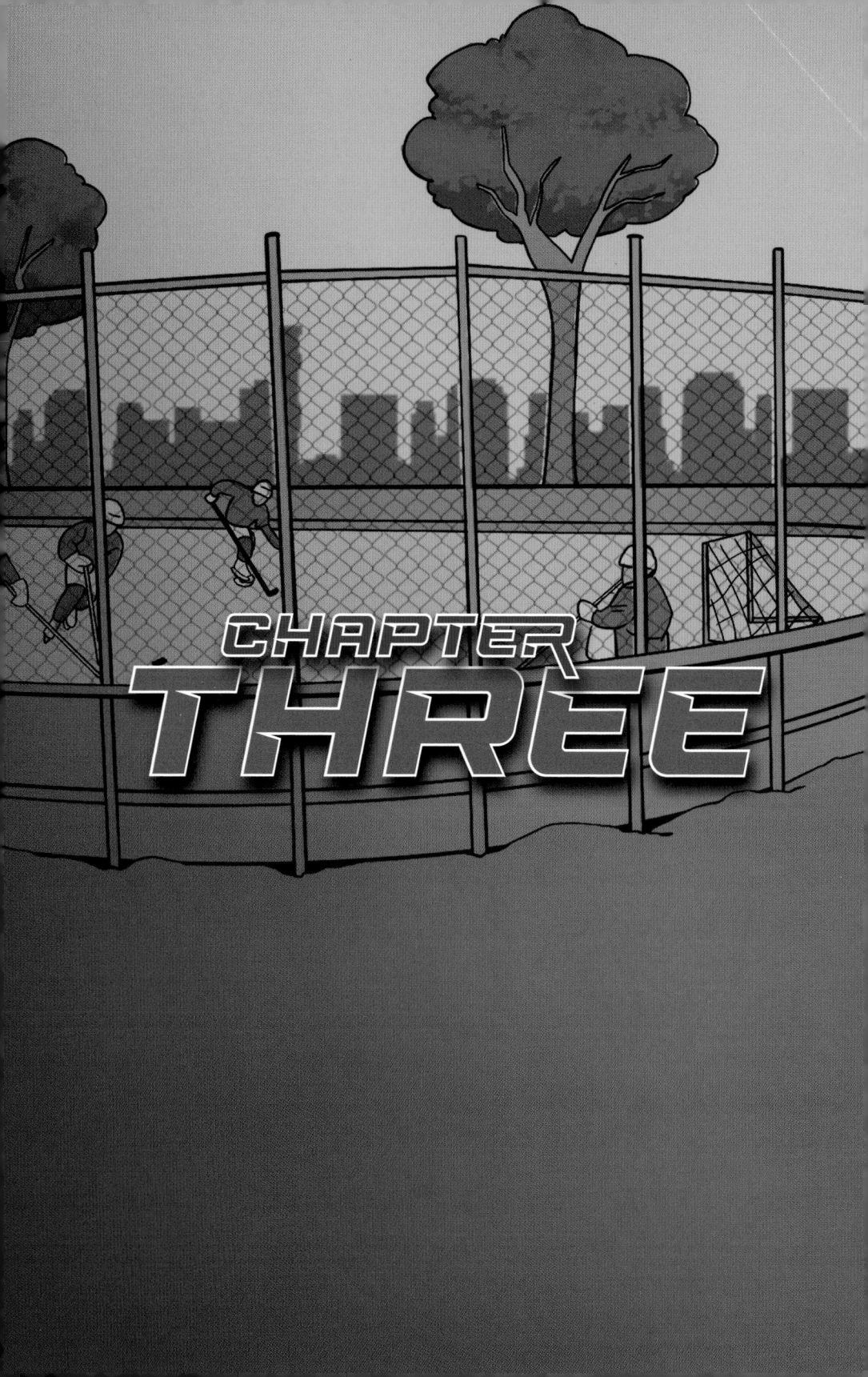

AS YOU CAN SEE, THAT NEWS HIT ME LIKE A PILLOWCASE FILLED WITH BRICKS.
MY MOM AND DAD WERE OBVIOUSLY HAPPY. THEY WORKED HARD FOR THIS AND GETTING THE PAPERWORK CAME RATHER SWIFTLY, SURPRISINGLY SO.
SECRETLY, EDWARD WAS PRAYING AND HOPING WE'D GET DENIED.
SO YOU CAN IMAGINE HIS DISAPPOINTMENT.
I JUST KEPT REPLAYING MY PARENTS' WORDS IN MY HEAD...
I KNOW THIS IS HOME, BUT NEITHER OF YOU HAS A FUTURE HERE. WE NEED TO LEAVE THIS COUNTRY FOR YOU TO BE ABLE TO ***SUCCEED AND PROSPER*** IN LIFE.
NO MATTER WHAT HAPPENS, YOUR MOTHER AND I ARE GOING TO BUILD A BETTER LIFE FOR THE TWO OF YOU.
NO MATTER WHAT...

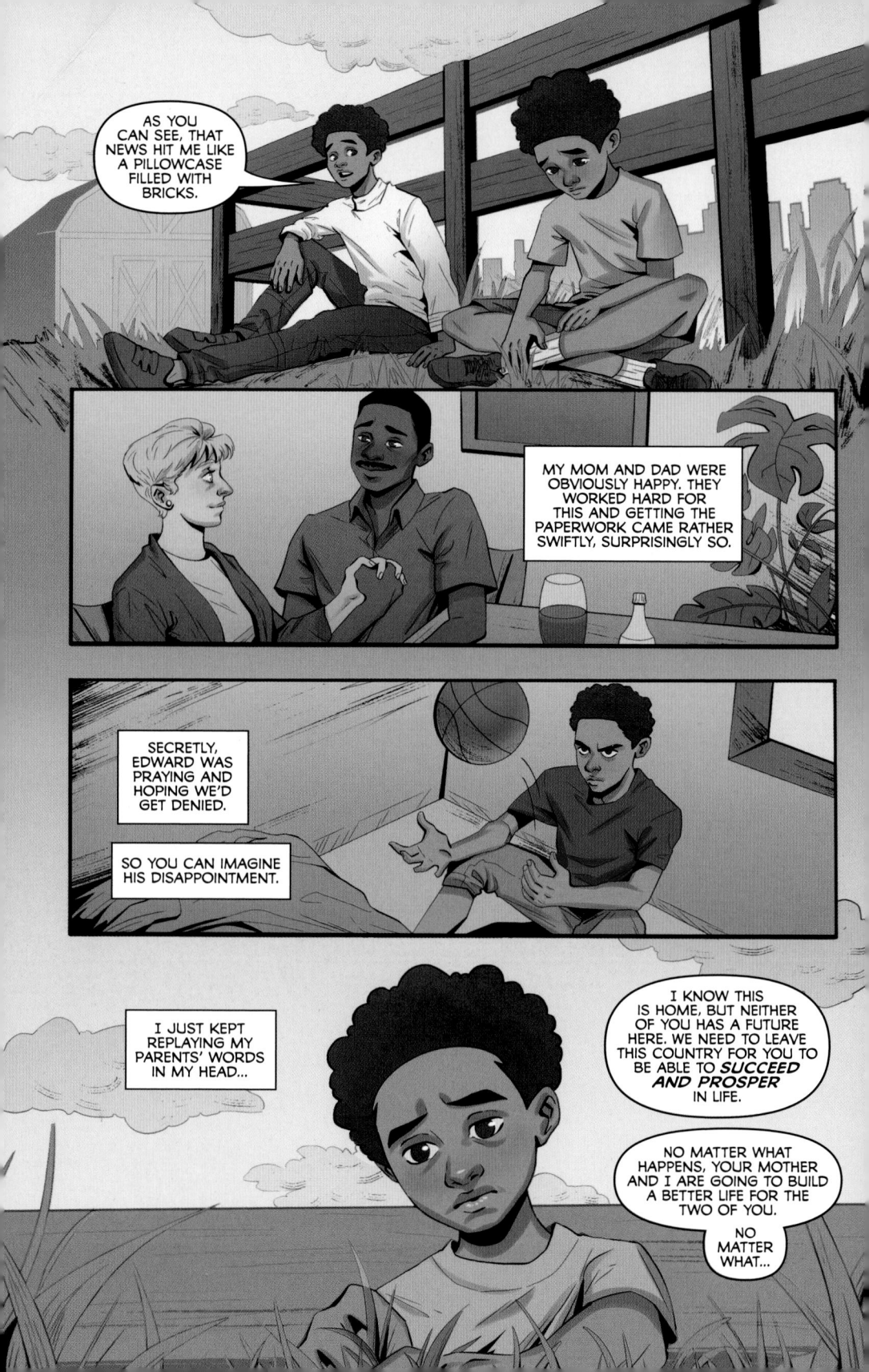

WHILE I WAS YOUNG, YEAH, I WAS ABLE TO UNDERSTAND *WHY* THIS NEEDED TO HAPPEN...
...IT DIDN'T MAKE IT HURT ANY LESS, THOUGH.
<HEY, YOU. COME HELP YOUR DEDUSHKA!>
DID GOING AWAY TO CANADA MEAN NOT SPENDING TIME WITH MY DEDUSHKA?
I LOVE MY DEDUSHKA.
WAS THIS GOING TO BE MY LAST TIME ON HIS FARM?

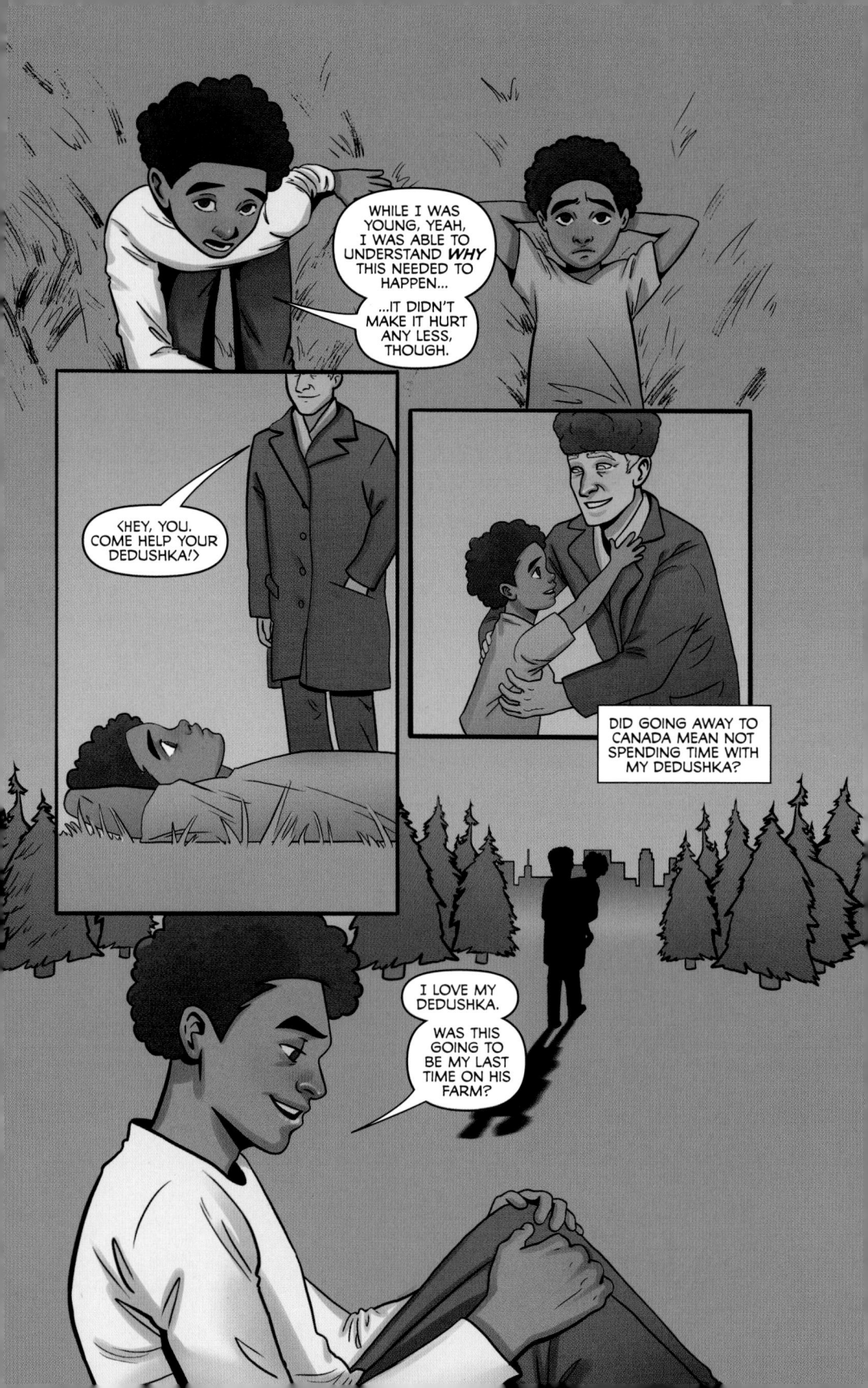

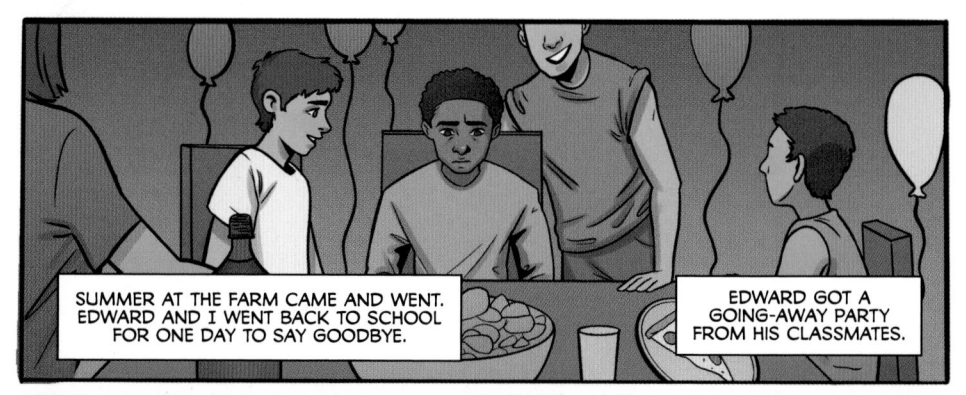

SUMMER AT THE FARM CAME AND WENT. EDWARD AND I WENT BACK TO SCHOOL FOR ONE DAY TO SAY GOODBYE.

EDWARD GOT A GOING-AWAY PARTY FROM HIS CLASSMATES.

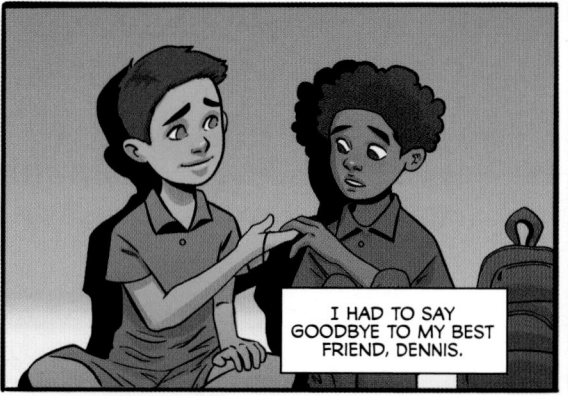

I HAD TO SAY GOODBYE TO MY BEST FRIEND, DENNIS.

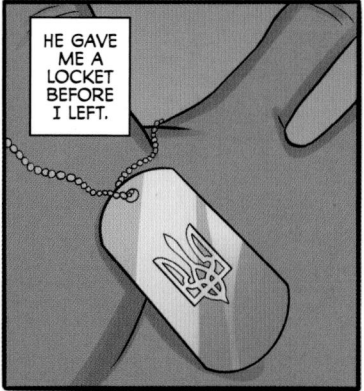

HE GAVE ME A LOCKET BEFORE I LEFT.

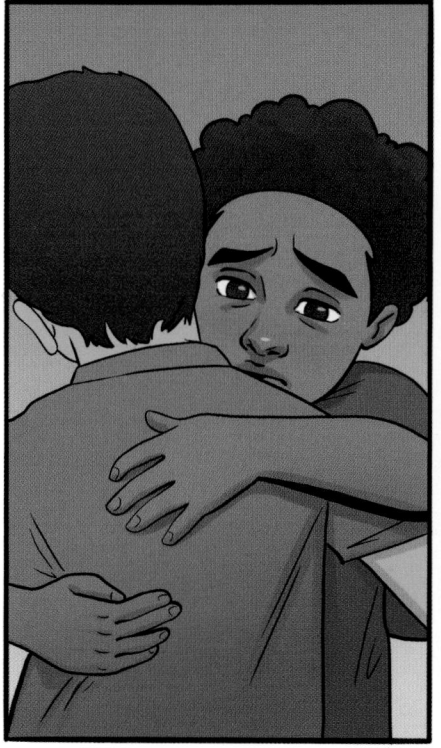

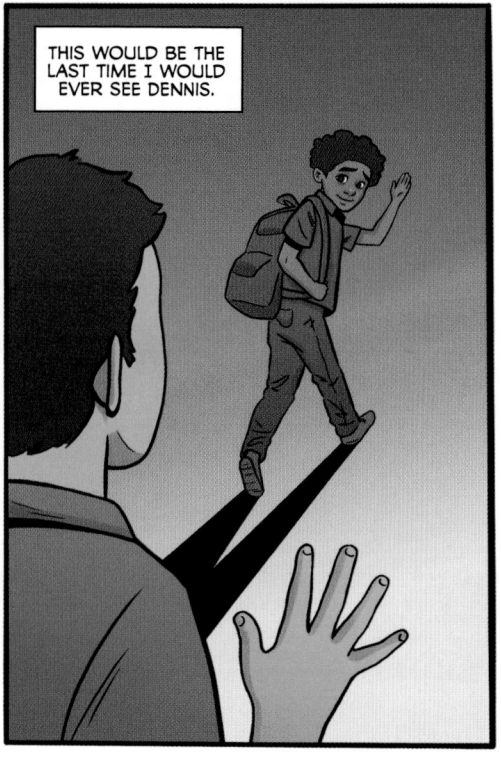

THIS WOULD BE THE LAST TIME I WOULD EVER SEE DENNIS.

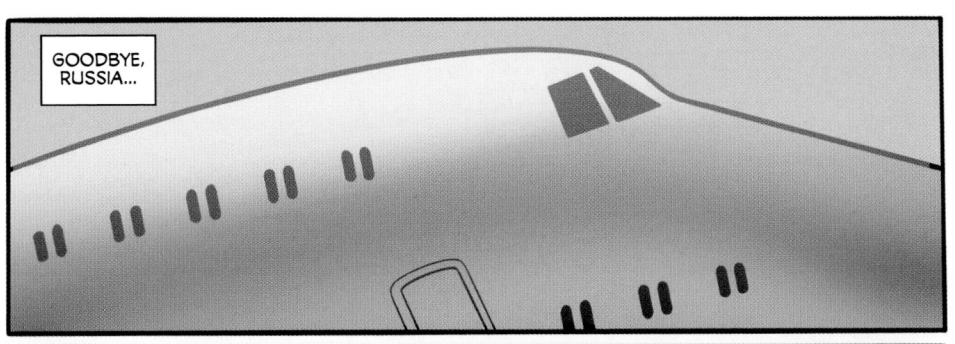

GOODBYE, RUSSIA...

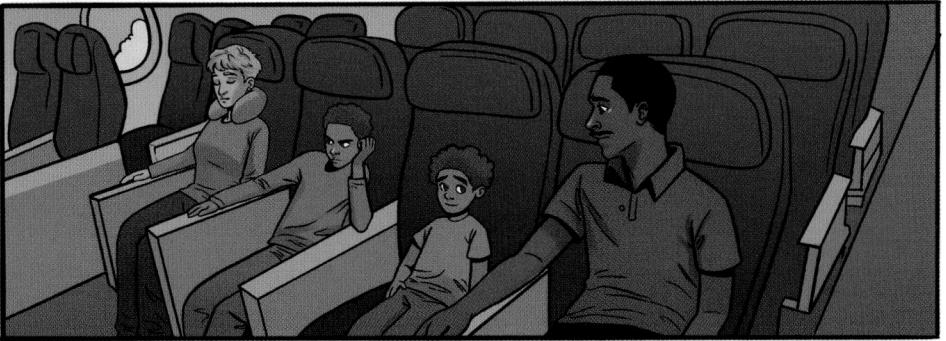

...

...CANADA...

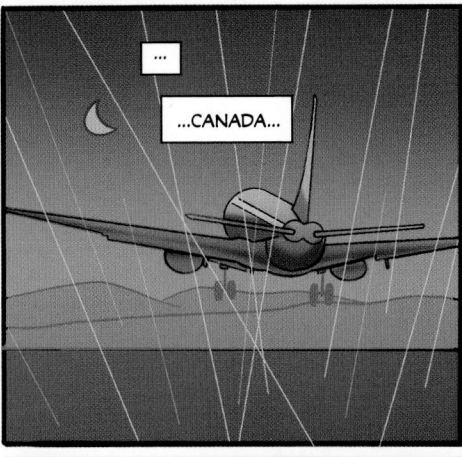

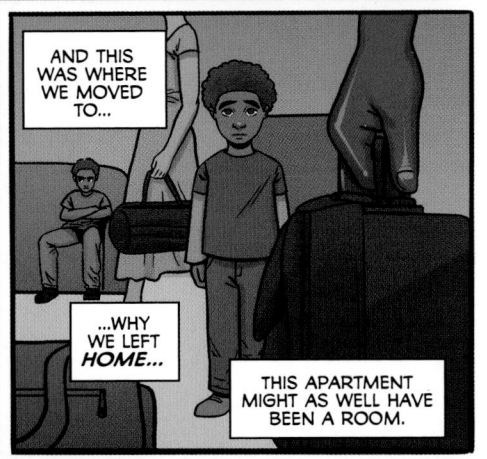

AND THIS WAS WHERE WE MOVED TO...

...WHY WE LEFT *HOME*...

THIS APARTMENT MIGHT AS WELL HAVE BEEN A ROOM.

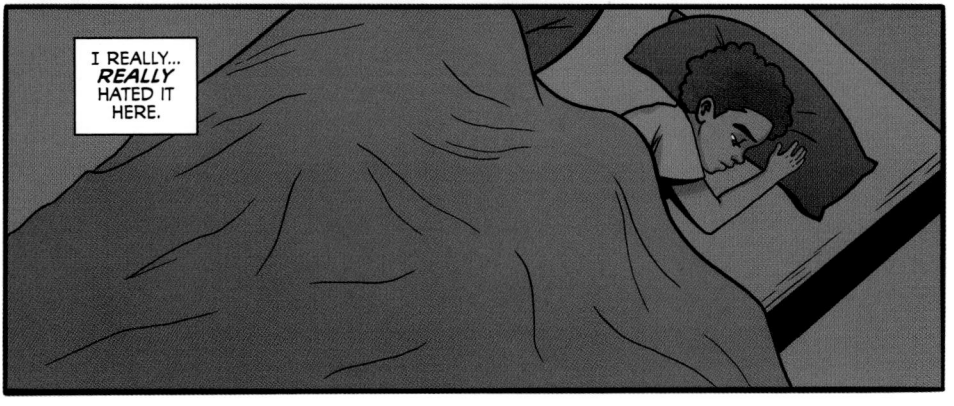

I REALLY... *REALLY* HATED IT HERE.

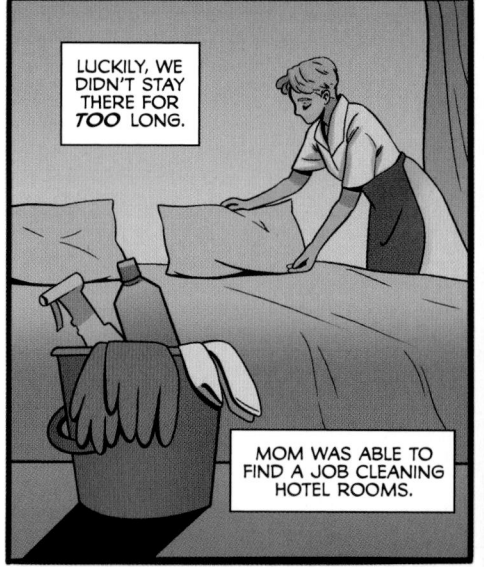

LUCKILY, WE DIDN'T STAY THERE FOR **TOO** LONG.

MOM WAS ABLE TO FIND A JOB CLEANING HOTEL ROOMS.

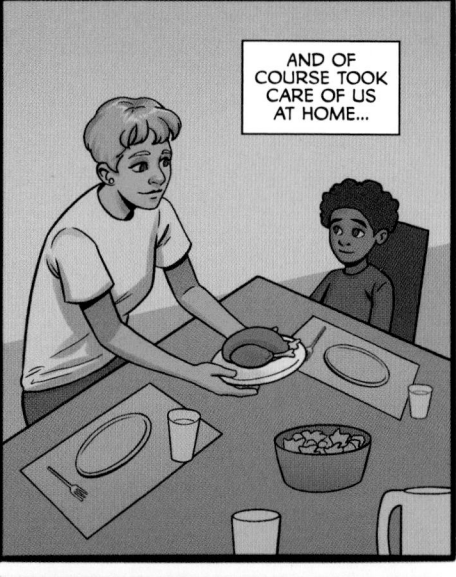

AND OF COURSE TOOK CARE OF US AT HOME...

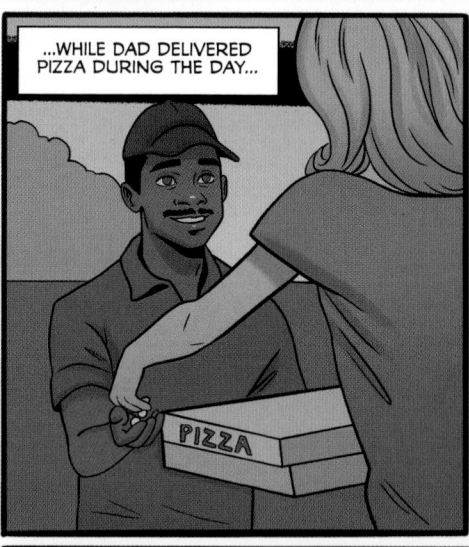

...WHILE DAD DELIVERED PIZZA DURING THE DAY...

PIZZA

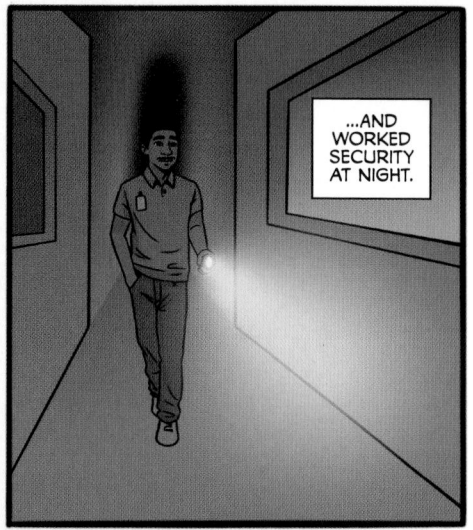

...AND WORKED SECURITY AT NIGHT.

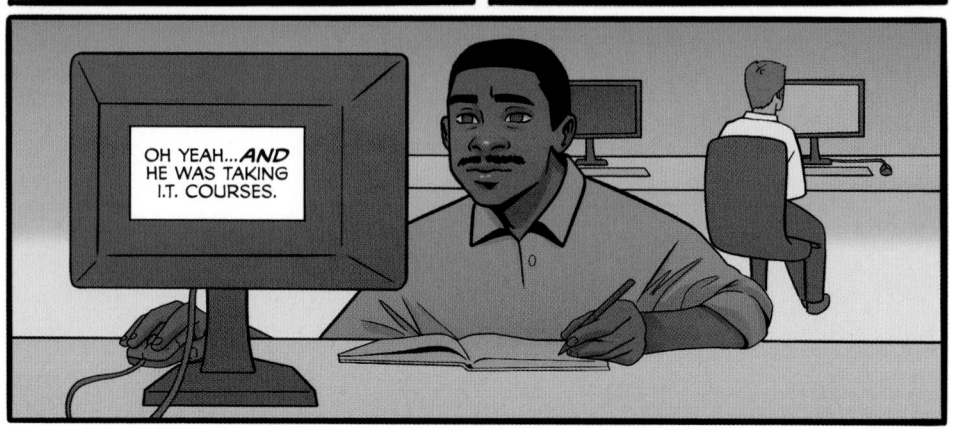

OH YEAH...**AND** HE WAS TAKING I.T. COURSES.

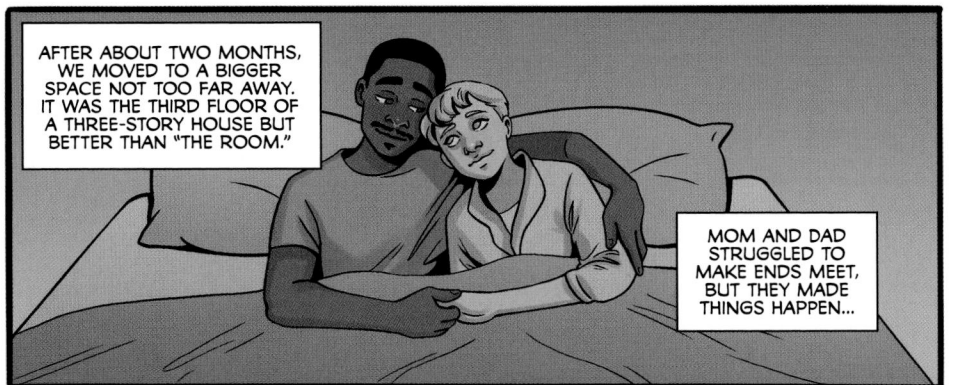

AFTER ABOUT TWO MONTHS, WE MOVED TO A BIGGER SPACE NOT TOO FAR AWAY. IT WAS THE THIRD FLOOR OF A THREE-STORY HOUSE BUT BETTER THAN "THE ROOM."

MOM AND DAD STRUGGLED TO MAKE ENDS MEET, BUT THEY MADE THINGS HAPPEN...

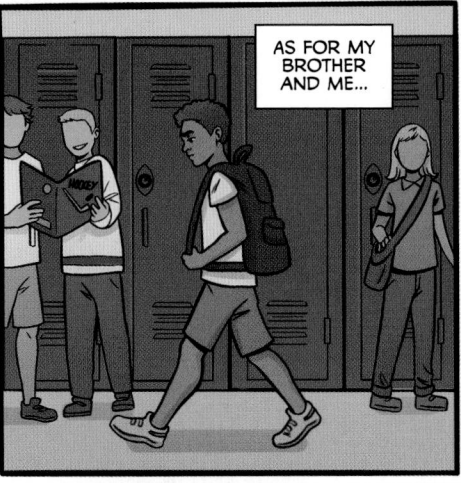

AS FOR MY BROTHER AND ME...

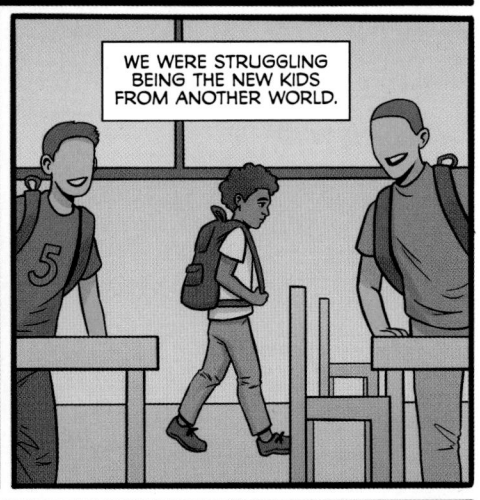

WE WERE STRUGGLING BEING THE NEW KIDS FROM ANOTHER WORLD.

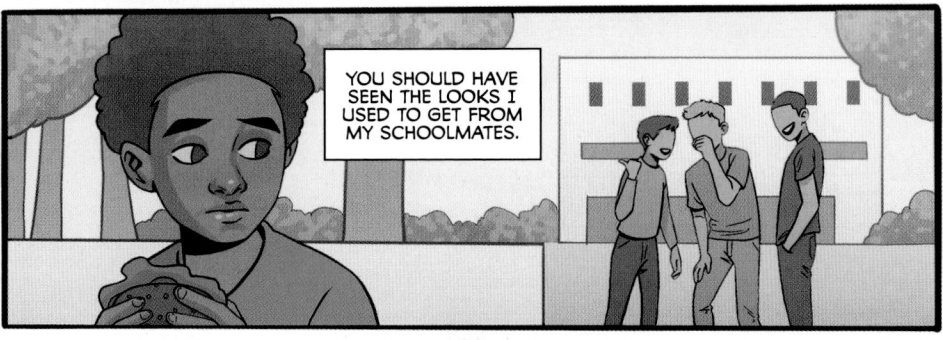

YOU SHOULD HAVE SEEN THE LOOKS I USED TO GET FROM MY SCHOOLMATES.

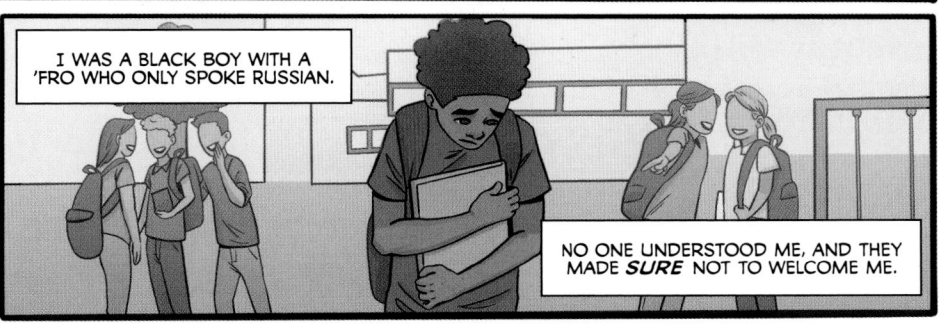

I WAS A BLACK BOY WITH A 'FRO WHO ONLY SPOKE RUSSIAN.

NO ONE UNDERSTOOD ME, AND THEY MADE *SURE* NOT TO WELCOME ME.

I HAD TO GO INTO ESL.
THE "ENGLISH AS A SECOND LANGUAGE" PROGRAM AT OUR SCHOOL.
WE WERE, FOR THE MOST PART, SEGREGATED FROM THE MAIN KIDS.
AND MAN, THE WAY ***THOSE*** KIDS SAW US OTHER KIDS WHO WERE GOING THROUGH ESL...
...SOME CHILDREN CAN BE SO NASTY.
OF THE
FOB?
WHILE I COULDN'T UNDERSTAND A SINGLE WORD BEING SAID TO ME...
...I WOULD COME TO LEARN THAT FOB MEANT "FRESH OFF THE BOAT."
WHICH WAS ***REALLY*** MEAN AND DEROGATORY.
EXCELLENT JOB, AKIM!
100%
AND HERE I WAS, READING AND DOING MATH AT A HIGHER LEVEL THAN MOST OF THE KIDS WHO CALLED ME "FOB."
AS MY ENGLISH WOULD GET ***A LITTLE*** BETTER—BUT NOT BY MUCH...
ALL THE TEASING AND MEANNESS WOULD LEAD TO...

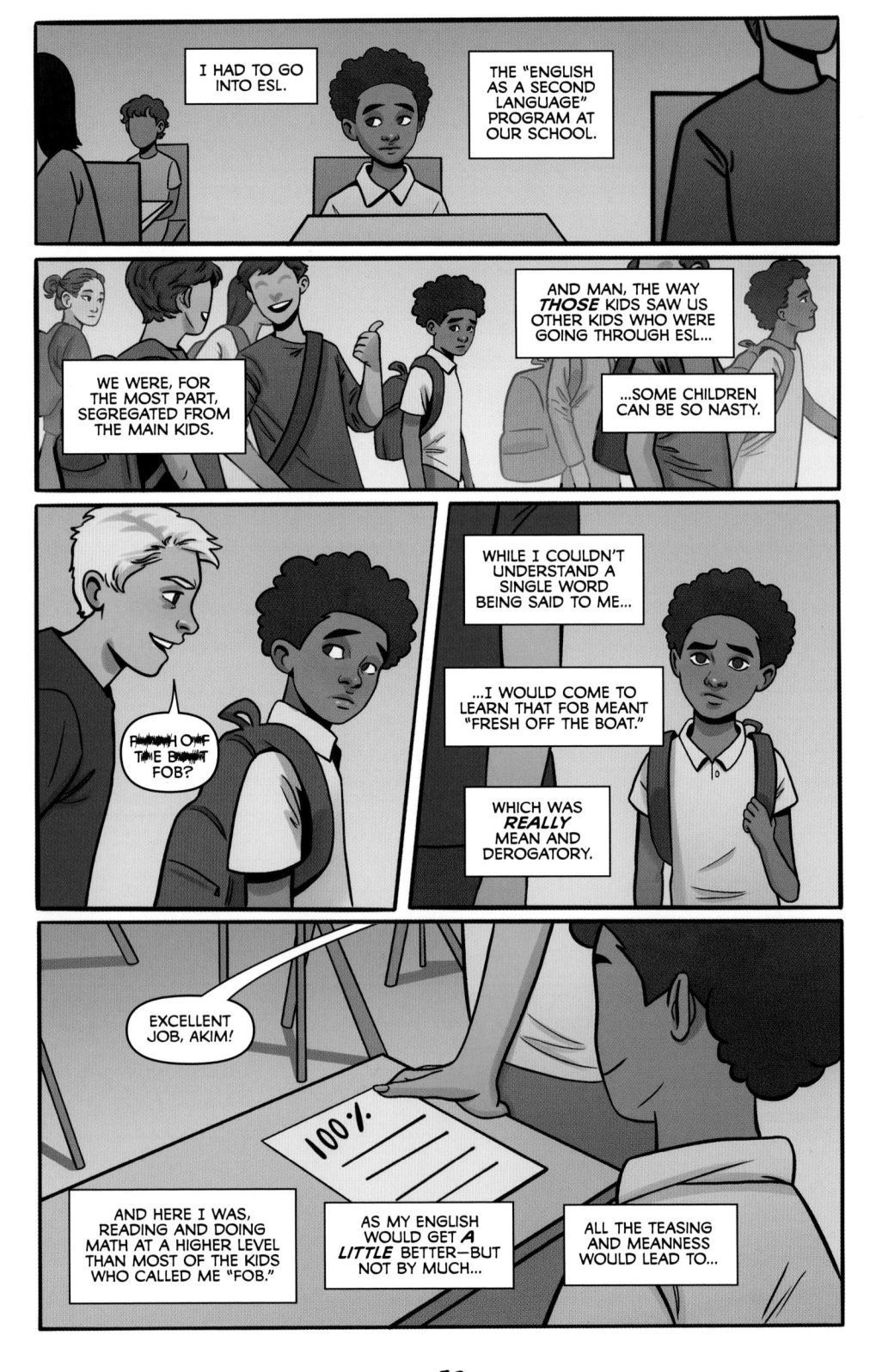

...THIS...

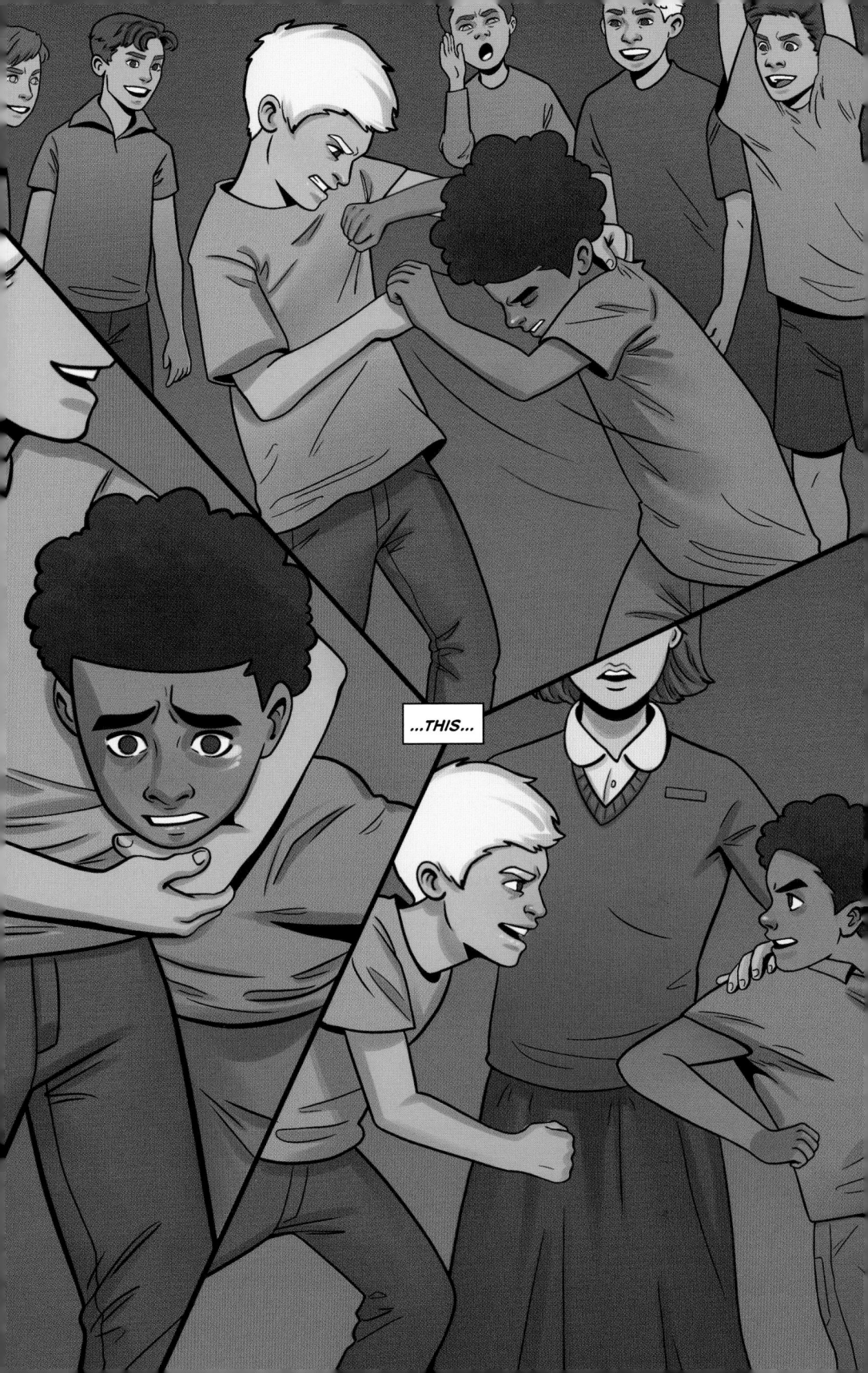

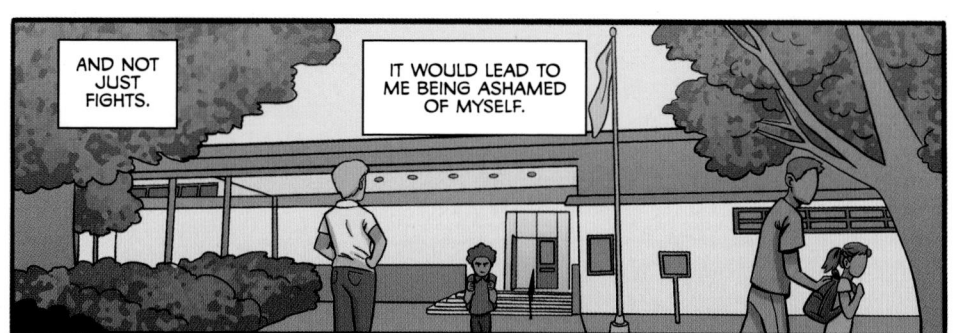

AND NOT JUST FIGHTS.

IT WOULD LEAD TO ME BEING ASHAMED OF MYSELF.

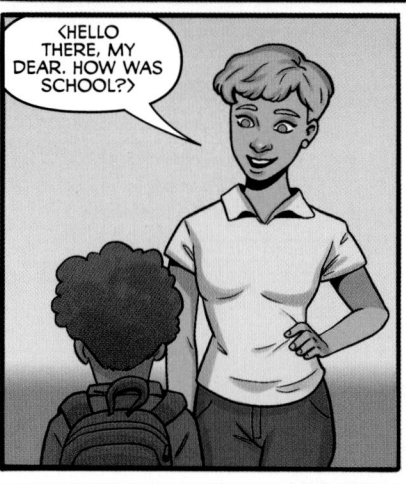

⟨HELLO THERE, MY DEAR. HOW WAS SCHOOL?⟩

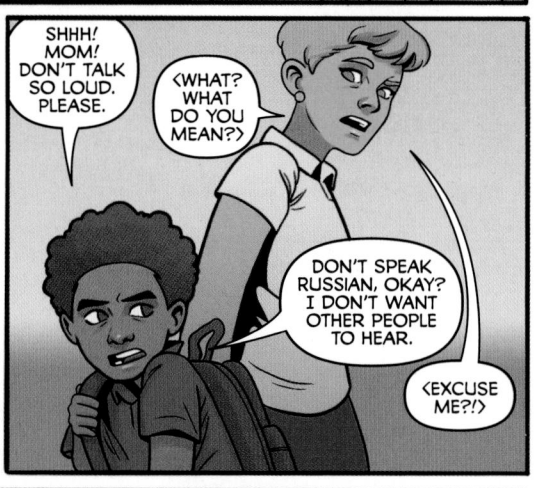

SHHH! MOM! DON'T TALK SO LOUD. PLEASE.

⟨WHAT? WHAT DO YOU MEAN?⟩

DON'T SPEAK RUSSIAN, OKAY? I DON'T WANT OTHER PEOPLE TO HEAR.

⟨EXCUSE ME?!⟩

CAN WE JUST GO? PLEASE?

⟨AKIM. WHY SHOULDN'T I SPEAK MY LANGUAGE? I AM RUSSIAN. I *SPEAK* RUSSIAN.⟩

⟨AND I WANT YOU TO SPEAK RUSSIAN WITH ME.⟩

54

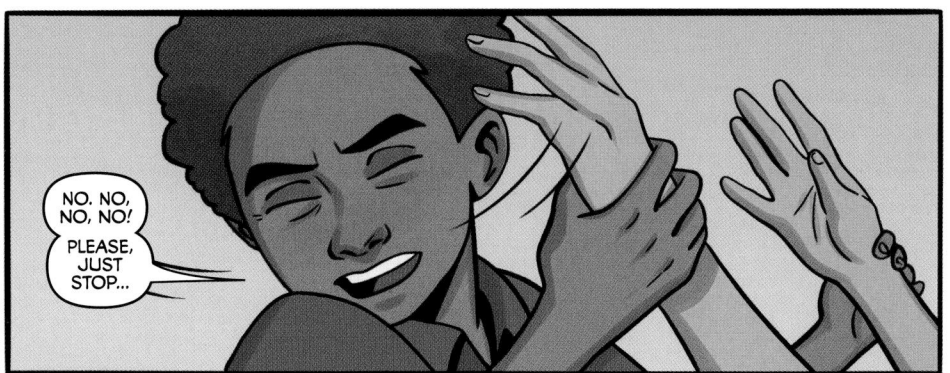

NO. NO, NO, NO! PLEASE, JUST STOP...

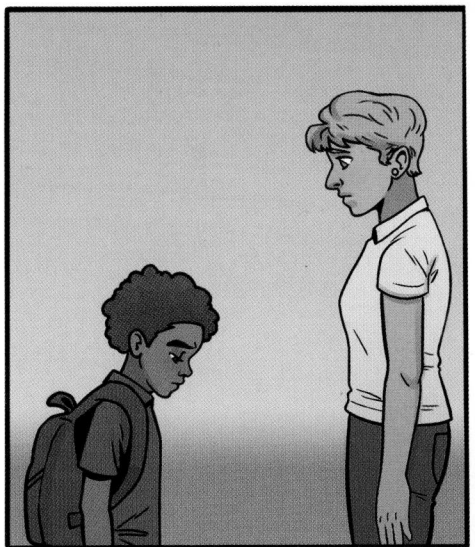

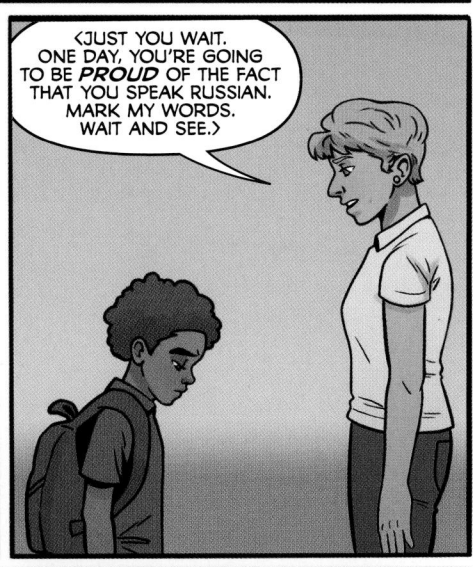

<JUST YOU WAIT. ONE DAY, YOU'RE GOING TO BE *PROUD* OF THE FACT THAT YOU SPEAK RUSSIAN. MARK MY WORDS. WAIT AND SEE.>

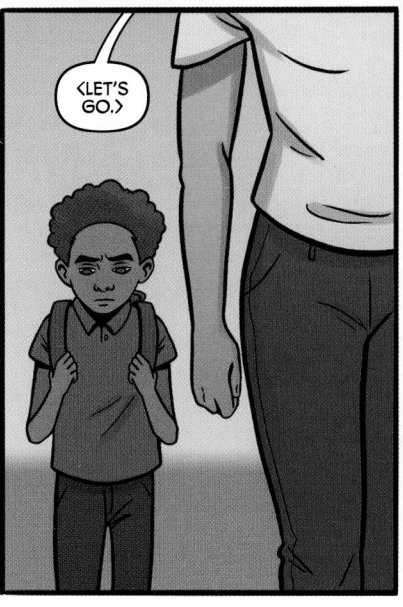

<LET'S GO.>

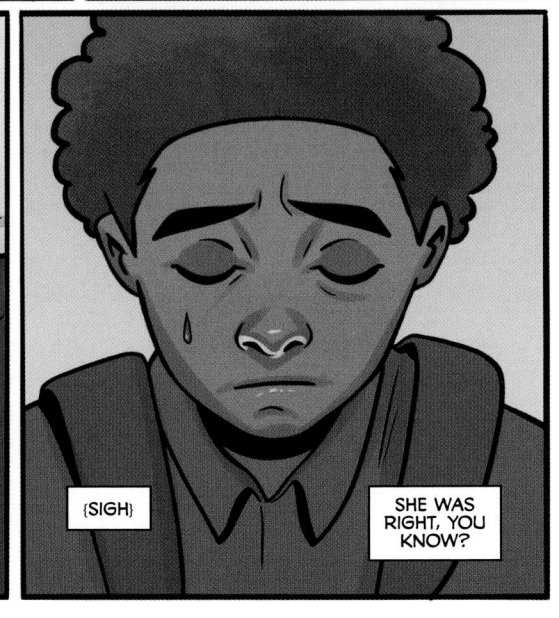

{SIGH}

SHE WAS RIGHT, YOU KNOW?

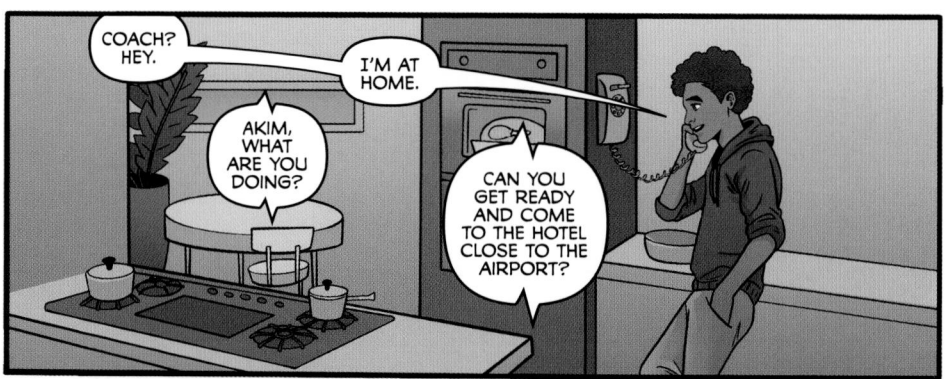

COACH? HEY.

I'M AT HOME.

AKIM, WHAT ARE YOU DOING?

CAN YOU GET READY AND COME TO THE HOTEL CLOSE TO THE AIRPORT?

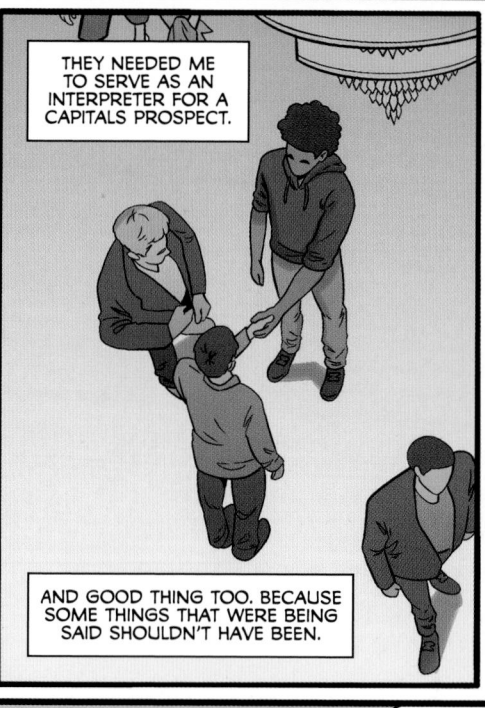

THEY NEEDED ME TO SERVE AS AN INTERPRETER FOR A CAPITALS PROSPECT.

AND GOOD THING TOO. BECAUSE SOME THINGS THAT WERE BEING SAID SHOULDN'T HAVE BEEN.

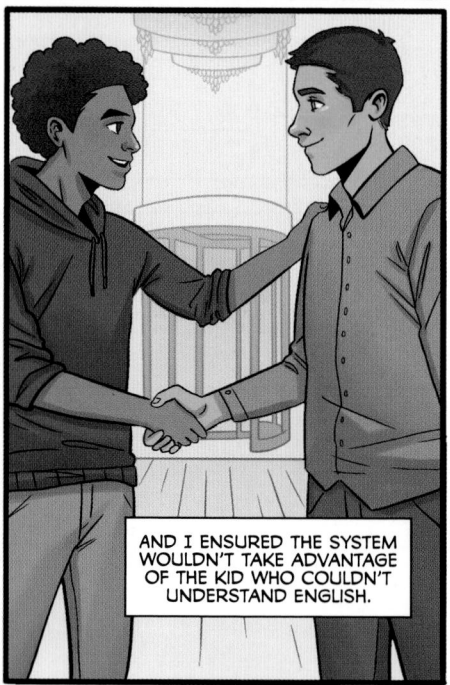

AND I ENSURED THE SYSTEM WOULDN'T TAKE ADVANTAGE OF THE KID WHO COULDN'T UNDERSTAND ENGLISH.

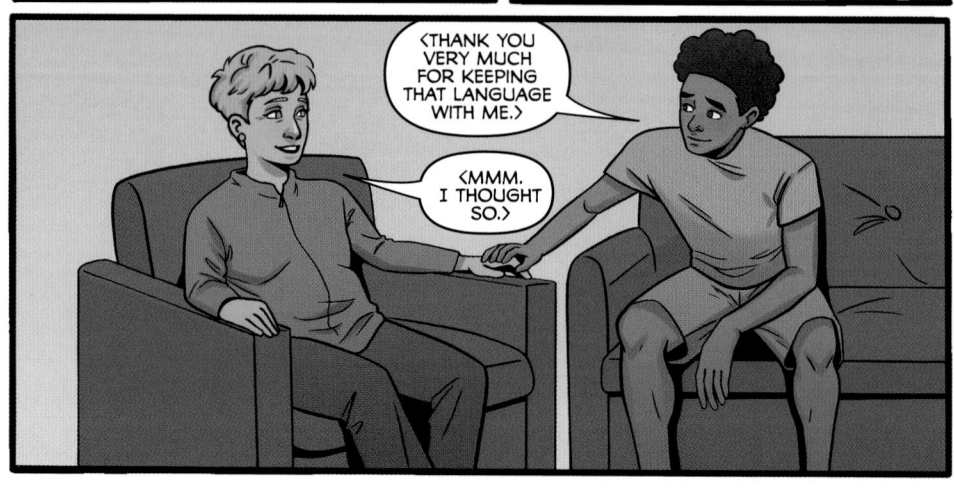

〈THANK YOU VERY MUCH FOR KEEPING THAT LANGUAGE WITH ME.〉

〈MMM. I THOUGHT SO.〉

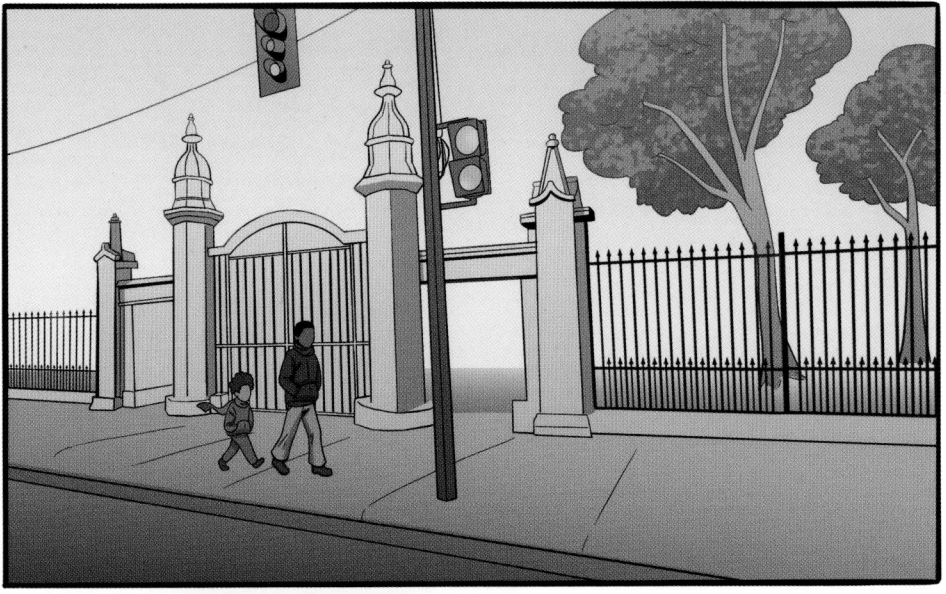

PASS IT! PASS IT OVER HERE!!

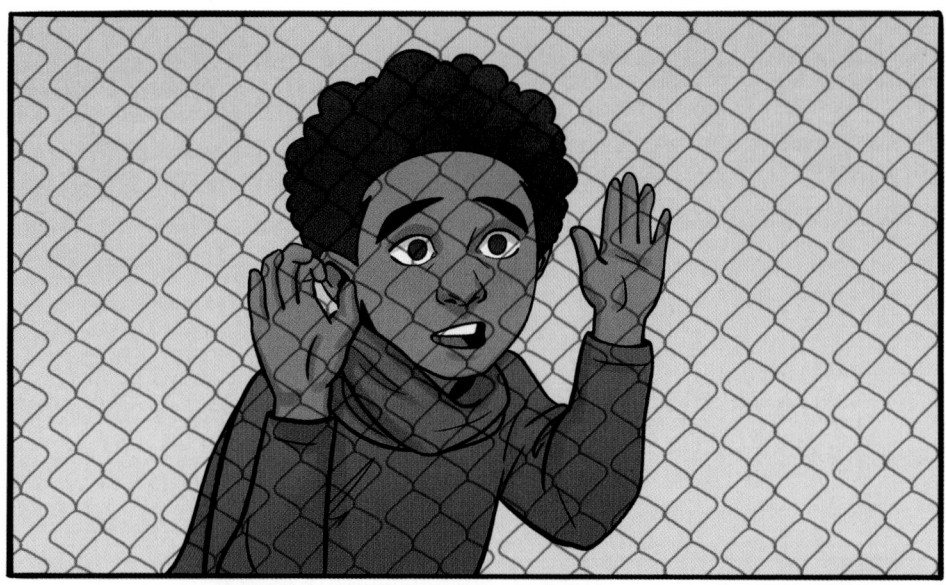

AKIM! LET'S GO!
AND HE SCORES!!!

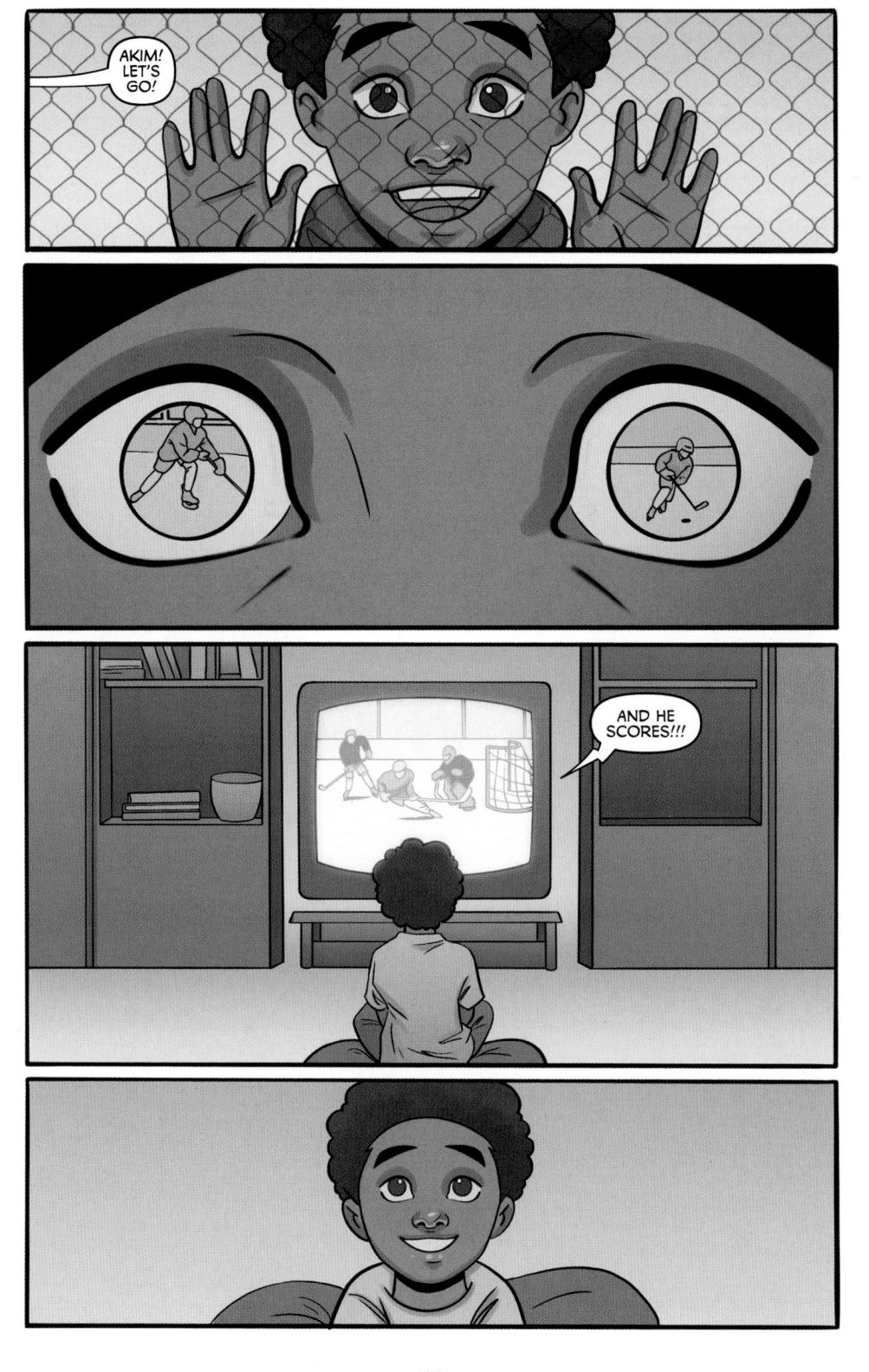

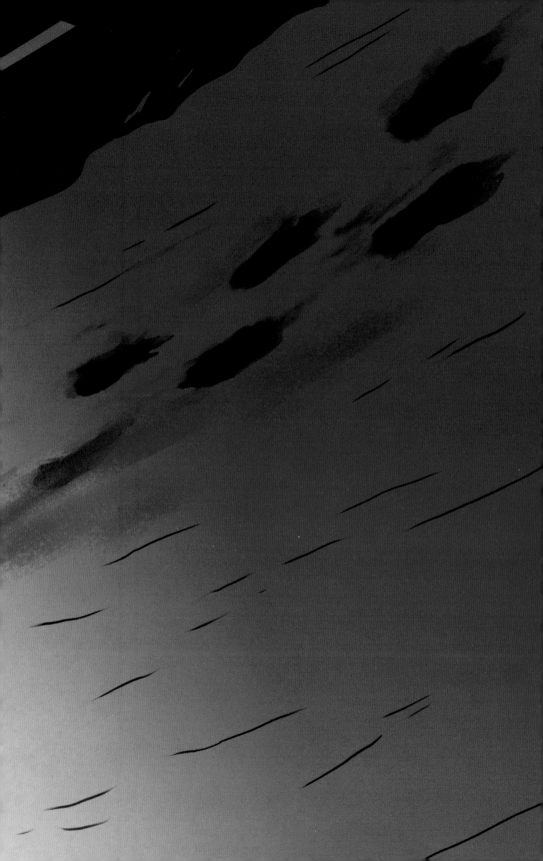

CHAPTER
FOUR

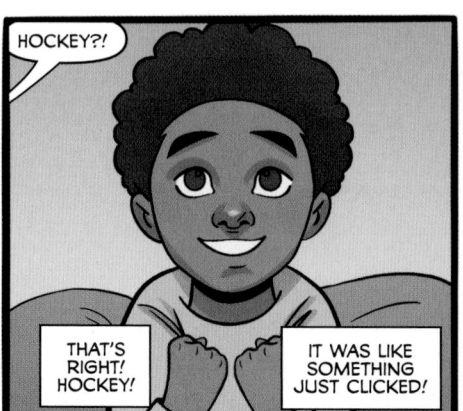

HOCKEY?!

THAT'S RIGHT! HOCKEY!

IT WAS LIKE SOMETHING JUST CLICKED!

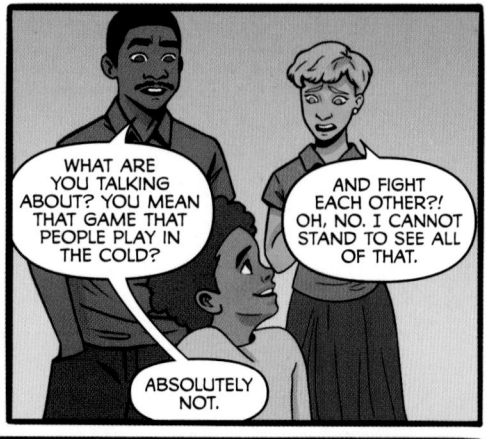

WHAT ARE YOU TALKING ABOUT? YOU MEAN THAT GAME THAT PEOPLE PLAY IN THE COLD?

AND FIGHT EACH OTHER?! OH, NO. I CANNOT STAND TO SEE ALL OF THAT.

ABSOLUTELY NOT.

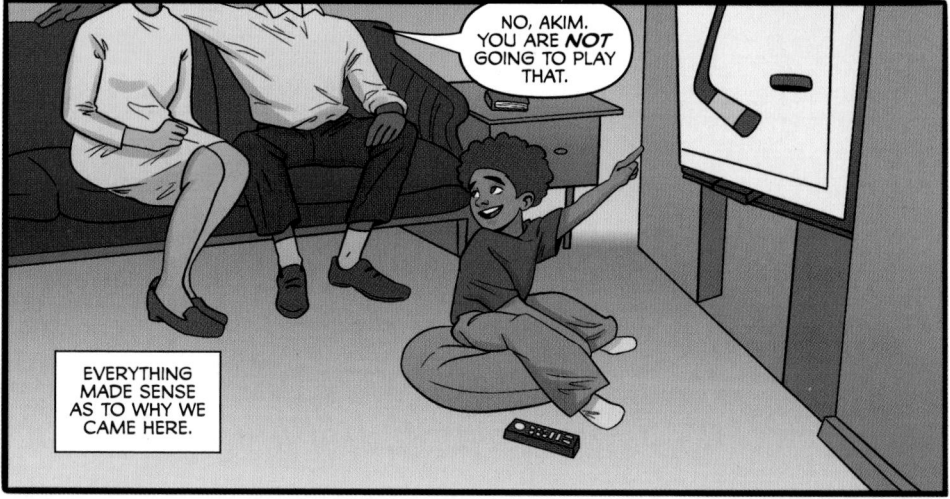

NO, AKIM. YOU ARE *NOT* GOING TO PLAY THAT.

EVERYTHING MADE SENSE AS TO WHY WE CAME HERE.

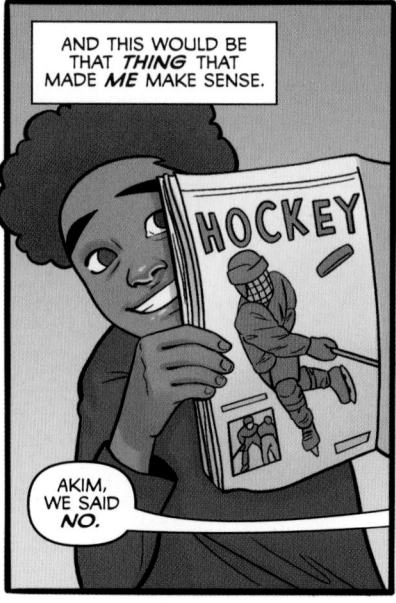

AND THIS WOULD BE THAT *THING* THAT MADE *ME* MAKE SENSE.

HOCKEY

AKIM, WE SAID *NO.*

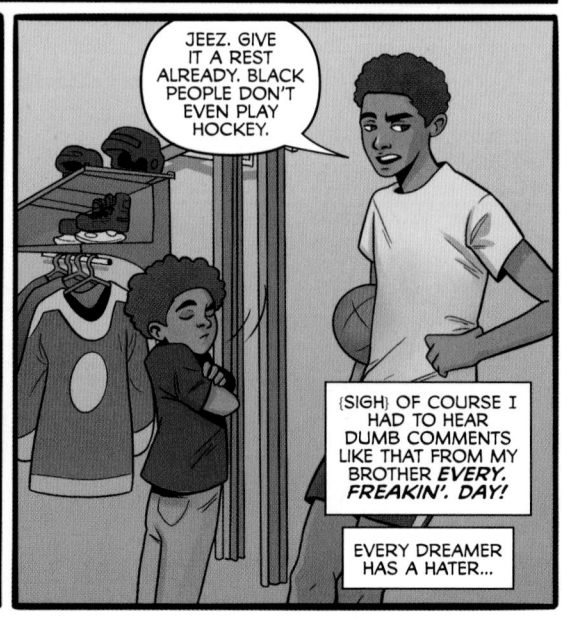

JEEZ. GIVE IT A REST ALREADY. BLACK PEOPLE DON'T EVEN PLAY HOCKEY.

{SIGH} OF COURSE I HAD TO HEAR DUMB COMMENTS LIKE THAT FROM MY BROTHER *EVERY. FREAKIN'. DAY!*

EVERY DREAMER HAS A HATER...

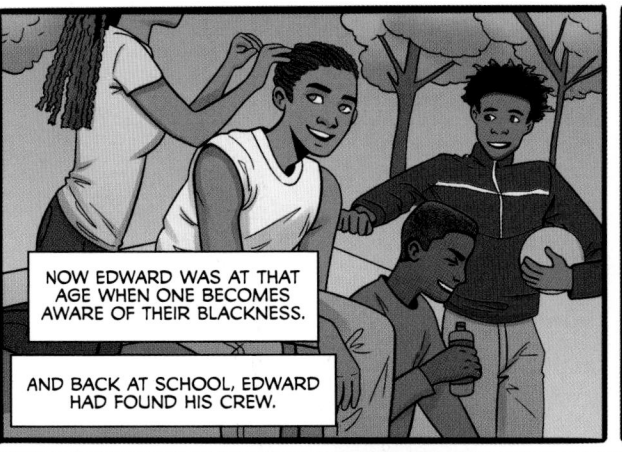

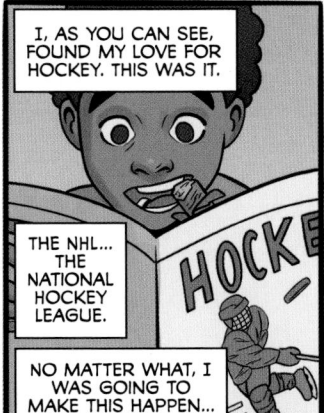

NOW EDWARD WAS AT THAT AGE WHEN ONE BECOMES AWARE OF THEIR BLACKNESS.

AND BACK AT SCHOOL, EDWARD HAD FOUND HIS CREW.

I, AS YOU CAN SEE, FOUND MY LOVE FOR HOCKEY. THIS WAS IT.

THE NHL... THE NATIONAL HOCKEY LEAGUE.

NO MATTER WHAT, I WAS GOING TO MAKE THIS HAPPEN...

...EVEN IF IT MEANT BUGGING AND BOTHERING AND PESTERING MY PARENTS EVERY SINGLE DAY.

I DON'T UNDERSTAND, AKIM. THIS IS SO EXPENSIVE. WHY DON'T YOU JUST STICK TO SOCCER? YOU'RE GOOD AT SOCCER.

OH YEAH...I ALSO LOVED SOCCER. I WAS REALLY GREAT AT IT TOO.

MOMMMM! WHAT ARE YOU DOING? THIS IS *MY* BOOK. ONLY *I'M* ALLOWED TO BREAK THE FOURTH WALL.

OH! I'M SO SORRY, DEAR.

BUT ALL I'M SAYING IS YOU *WERE* BETTER AT SOCCER.

{SIGH}

HE WAS BETTER AT SOCCER THAN HE WAS AT HOCKEY, IF YOU ASK ME. SO MUCH BETTER. I JUST DON'T UNDERSTAND WHY HOCKEY OVER SOCCER!

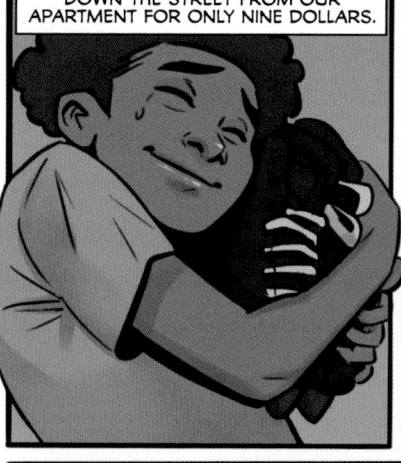

MOM AND POPS GOT ME THE PAIR OF SKATES AT THE YARD SALE JUST DOWN THE STREET FROM OUR APARTMENT FOR ONLY NINE DOLLARS.

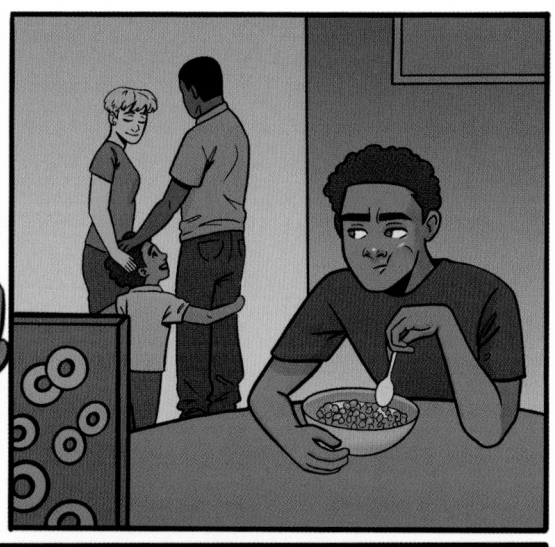

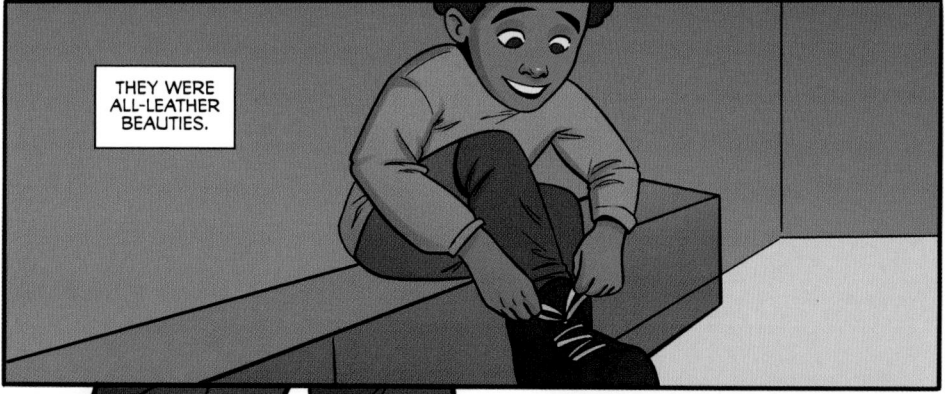

THEY WERE ALL-LEATHER BEAUTIES.

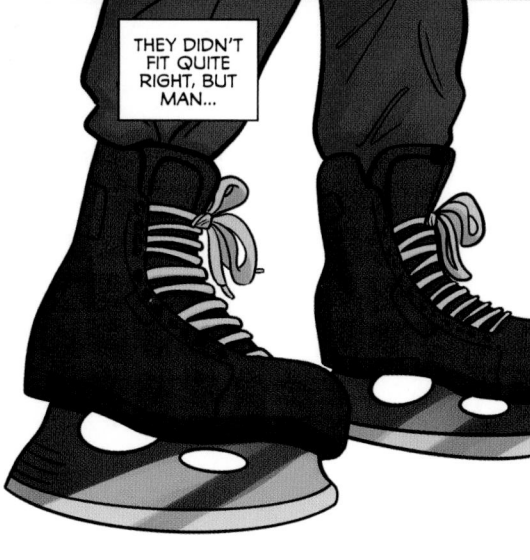

THEY DIDN'T FIT QUITE RIGHT, BUT MAN...

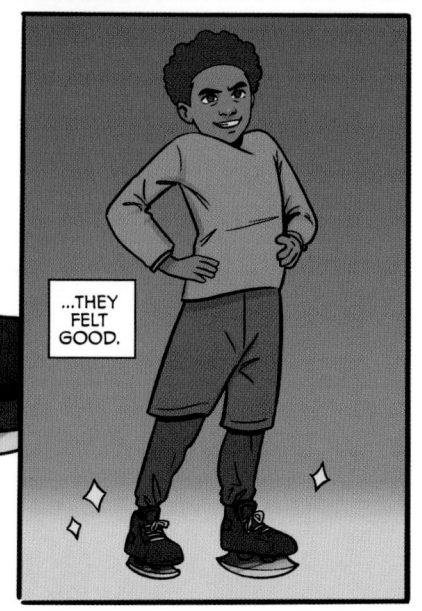

...THEY FELT GOOD.

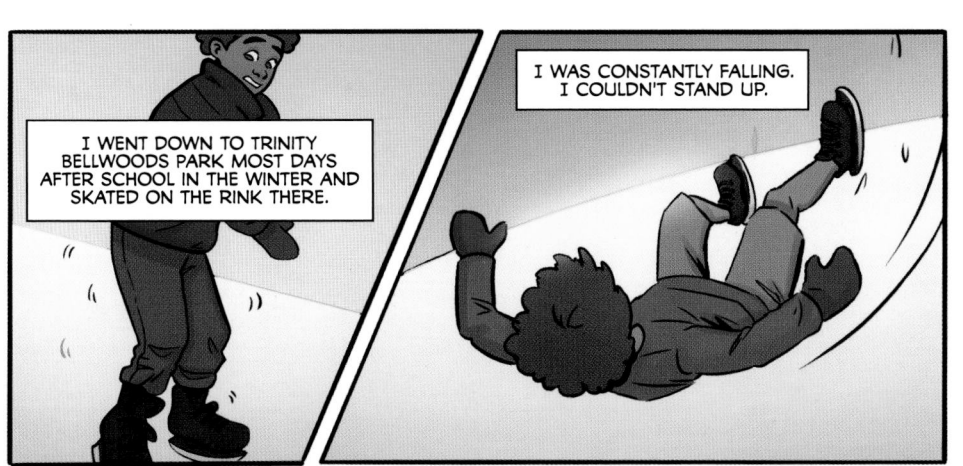

I WENT DOWN TO TRINITY BELLWOODS PARK MOST DAYS AFTER SCHOOL IN THE WINTER AND SKATED ON THE RINK THERE.

I WAS CONSTANTLY FALLING. I COULDN'T STAND UP.

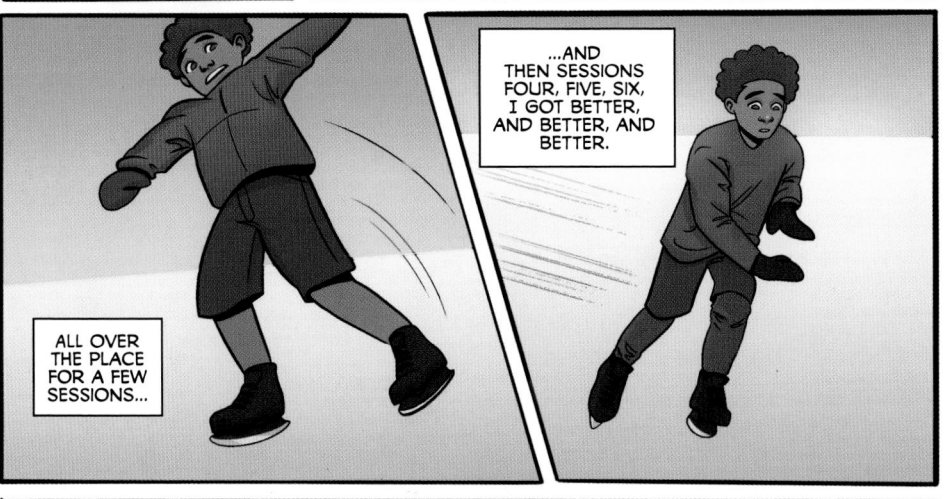

ALL OVER THE PLACE FOR A FEW SESSIONS...

...AND THEN SESSIONS FOUR, FIVE, SIX, I GOT BETTER, AND BETTER, AND BETTER.

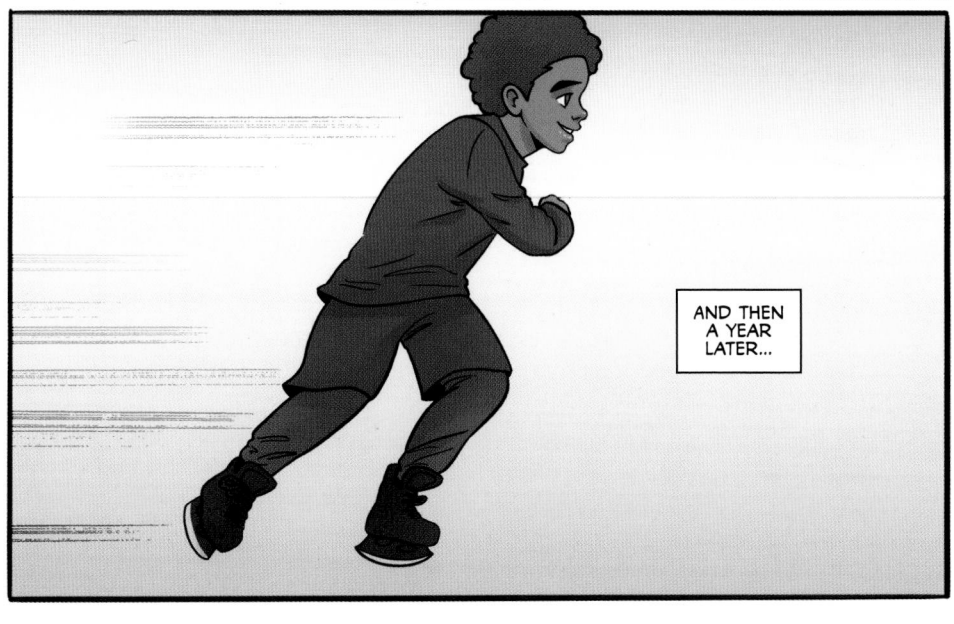

AND THEN A YEAR LATER...

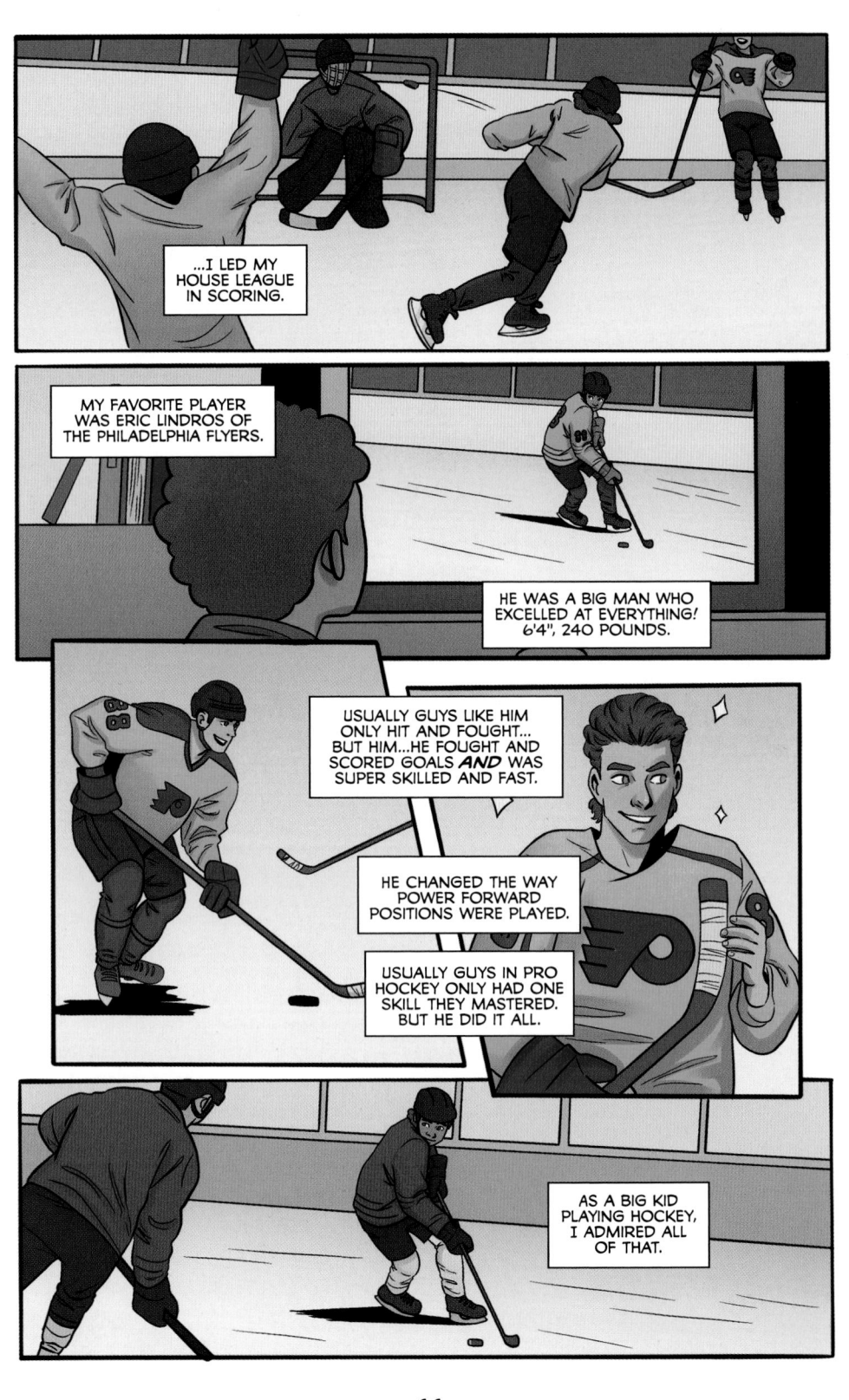

...I LED MY HOUSE LEAGUE IN SCORING.

MY FAVORITE PLAYER WAS ERIC LINDROS OF THE PHILADELPHIA FLYERS.

HE WAS A BIG MAN WHO EXCELLED AT EVERYTHING! 6'4", 240 POUNDS.

USUALLY GUYS LIKE HIM ONLY HIT AND FOUGHT... BUT HIM...HE FOUGHT AND SCORED GOALS *AND* WAS SUPER SKILLED AND FAST.

HE CHANGED THE WAY POWER FORWARD POSITIONS WERE PLAYED.

USUALLY GUYS IN PRO HOCKEY ONLY HAD ONE SKILL THEY MASTERED. BUT HE DID IT ALL.

AS A BIG KID PLAYING HOCKEY, I ADMIRED ALL OF THAT.

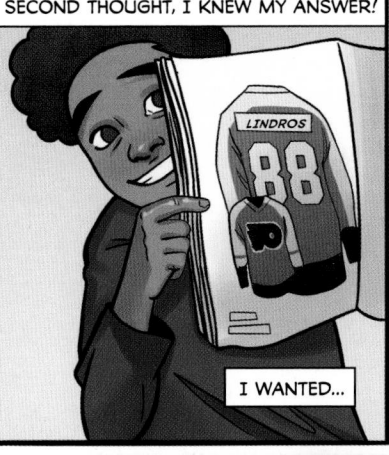

WHEN MY PARENTS ASKED ME WHAT I WANTED FOR CHRISTMAS, WITHOUT A SECOND THOUGHT, I KNEW MY ANSWER!

LINDROS
88

I WANTED...

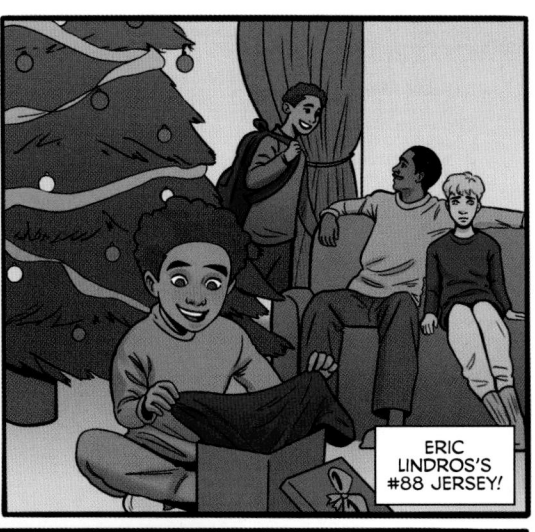

ERIC LINDROS'S #88 JERSEY!

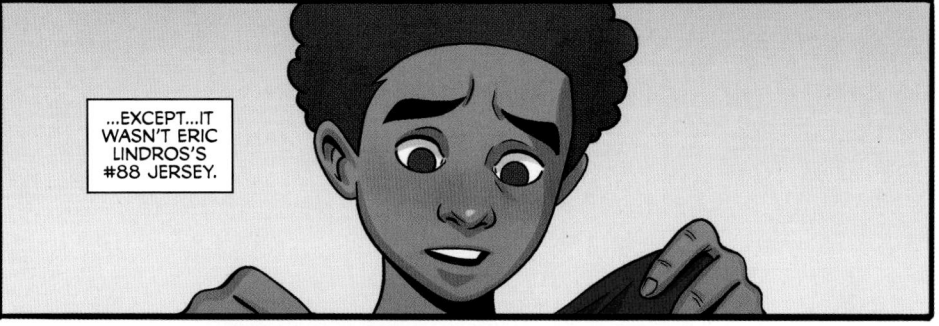

...EXCEPT...IT WASN'T ERIC LINDROS'S #88 JERSEY.

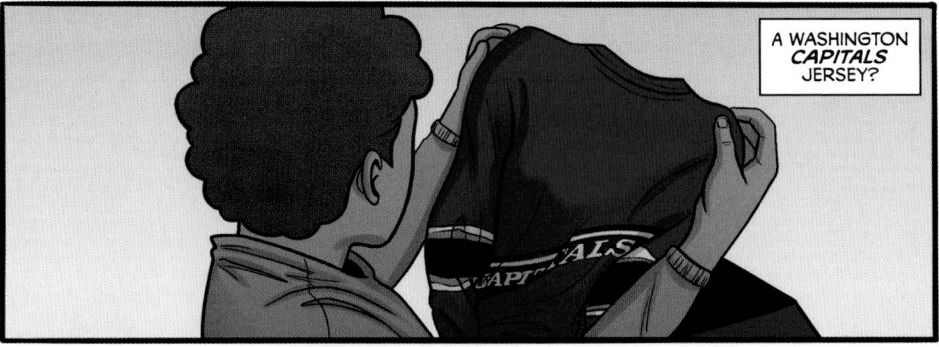

A WASHINGTON *CAPITALS* JERSEY?

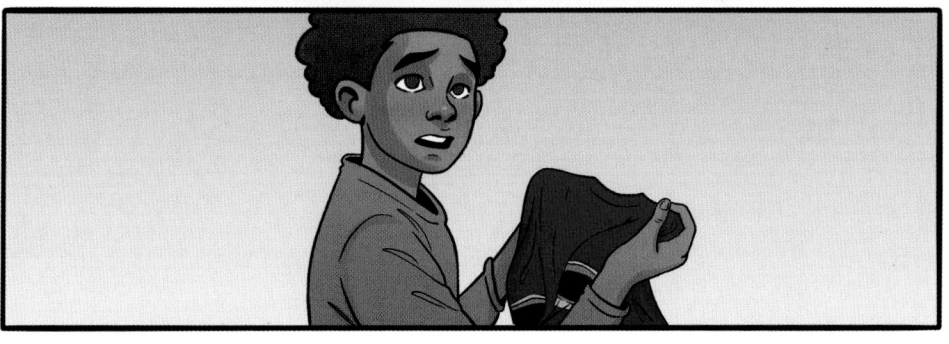

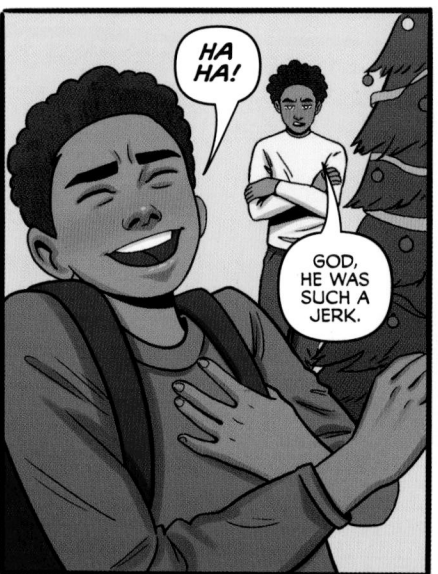

HA HA!

GOD, HE WAS SUCH A JERK.

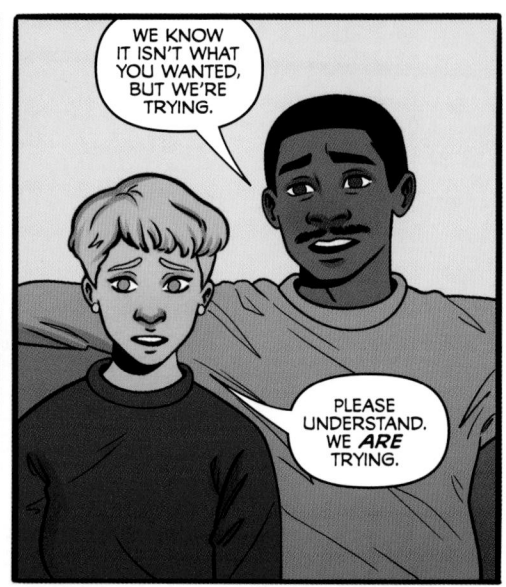

WE KNOW IT ISN'T WHAT YOU WANTED, BUT WE'RE TRYING.

PLEASE UNDERSTAND. WE *ARE* TRYING.

OH MY GOD!

$130

YEAH...I KNOW.

YEAH, I WAS DISAPPOINTED.

BUT I STILL FELT BAD AT THE SAME TIME 'CAUSE I KNEW MY PARENTS WERE DOING THEIR BEST.

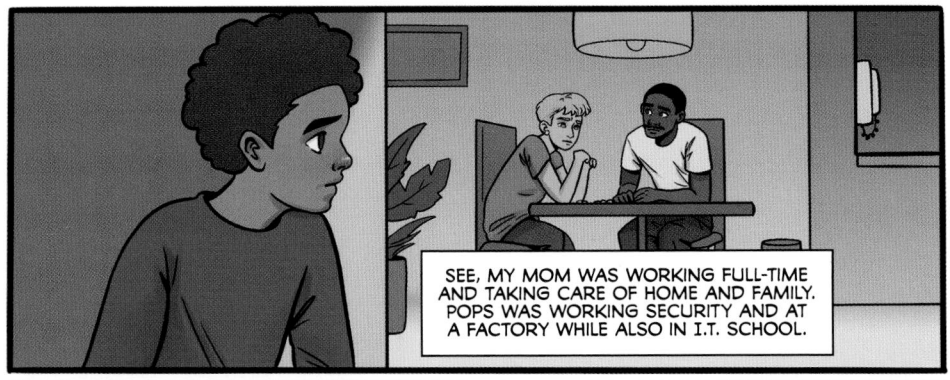

SEE, MY MOM WAS WORKING FULL-TIME AND TAKING CARE OF HOME AND FAMILY. POPS WAS WORKING SECURITY AND AT A FACTORY WHILE ALSO IN I.T. SCHOOL.

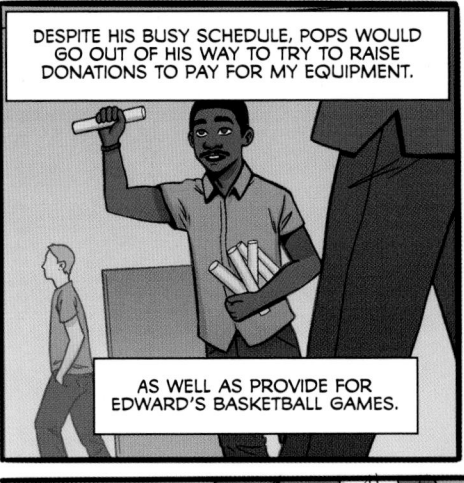

DESPITE HIS BUSY SCHEDULE, POPS WOULD GO OUT OF HIS WAY TO TRY TO RAISE DONATIONS TO PAY FOR MY EQUIPMENT.

AS WELL AS PROVIDE FOR EDWARD'S BASKETBALL GAMES.

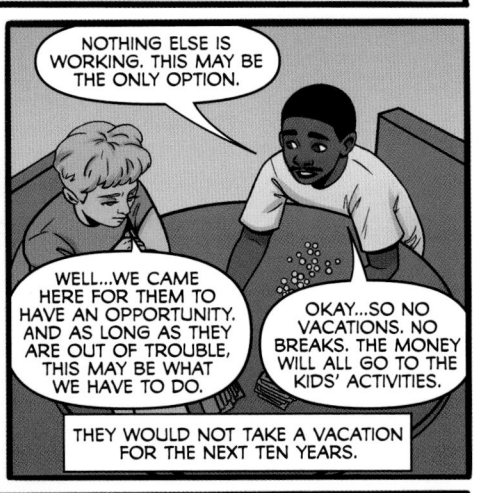

NOTHING ELSE IS WORKING. THIS MAY BE THE ONLY OPTION.

WELL...WE CAME HERE FOR THEM TO HAVE AN OPPORTUNITY. AND AS LONG AS THEY ARE OUT OF TROUBLE, THIS MAY BE WHAT WE HAVE TO DO.

OKAY...SO NO VACATIONS. NO BREAKS. THE MONEY WILL ALL GO TO THE KIDS' ACTIVITIES.

THEY WOULD NOT TAKE A VACATION FOR THE NEXT TEN YEARS.

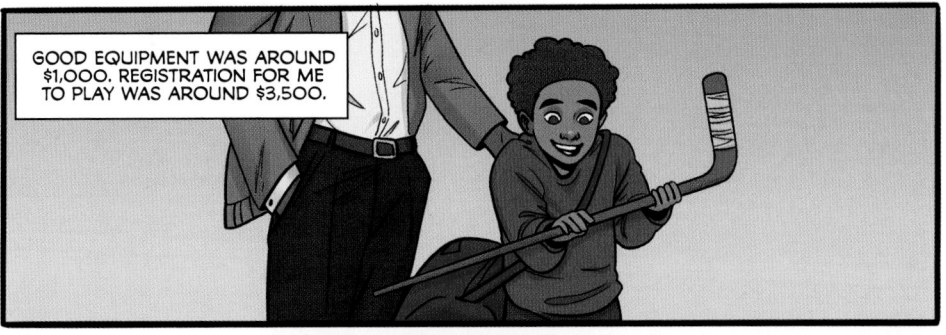

GOOD EQUIPMENT WAS AROUND $1,000. REGISTRATION FOR ME TO PLAY WAS AROUND $3,500.

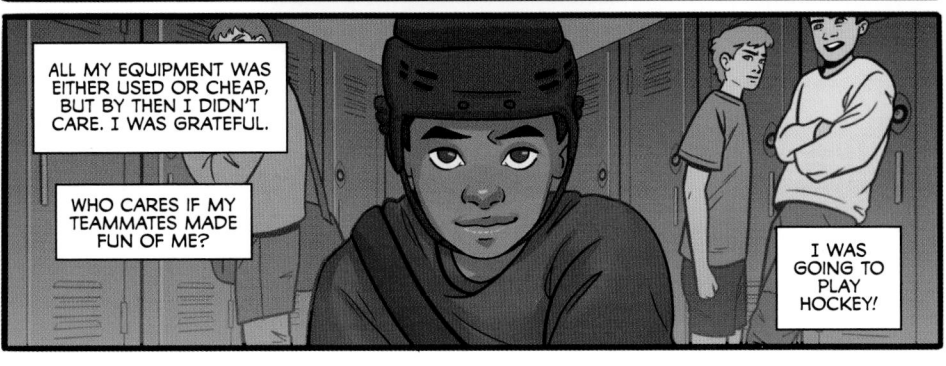

ALL MY EQUIPMENT WAS EITHER USED OR CHEAP, BUT BY THEN I DIDN'T CARE. I WAS GRATEFUL.

WHO CARES IF MY TEAMMATES MADE FUN OF ME?

I WAS GOING TO PLAY HOCKEY!

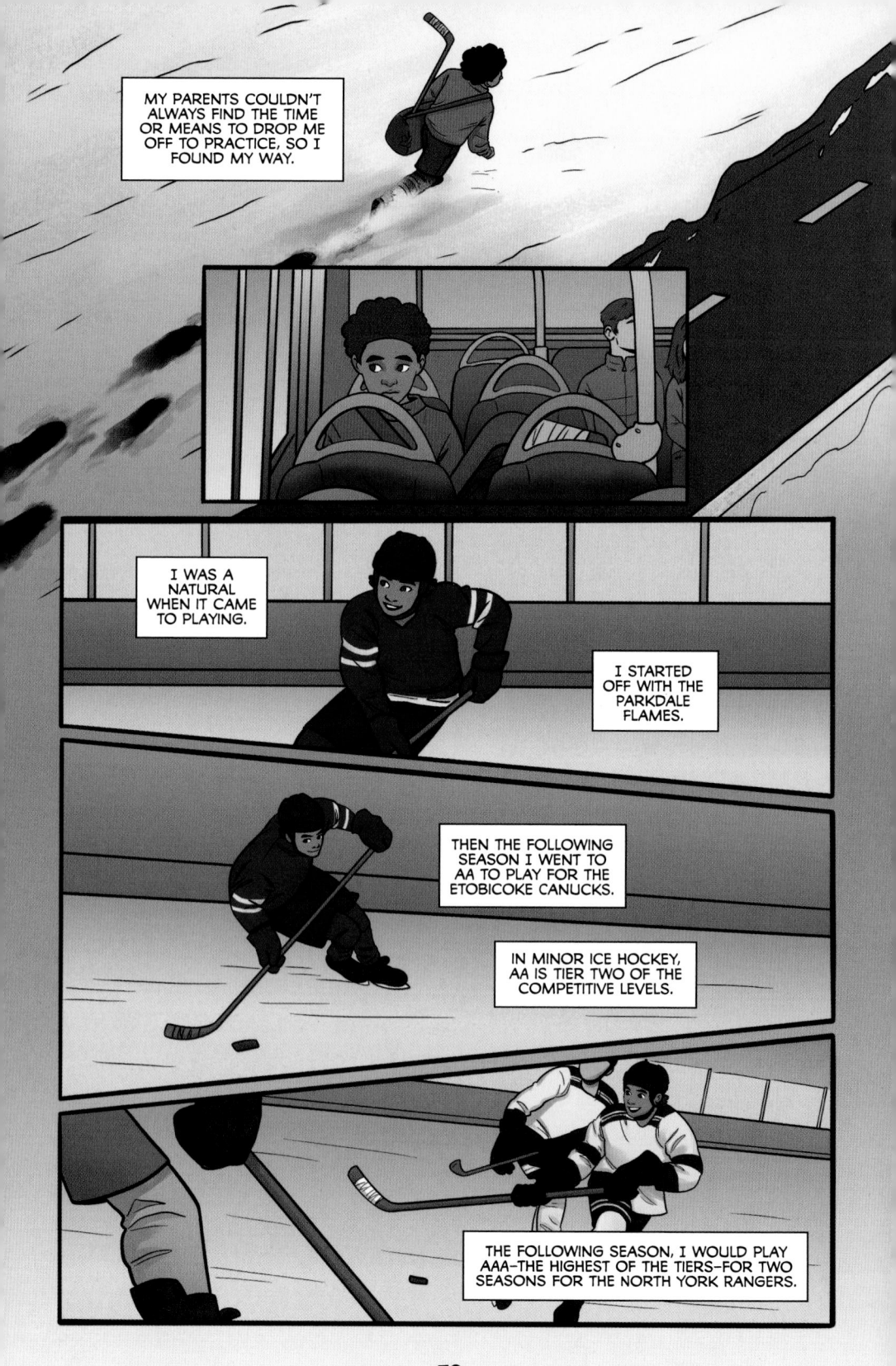

MY PARENTS COULDN'T ALWAYS FIND THE TIME OR MEANS TO DROP ME OFF TO PRACTICE, SO I FOUND MY WAY.

I WAS A NATURAL WHEN IT CAME TO PLAYING.

I STARTED OFF WITH THE PARKDALE FLAMES.

THEN THE FOLLOWING SEASON I WENT TO AA TO PLAY FOR THE ETOBICOKE CANUCKS.

IN MINOR ICE HOCKEY, AA IS TIER TWO OF THE COMPETITIVE LEVELS.

THE FOLLOWING SEASON, I WOULD PLAY AAA—THE HIGHEST OF THE TIERS—FOR TWO SEASONS FOR THE NORTH YORK RANGERS.

THEN I WENT TO THE POWERHOUSE TORONTO MARLIES FROM AGE THIRTEEN TO FIFTEEN...
...AND THEN FINALLY I WAS DRAFTED INTO THE OHL—THE ONTARIO HOCKEY LEAGUE—BY THE WINDSOR SPITFIRES.
I KNOW I'M SKIPPING AHEAD A BIT, BUT YOU HAVE TO ADMIT, I WAS MOVING AT A PRETTY COOL AND SURPRISING PACE.
MY LOVE FOR THIS GREW EVERY DAY, AND EVERY DAY I GOT CLOSER TO MY DREAM OF PLAYING FOR THE NATIONAL HOCKEY LEAGUE.

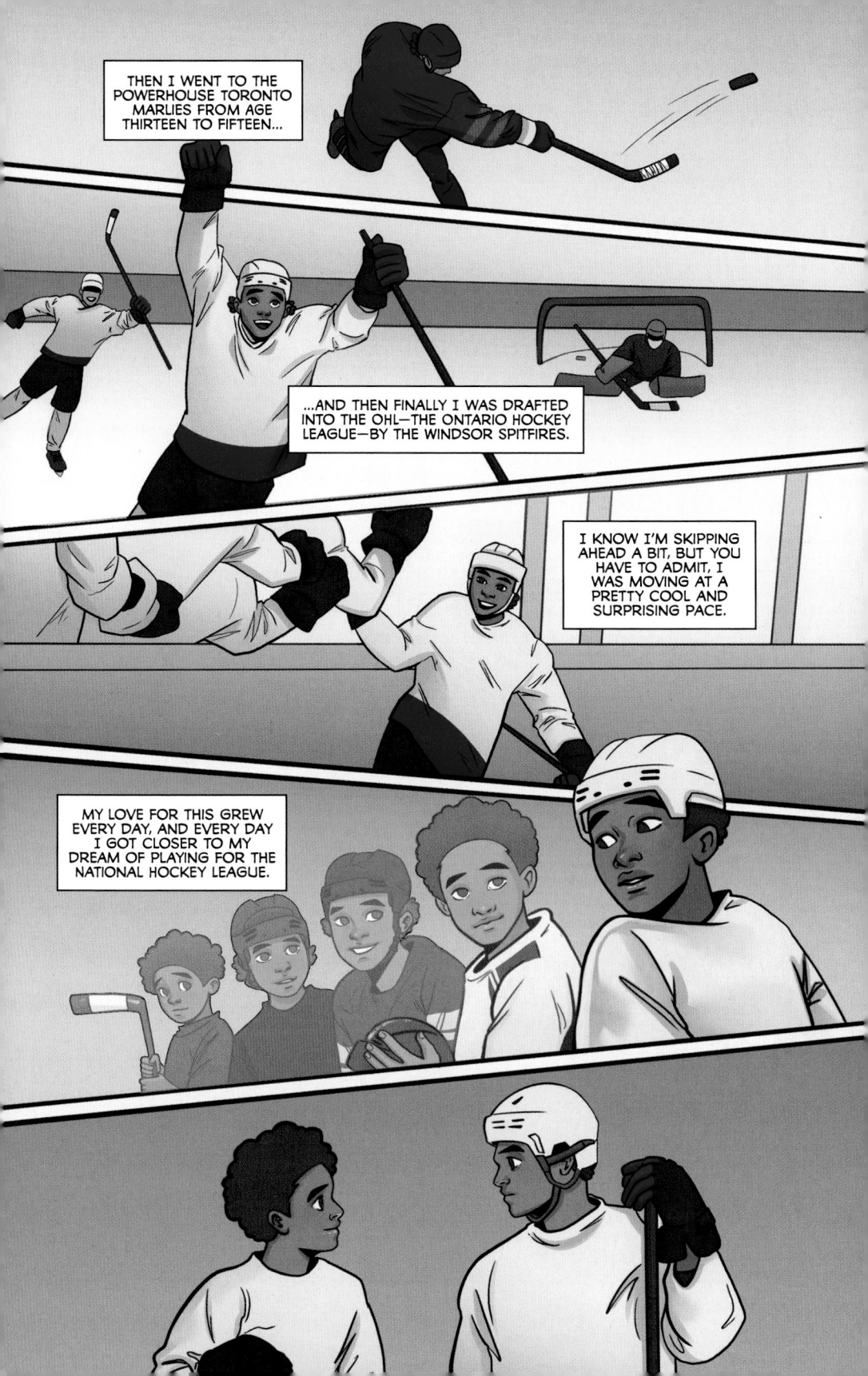

WHEN I WAS TWELVE, I WAS PART OF A SUMMER TEAM BEFORE I BECAME A MEMBER OF THE TORONTO MARLIES.
THAT WAS WHEN ***THIS*** HAPPENED...
HOW MANY TIMES ARE WE GOING TO LET THIS N[redacted]R SCORE?!?
HEY...YOU OKAY?
... I'M FINE.
... ALL RIGHT.

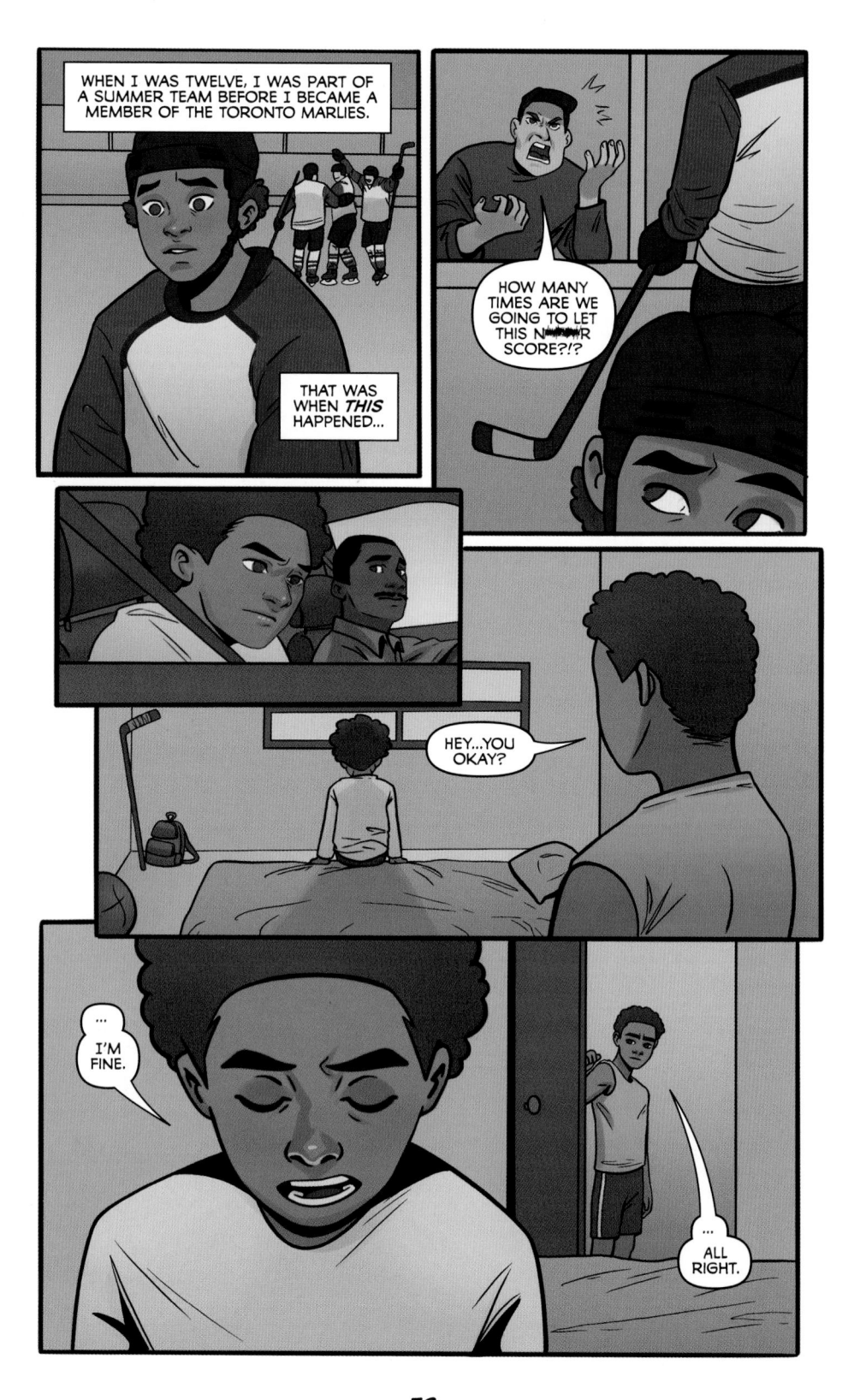

I SAID BEFORE THAT SOMETIMES PLAYING WITH A TEAM MADE ME FEEL ALONE.

YEAH, I STARTED GAINING RESPECT. BUT I DIDN'T FEEL LIKE IT WAS FOR WHO I WAS...

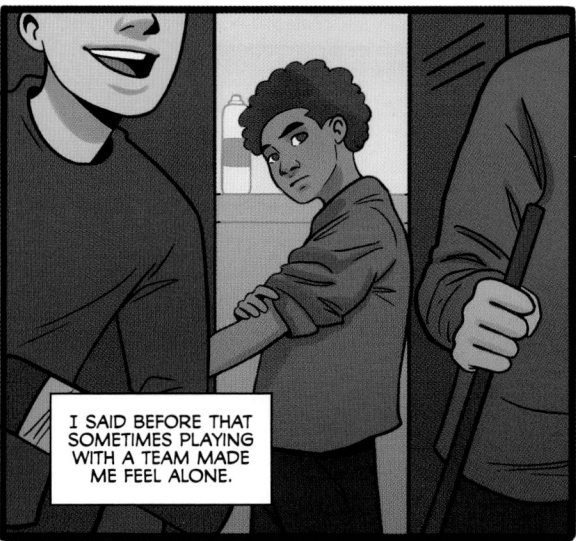

...BUT FOR WHAT I COULD DO ON THE ICE. SO IT BECAME LIKE A PRESTIGE THING.

YOU WALK IN THE ARENA, AND YOU'RE ONE OF THE BETTER PLAYERS IN THE AGE GROUP, RIGHT?

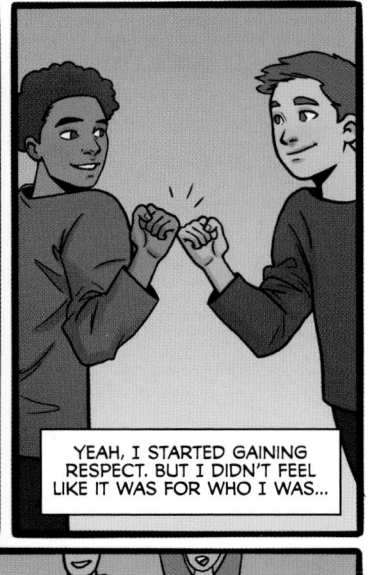

SO YOU GET AUTOMATIC RESPECT FROM OTHER KIDS AND PARENTS AND OTHERS.

THROUGHOUT THE YEARS, IT'D FEEL VERY MUCH LIKE..."WELL, YOU DON'T FIT INTO OUR CLUB. HE'S DIFFERENT. HE TALKS DIFFERENT. THE MUSIC HE LISTENS TO IS DIFFERENT. HIS APPEARANCE IS DIFFERENT..."

BUT OUTSIDE OF THE ICE, WHEN I WASN'T REALLY NEEDED BEYOND INTIMIDATING THE OPPOSING TEAM AND HITTING THE PUCK, I JUST FELT...DIFFERENT.

SO MAYBE EDWARD WAS RIGHT...

EDWARD ***WAS*** RIGHT...RIGHT?
THIS WASN'T A SPORT FOR PEOPLE LIKE US.
WAIT, WHA–
WHOA! DID YOU GUYS JUST SEE WHAT I SAW?!
HIS NAME WAS AARON ATWELL AND HE WAS A PLAYER FOR ANOTHER TEAM.
ARE YOU COMING BY LATER? THERE'S A FEW OF US GOING TO PLAY SOME SOCCER.
OH YEAH, I'M COMING!
WE ACTUALLY GOT CLOSE PRETTY FAST.
WE TRIED TO PLAY ON THE SAME TEAMS THROUGH THE YEARS, BUT IT WASN'T UNTIL WE BOTH GOT ON THE MARLIES THAT WE FINALLY BECAME TEAMMATES.
AND HE WOULD BECOME ONE OF MY BEST FRIENDS.
IN YOUR FACE, EDWARD!

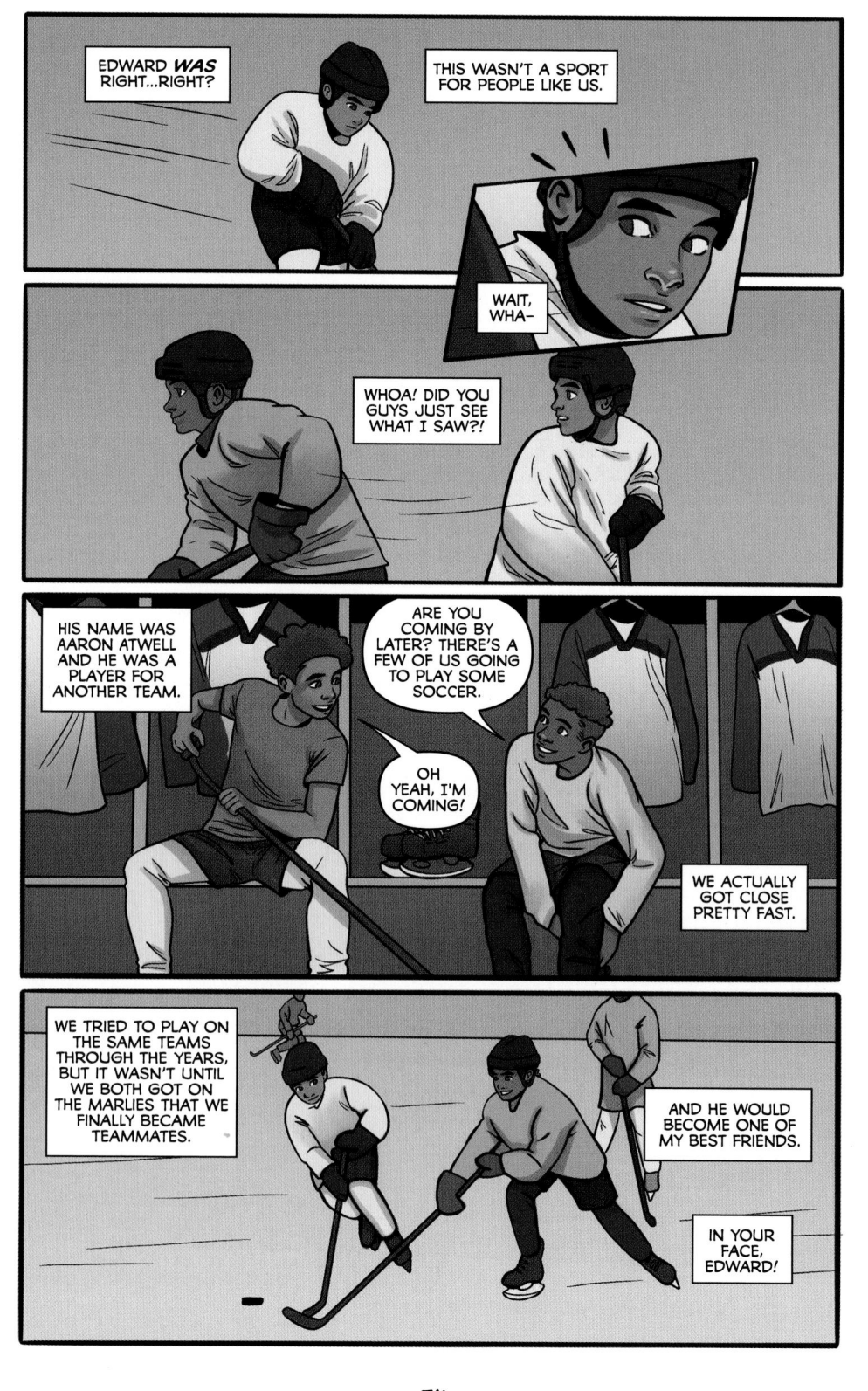

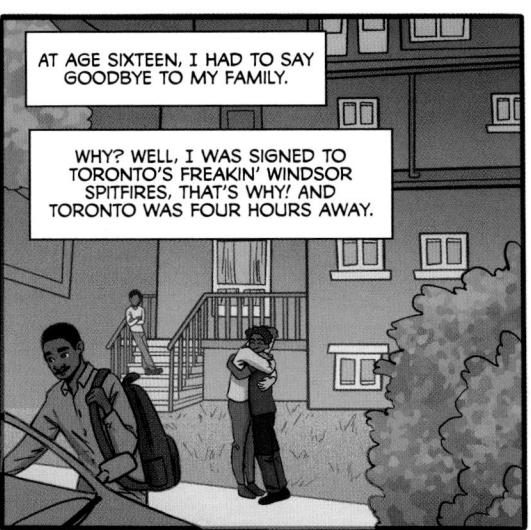

AT AGE SIXTEEN, I HAD TO SAY GOODBYE TO MY FAMILY.

WHY? WELL, I WAS SIGNED TO TORONTO'S FREAKIN' WINDSOR SPITFIRES, THAT'S WHY! AND TORONTO WAS FOUR HOURS AWAY.

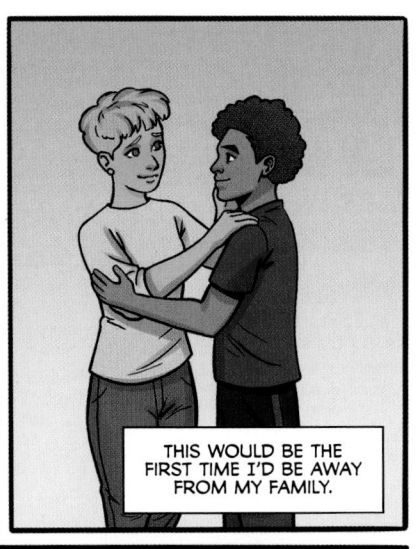

THIS WOULD BE THE FIRST TIME I'D BE AWAY FROM MY FAMILY.

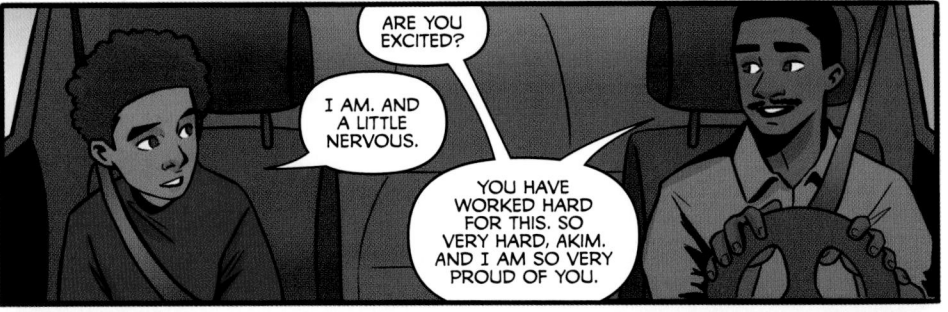

I WAS BOTH THRILLED AND SCARED.

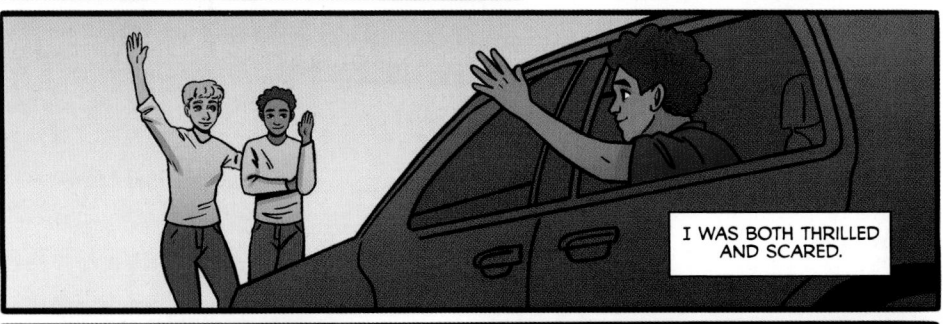

ARE YOU EXCITED?

I AM. AND A LITTLE NERVOUS.

YOU HAVE WORKED HARD FOR THIS. SO VERY HARD, AKIM. AND I AM SO VERY PROUD OF YOU.

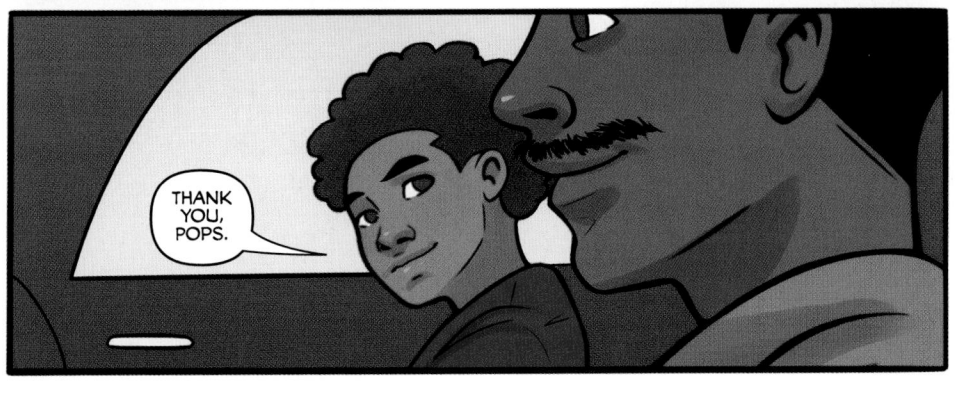

THANK YOU, POPS.

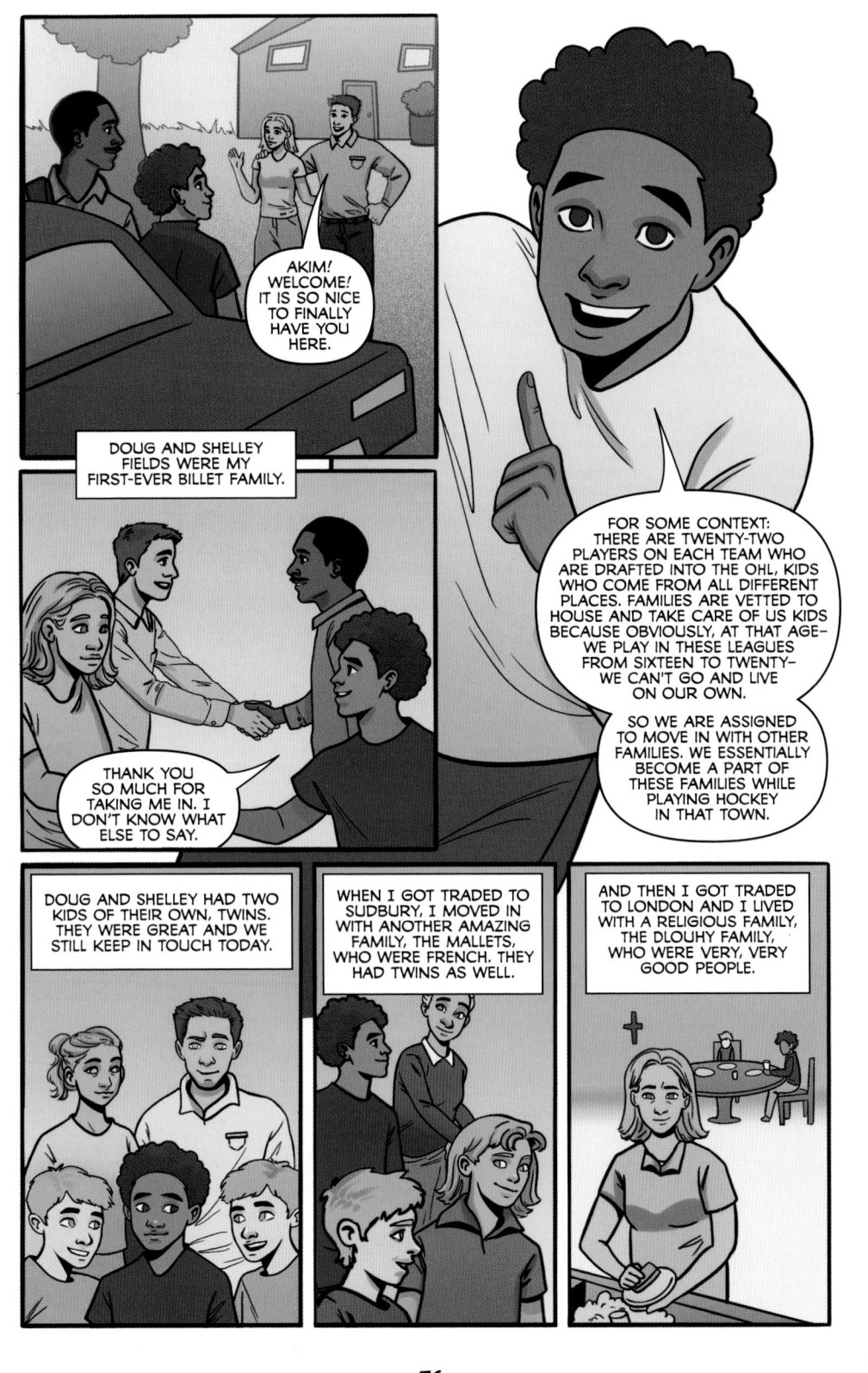

AKIM! WELCOME! IT IS SO NICE TO FINALLY HAVE YOU HERE.

DOUG AND SHELLEY FIELDS WERE MY FIRST-EVER BILLET FAMILY.

FOR SOME CONTEXT: THERE ARE TWENTY-TWO PLAYERS ON EACH TEAM WHO ARE DRAFTED INTO THE OHL, KIDS WHO COME FROM ALL DIFFERENT PLACES. FAMILIES ARE VETTED TO HOUSE AND TAKE CARE OF US KIDS BECAUSE OBVIOUSLY, AT THAT AGE— WE PLAY IN THESE LEAGUES FROM SIXTEEN TO TWENTY— WE CAN'T GO AND LIVE ON OUR OWN.

SO WE ARE ASSIGNED TO MOVE IN WITH OTHER FAMILIES. WE ESSENTIALLY BECOME A PART OF THESE FAMILIES WHILE PLAYING HOCKEY IN THAT TOWN.

THANK YOU SO MUCH FOR TAKING ME IN. I DON'T KNOW WHAT ELSE TO SAY.

DOUG AND SHELLEY HAD TWO KIDS OF THEIR OWN, TWINS. THEY WERE GREAT AND WE STILL KEEP IN TOUCH TODAY.

WHEN I GOT TRADED TO SUDBURY, I MOVED IN WITH ANOTHER AMAZING FAMILY, THE MALLETS, WHO WERE FRENCH. THEY HAD TWINS AS WELL.

AND THEN I GOT TRADED TO LONDON AND I LIVED WITH A RELIGIOUS FAMILY, THE DLOUHY FAMILY, WHO WERE VERY, VERY GOOD PEOPLE.

MY FIRST BILLET FAMILY, THE FIELDS, WERE ABSOLUTELY AMAZING.
OH, ARE YOU CURIOUS ABOUT THEIR VETTING INTERVIEW? GLAD YOU ASKED...
...I JUST WANT TO LET YOU KNOW THE KID THAT YOU'RE GETTING IS BLACK. ARE YOU OKAY WITH THAT?
WHAT? WHY ARE YOU TELLING US THAT?
WHY SHOULD THAT EVEN MATTER?
AND THAT WAS THE ASSISTANT COACH ASKING, LADIES AND GENTS.
THANK YOU, POPS.
YOU CALL ME AND YOUR MOTHER FOR ANYTHING, YOU HEAR? WE'RE JUST A FEW HOURS AWAY.
I KNOW. DRIVE SAFELY.
I ACTUALLY WASN'T THE ONLY ONE STAYING WITH THE FIELDS.
AKIM, THIS IS MIKE WEBER. HE'LL ALSO BE STAYING WITH US.
HEY, MAN! NICE TO MEET YOU. SO WE'RE GOING TO BE TEAMMATES!
GREAT TO MEET YOU, MAN. I CAN'T WAIT!

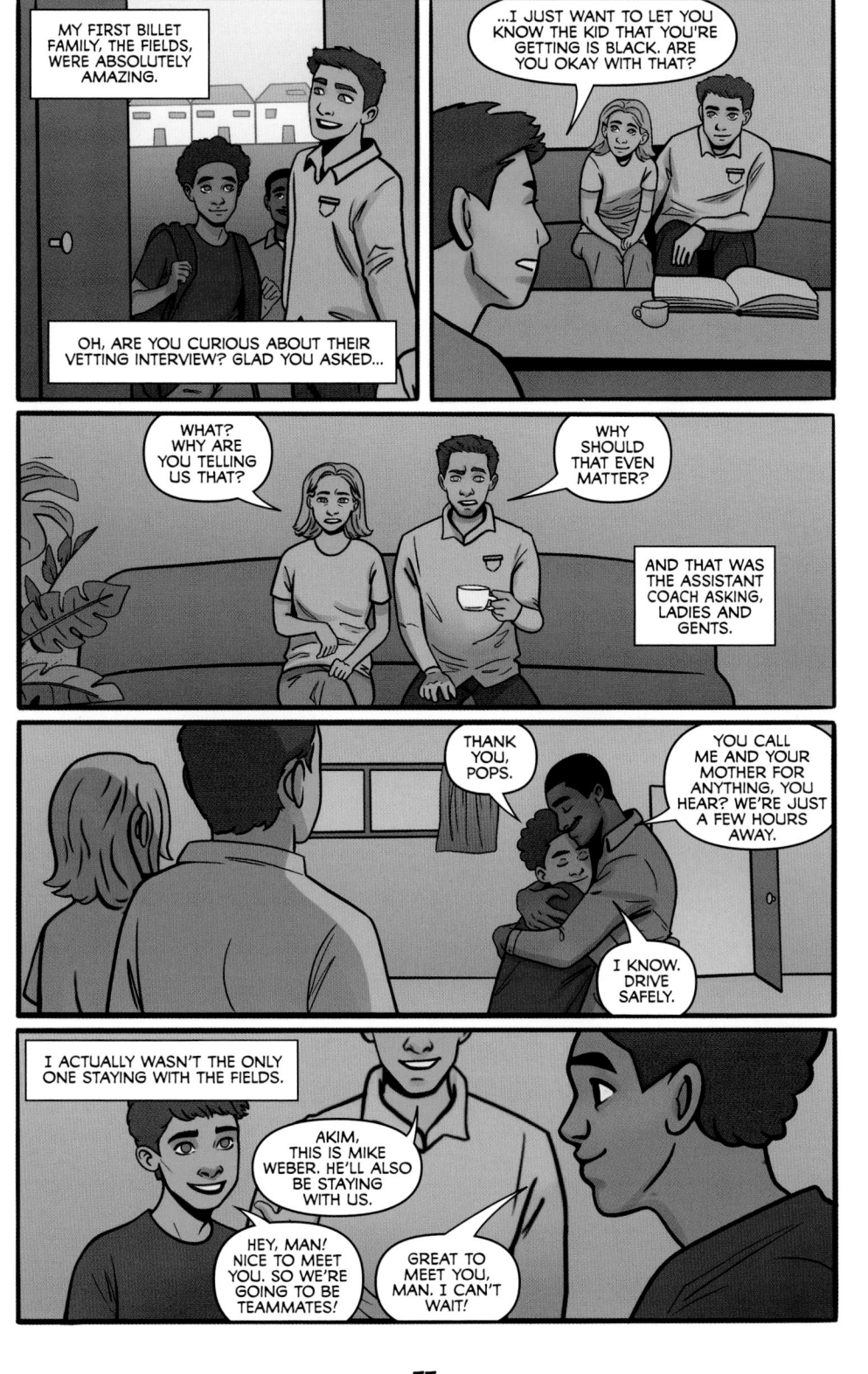

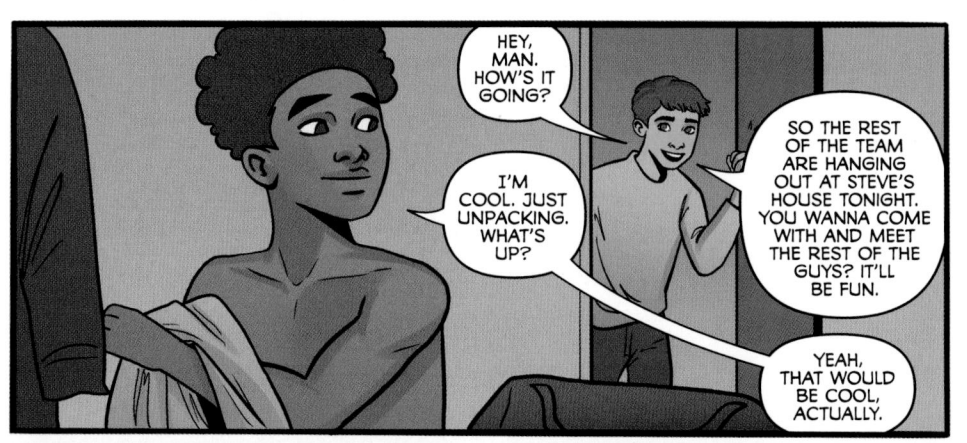

HEY, MAN. HOW'S IT GOING?

I'M COOL. JUST UNPACKING. WHAT'S UP?

SO THE REST OF THE TEAM ARE HANGING OUT AT STEVE'S HOUSE TONIGHT. YOU WANNA COME WITH AND MEET THE REST OF THE GUYS? IT'LL BE FUN.

YEAH, THAT WOULD BE COOL, ACTUALLY.

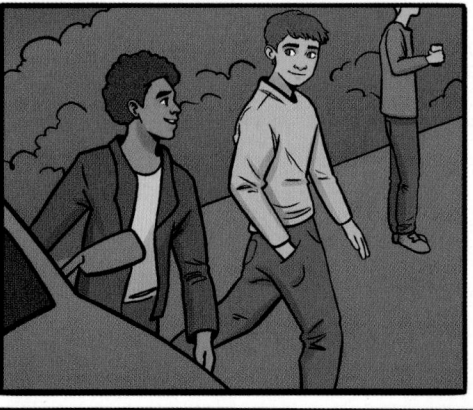

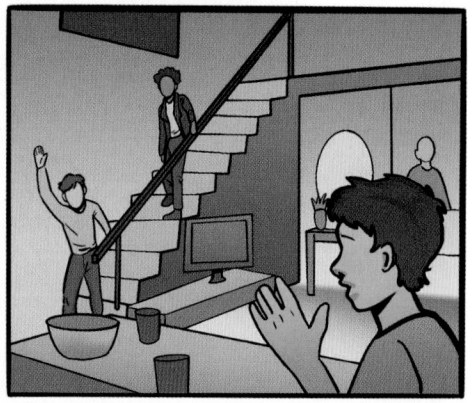

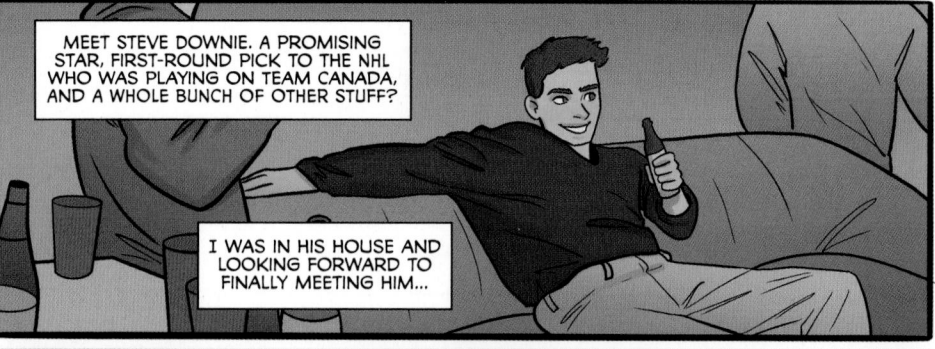

MEET STEVE DOWNIE. A PROMISING STAR, FIRST-ROUND PICK TO THE NHL WHO WAS PLAYING ON TEAM CANADA, AND A WHOLE BUNCH OF OTHER STUFF?

I WAS IN HIS HOUSE AND LOOKING FORWARD TO FINALLY MEETING HIM...

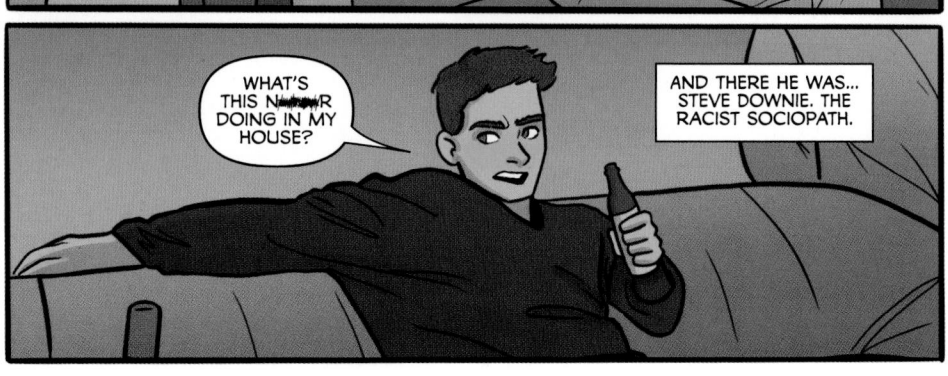

WHAT'S THIS N——R DOING IN MY HOUSE?

AND THERE HE WAS... STEVE DOWNIE. THE RACIST SOCIOPATH.

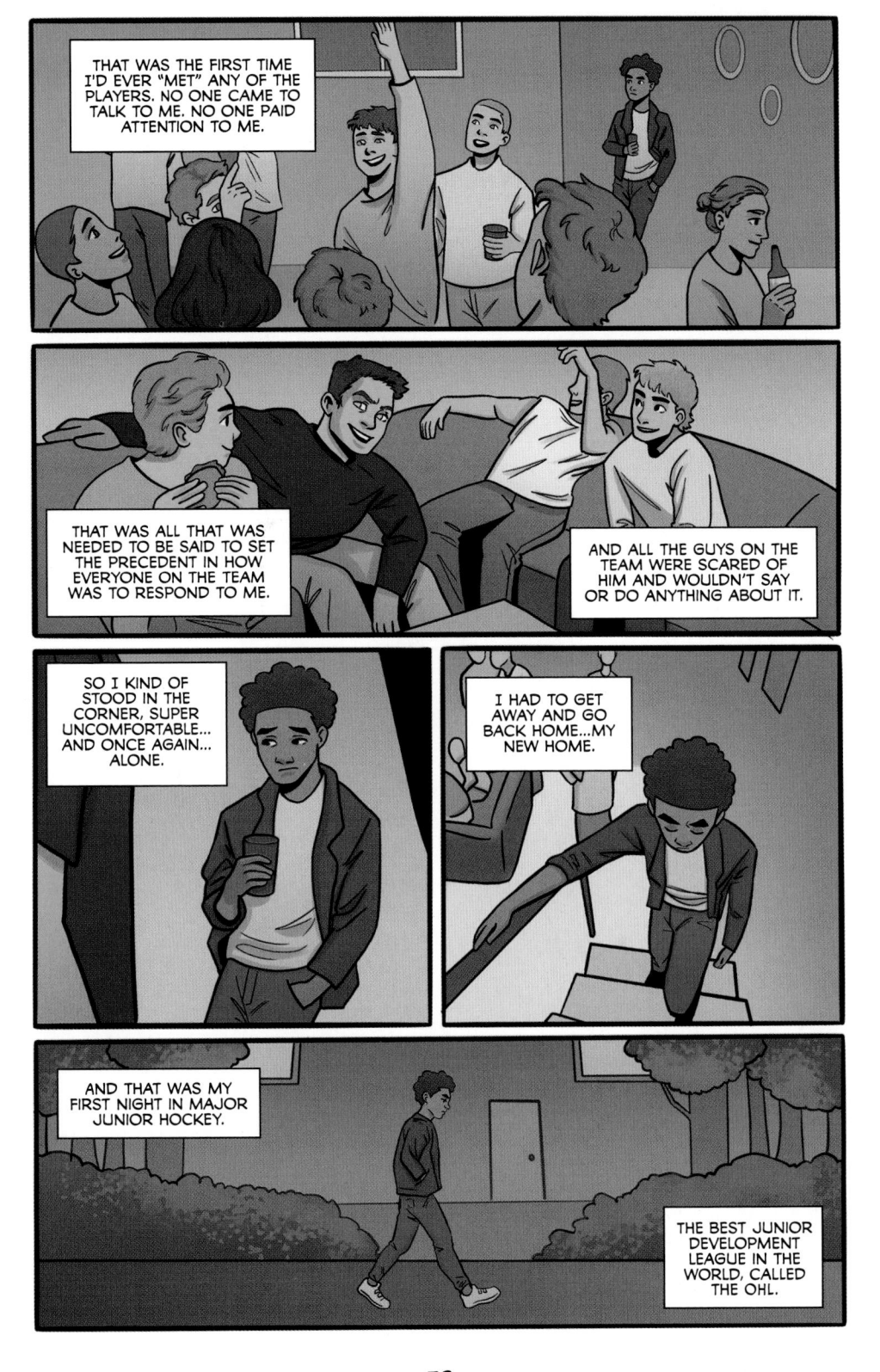

THAT WAS THE FIRST TIME I'D EVER "MET" ANY OF THE PLAYERS. NO ONE CAME TO TALK TO ME. NO ONE PAID ATTENTION TO ME.

THAT WAS ALL THAT WAS NEEDED TO BE SAID TO SET THE PRECEDENT IN HOW EVERYONE ON THE TEAM WAS TO RESPOND TO ME.

AND ALL THE GUYS ON THE TEAM WERE SCARED OF HIM AND WOULDN'T SAY OR DO ANYTHING ABOUT IT.

SO I KIND OF STOOD IN THE CORNER, SUPER UNCOMFORTABLE... AND ONCE AGAIN... ALONE.

I HAD TO GET AWAY AND GO BACK HOME...MY NEW HOME.

AND THAT WAS MY FIRST NIGHT IN MAJOR JUNIOR HOCKEY.

THE BEST JUNIOR DEVELOPMENT LEAGUE IN THE WORLD, CALLED THE OHL.

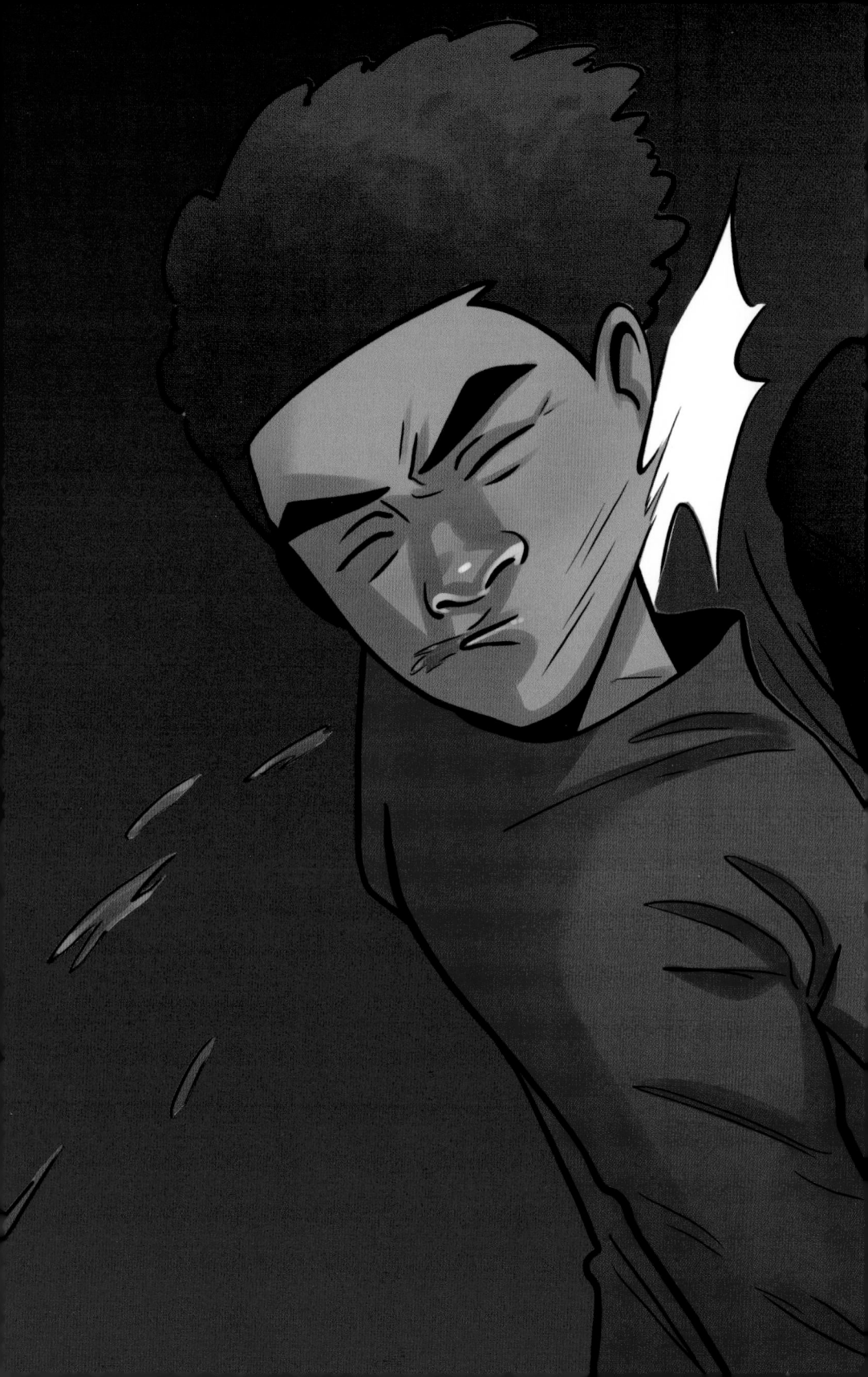

CHAPTER
FIVE

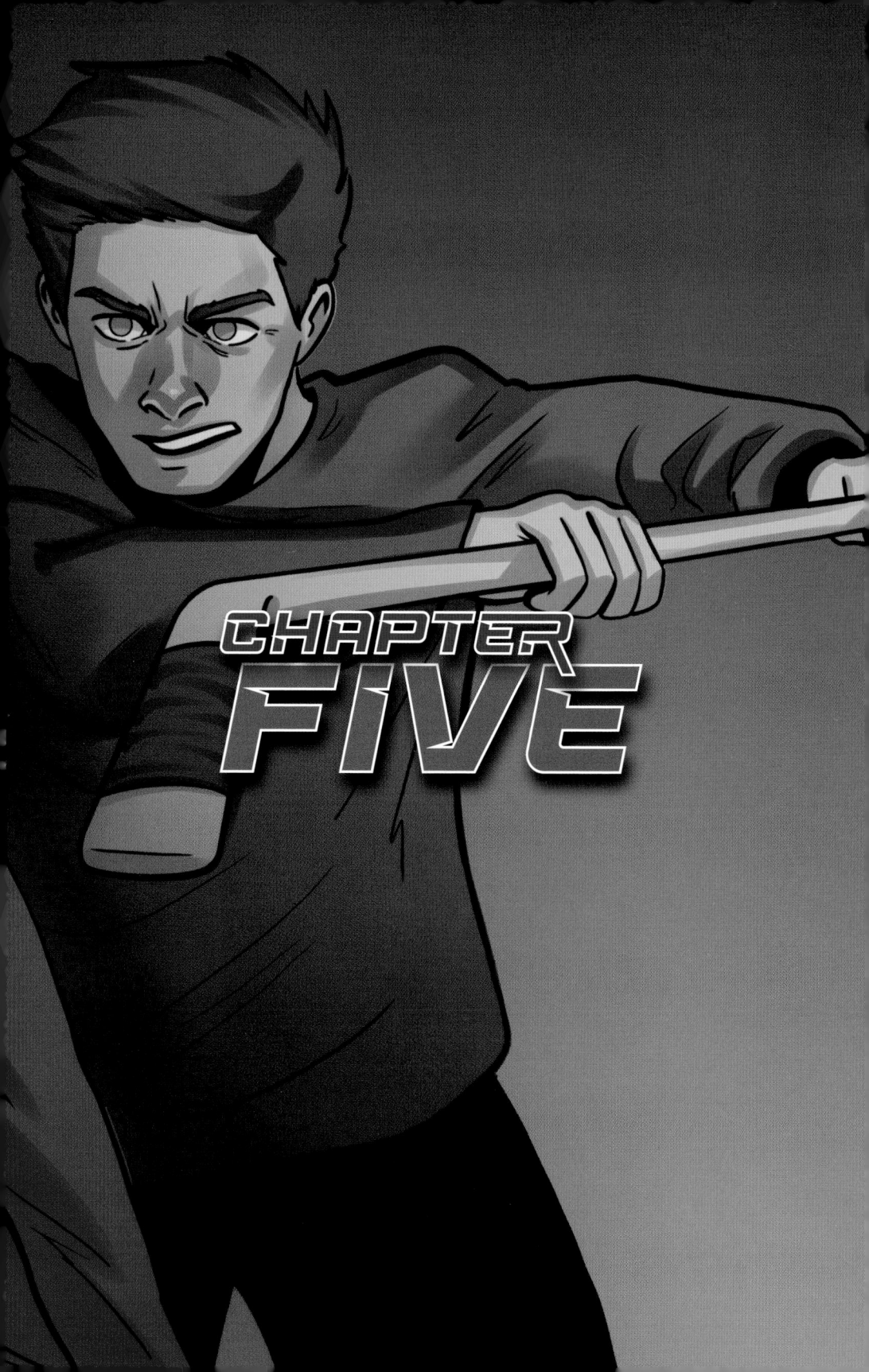

GET YOUR ASS BACK IN THERE. RIGHT. NOW.
NO!

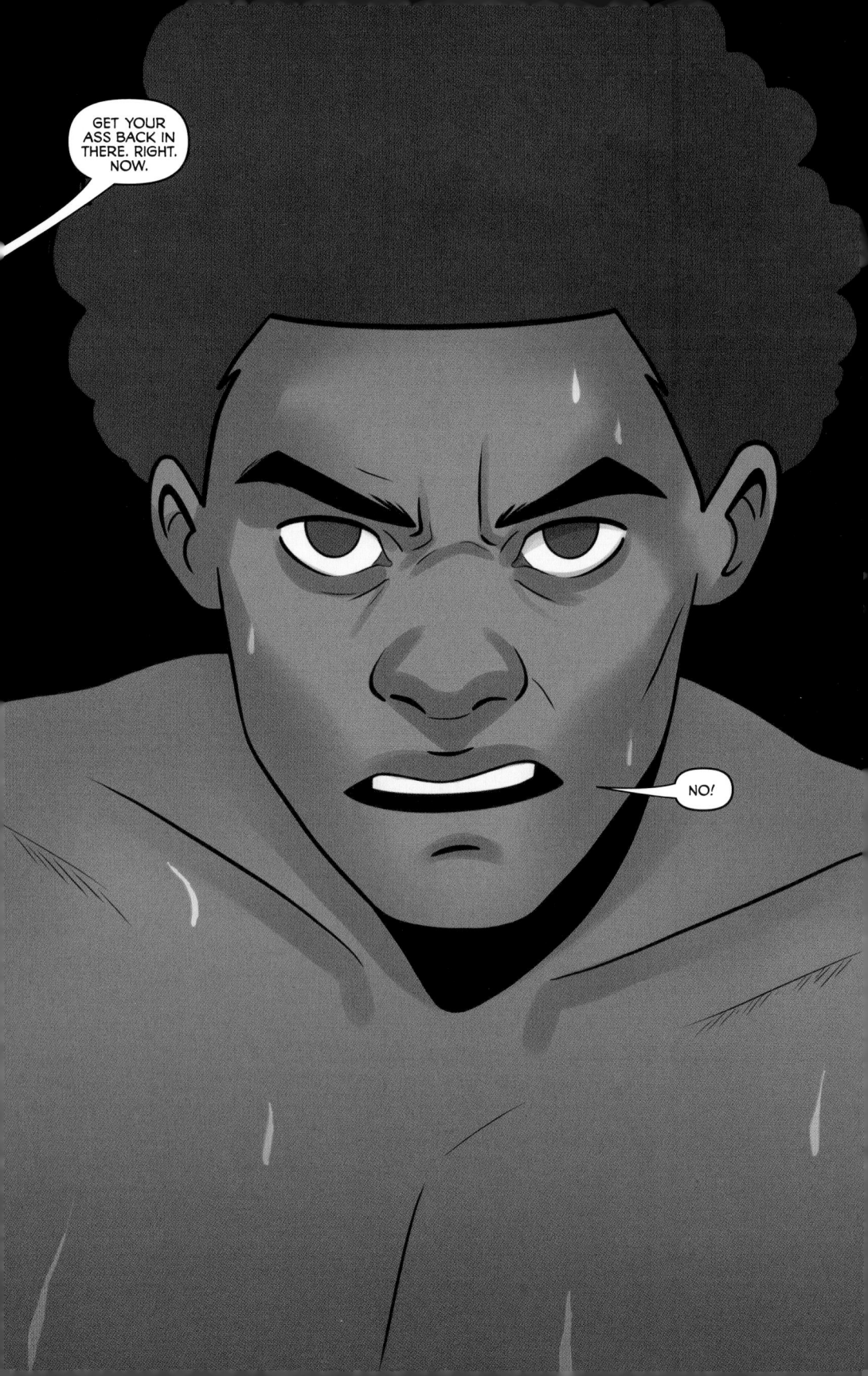

I HAD FINALLY GOTTEN INTO THE OHL.
TRAINED SO HARD TO GET A SPOT ON THE TEAM, ON MY WAY TO THE NHL.
AND HERE I WAS, BUTT NAKED FOR A STUPIDLY HORRIFIC RITUAL LED BY THIS FUTURE NHL STAR.
I'M NOT DOING THIS ANYMORE.
YEAH, YOU ARE.
STEVE DOWNIE.
SINCE I MET THIS GUY, IT WAS CONSTANT HARASSMENT AND MAKING MY TIME ON THIS TEAM A LIVING HELL.

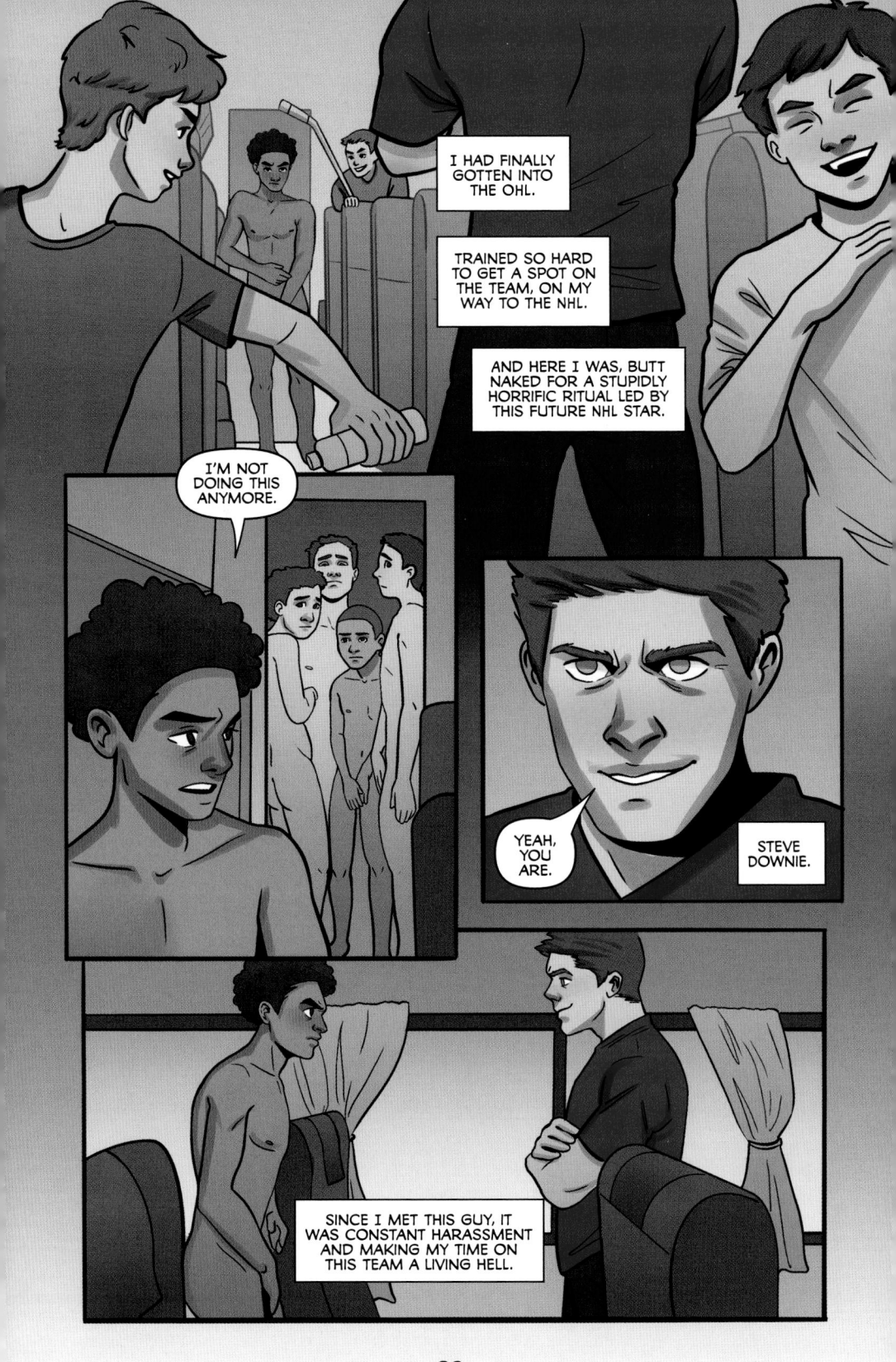

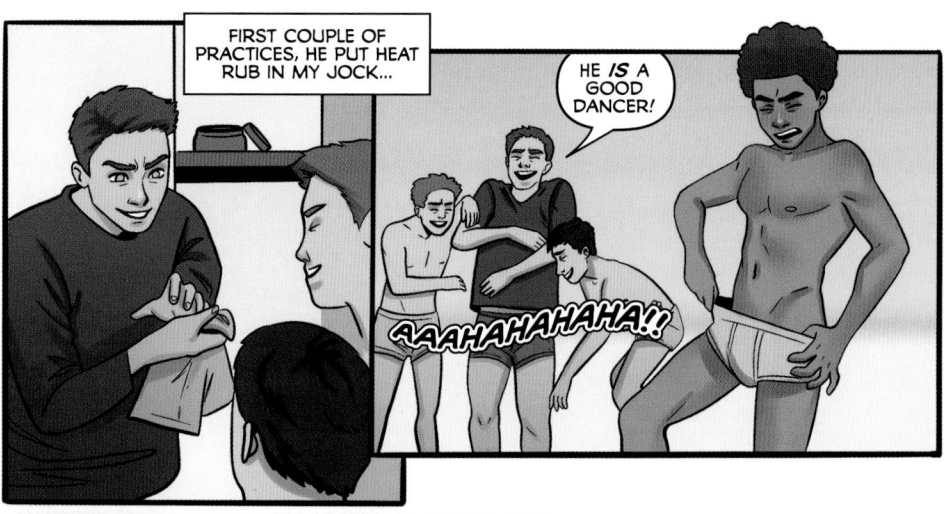

FIRST COUPLE OF PRACTICES, HE PUT HEAT RUB IN MY JOCK...

HE *IS* A GOOD DANCER!

AAAHAHAHAHA!!

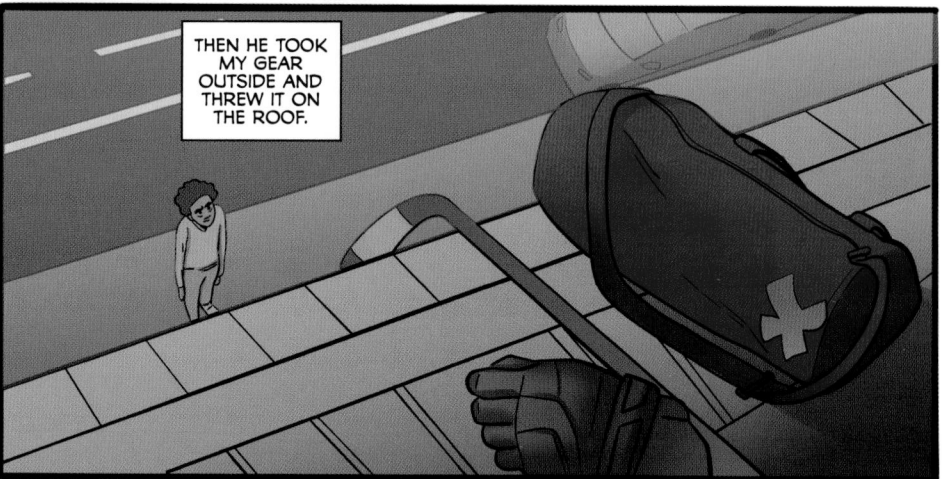

THEN HE TOOK MY GEAR OUTSIDE AND THREW IT ON THE ROOF.

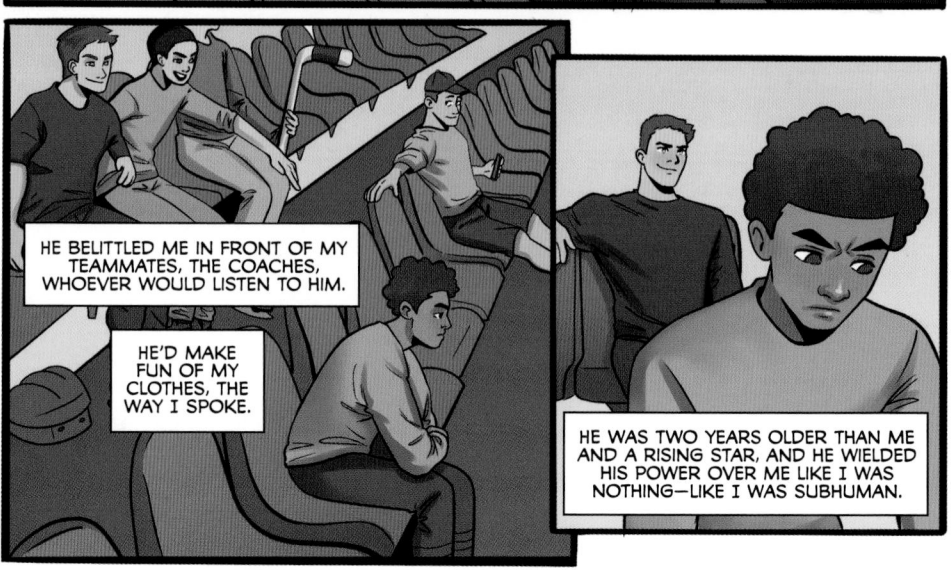

HE BELITTLED ME IN FRONT OF MY TEAMMATES, THE COACHES, WHOEVER WOULD LISTEN TO HIM.

HE'D MAKE FUN OF MY CLOTHES, THE WAY I SPOKE.

HE WAS TWO YEARS OLDER THAN ME AND A RISING STAR, AND HE WIELDED HIS POWER OVER ME LIKE I WAS NOTHING—LIKE I WAS SUBHUMAN.

IF YOU'VE HEARD OF ME, YOU'VE HEARD OF THE HAZING INCIDENT THAT TOOK PLACE THAT SEASON.
THEY FORCED US TO GET NAKED RIGHT OUTSIDE THE BATHROOM.
...AND THEN CRANKED THE HEAT UP.
I STARTED TO PANIC...
YO, LET ME OUT!
I STARTED GETTING CLAUSTROPHOBIC...
OPEN THE DOOR!!

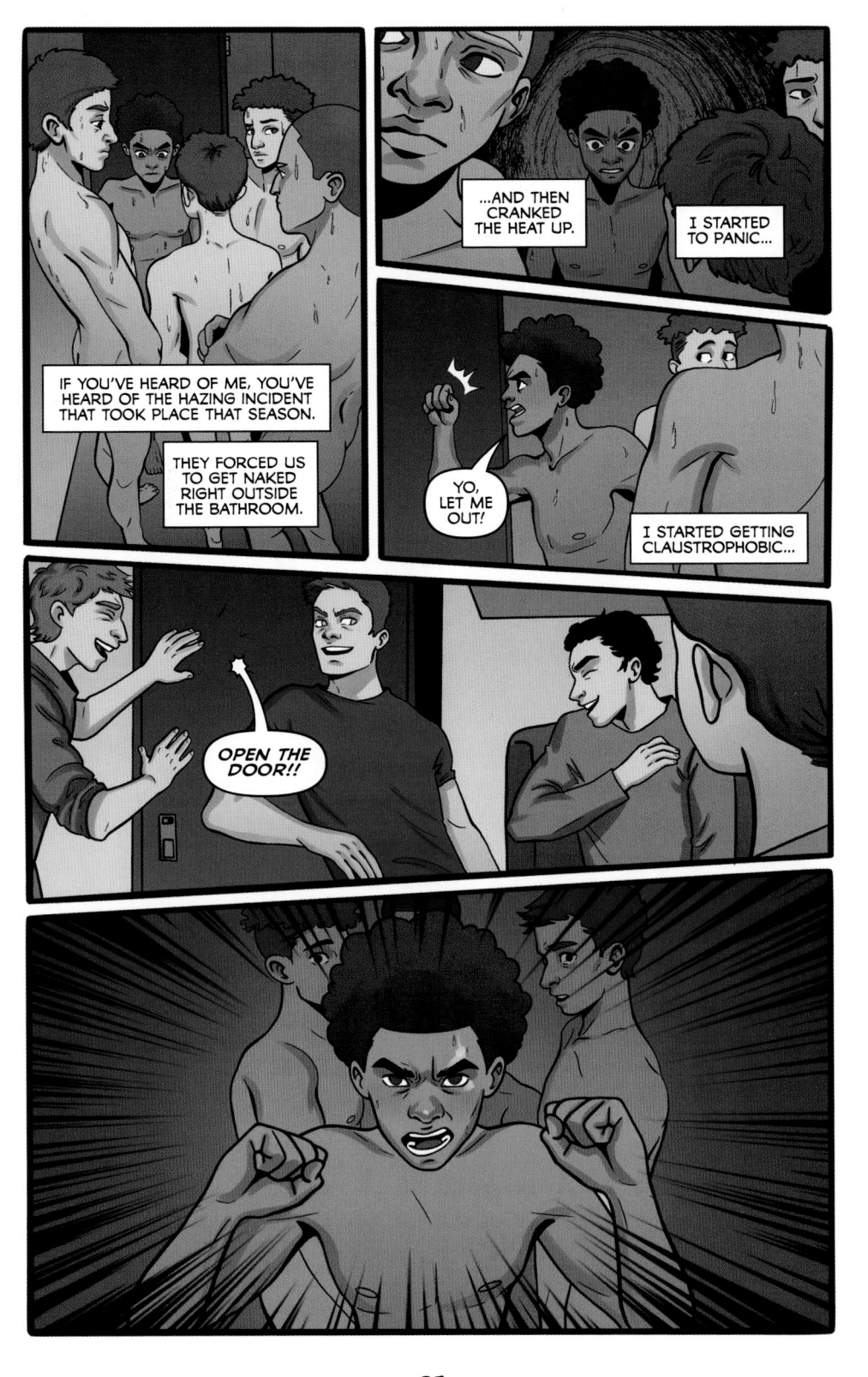

{HUFF}
{HUFF}
ALL RIGHT, YOU CAUGHT YOUR BREATH. NOW GET BACK IN THERE.
NO.
GET YOUR ASS BACK IN THERE. RIGHT. NOW.
NO!
I'M NOT DOING THIS ANYMORE.
YEAH, YOU ARE.

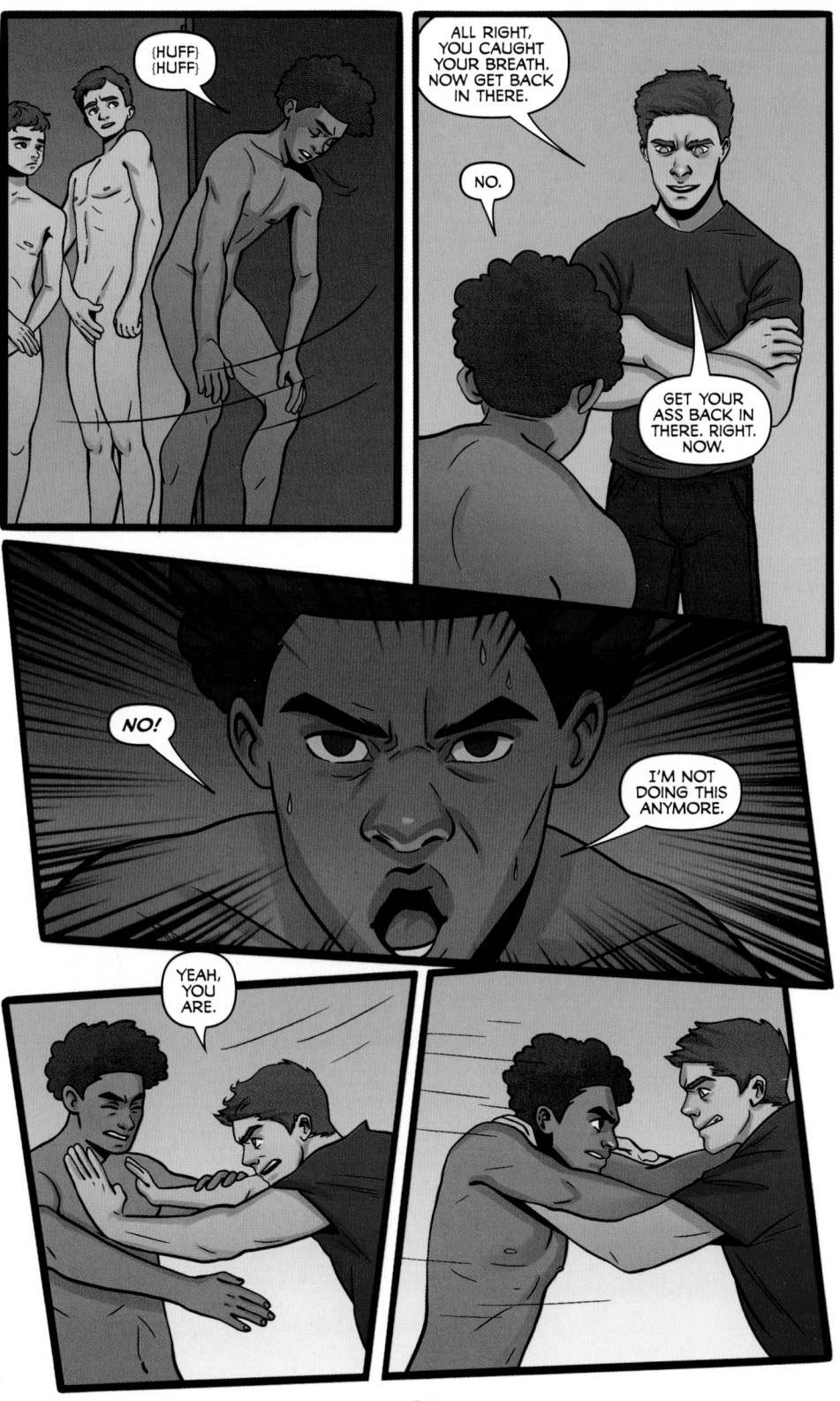

THANKS TO THIS GUY, THAT WAS THE WAY I WAS INTRODUCED TO THE ENTIRE HOCKEY WORLD.
I WAS THE KID WHO WOULDN'T GO ALONG WITH IT.
THE KID WHO DIDN'T "GET" THE CULTURE.
WATCH NEXT PRACTICE! WATCH YOUR F[redacted]NG BACK!
CAN YOU IMAGINE THE FEELING OF DREAMING THAT YOUR PARENTS WOULD FINALLY READ ABOUT YOU IN THE HEADLINES MAKING GOALS...
...BUT INSTEAD IT WAS ABOUT YOUR BOY GETTING IN A FIGHT BECAUSE HE REFUSED TO GO BACK INTO A BATHROOM NAKED WITH FOUR OTHER GUYS?

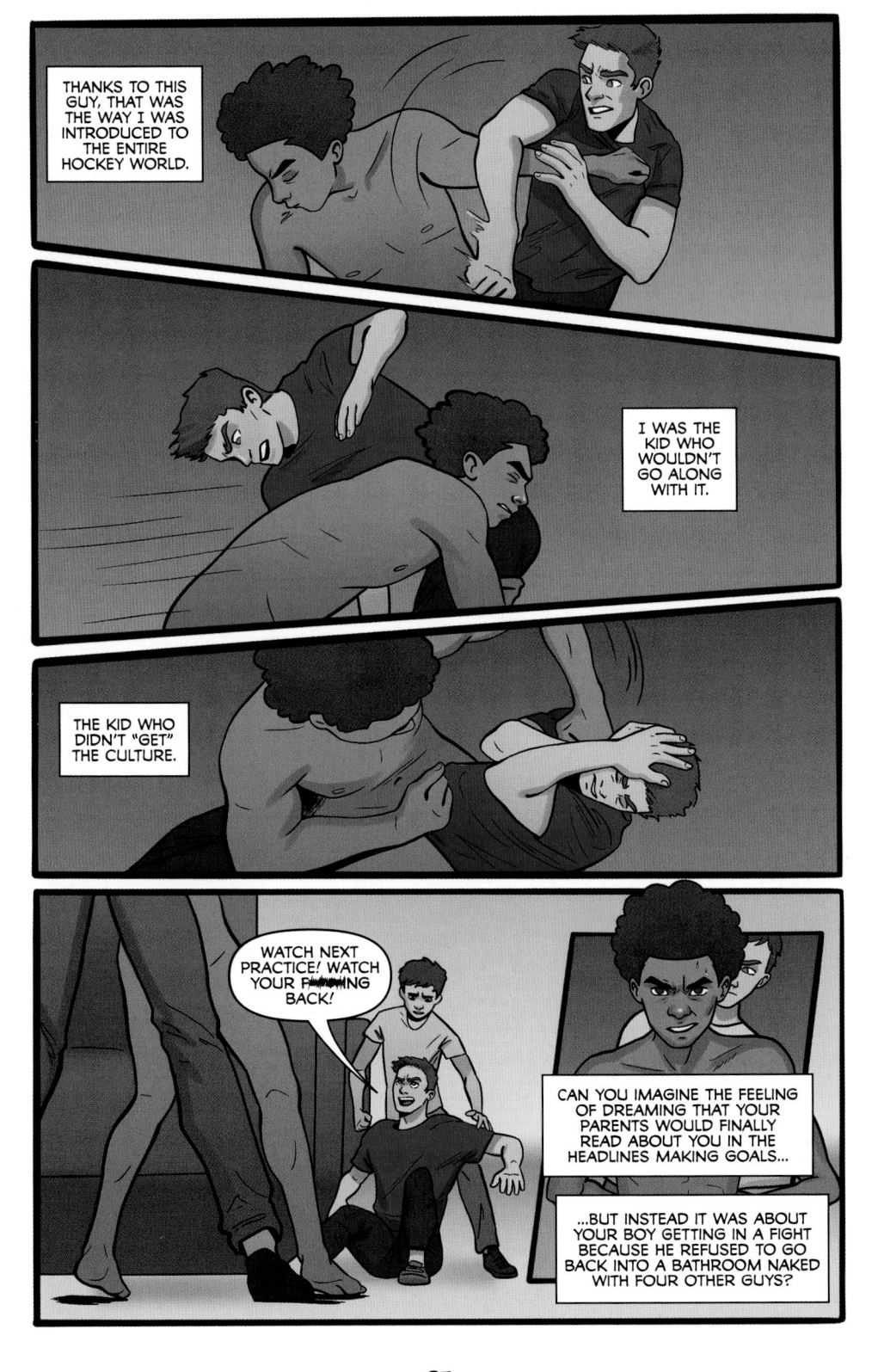

AND, SOMEHOW, THE WHOLE ISSUE WAS TREATED LIKE SOME SORT OF DISCUSSION. I READ HEADLINES LIKE...
WAS WHAT HAPPENED TO AKIM ALIU WRONG?
WHAT?
ONE NHL PLAYER CALLED IT...
AMUSING.
"AMUSING."
STRIPPING SIXTEEN-YEAR-OLD BOYS AND SHOVING THEM IN BATHROOMS AND CRANKING UP THE HEAT.
YOU KNOW WHAT I THINK IS AMUSING?
THE NHL'S TITLE FOR THEIR ANNUAL DIVERSITY CAMPAIGN, "HOCKEY IS FOR EVERYONE."
MAKES ME CRACK UP.
BECAUSE, RIGHT NOW, HOCKEY IS ***NOT*** FOR EVERYONE.
NHL
HOCKEY IS FOR EVERYONE
I LEARNED THAT WHEN I WAS SIXTEEN.

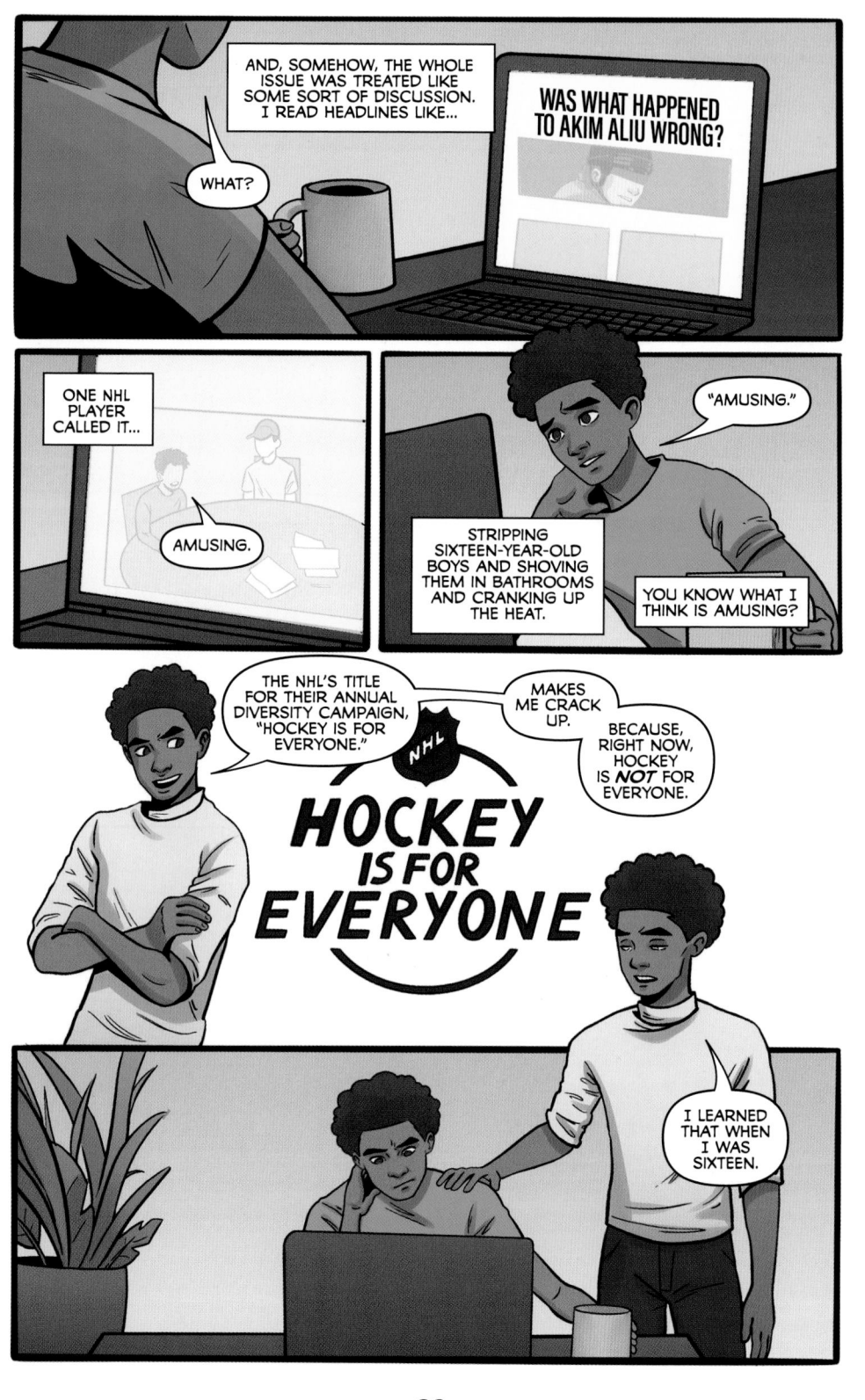

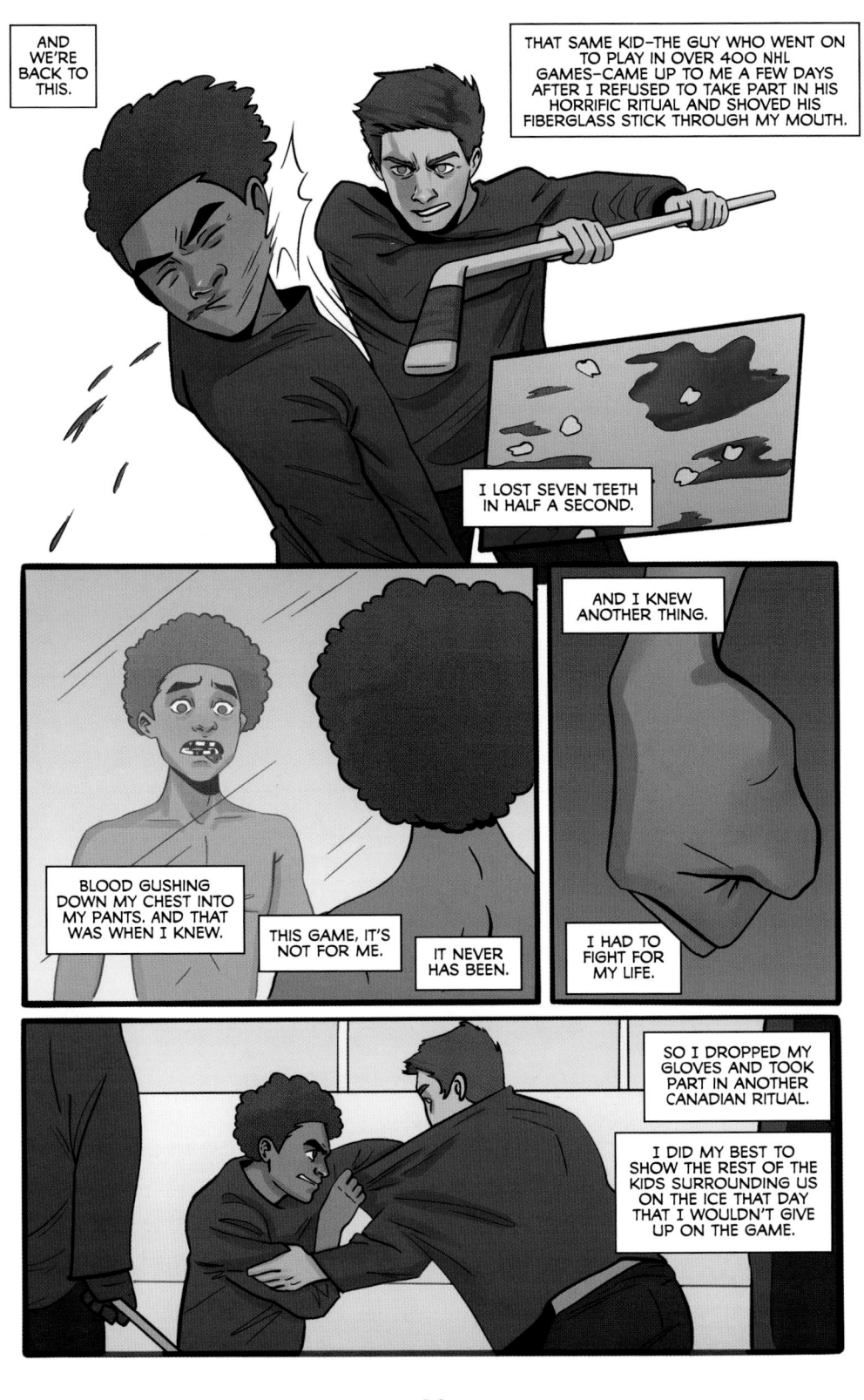

AND WE'RE BACK TO THIS.

THAT SAME KID—THE GUY WHO WENT ON TO PLAY IN OVER 400 NHL GAMES—CAME UP TO ME A FEW DAYS AFTER I REFUSED TO TAKE PART IN HIS HORRIFIC RITUAL AND SHOVED HIS FIBERGLASS STICK THROUGH MY MOUTH.

I LOST SEVEN TEETH IN HALF A SECOND.

AND I KNEW ANOTHER THING.

BLOOD GUSHING DOWN MY CHEST INTO MY PANTS. AND THAT WAS WHEN I KNEW.

THIS GAME, IT'S NOT FOR ME.

IT NEVER HAS BEEN.

I HAD TO FIGHT FOR MY LIFE.

SO I DROPPED MY GLOVES AND TOOK PART IN ANOTHER CANADIAN RITUAL.

I DID MY BEST TO SHOW THE REST OF THE KIDS SURROUNDING US ON THE ICE THAT DAY THAT I WOULDN'T GIVE UP ON THE GAME.

89

GOD, TAI. LOOK AT HIM. LOOK WHAT THEY DID TO OUR SON.

MOM...

THIS IS *NOT* SUPPOSED TO HAPPEN. THE *WHOLE* TEAM ON THE ICE, COACHES ARE THERE, AND THEY ALLOW *THIS* TO HAPPEN?

LOOK AT MY SON. THIS IS COMPLETELY UNACCEPTABLE. WHAT ARE YOU GOING TO DO ABOUT THIS DOWNIE BOY?

WE ARE DOING EVERYTHING WE CAN. WE ARE GOING TO INVESTIGATE...

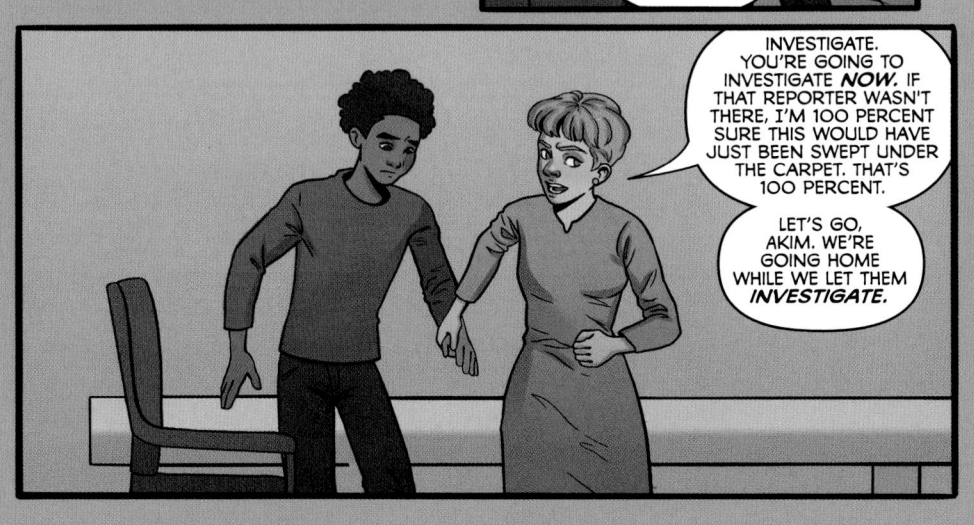

INVESTIGATE. YOU'RE GOING TO INVESTIGATE *NOW.* IF THAT REPORTER WASN'T THERE, I'M 100 PERCENT SURE THIS WOULD HAVE JUST BEEN SWEPT UNDER THE CARPET. THAT'S 100 PERCENT.

LET'S GO, AKIM. WE'RE GOING HOME WHILE WE LET THEM *INVESTIGATE.*

BUT IT WASN'T MY PARENTS DRIVING ME BACK...IT WAS THE TEAM OWNER, STEVE RIOLO.
ONE WOULD GUESS HE WANTED TO TALK TO ME IN HOPES OF ME NOT MAKING THIS ***THING*** WITH DOWNIE A BIG DEAL.
A MEANS TO COVER ONE'S BUTT.
YEAH, WE'LL FIGURE IT OUT, OKAY, BUDDY? WE'LL WORK IT OUT. DON'T WORRY ABOUT IT. EVERYTHING IS GOING TO WORK OUT.

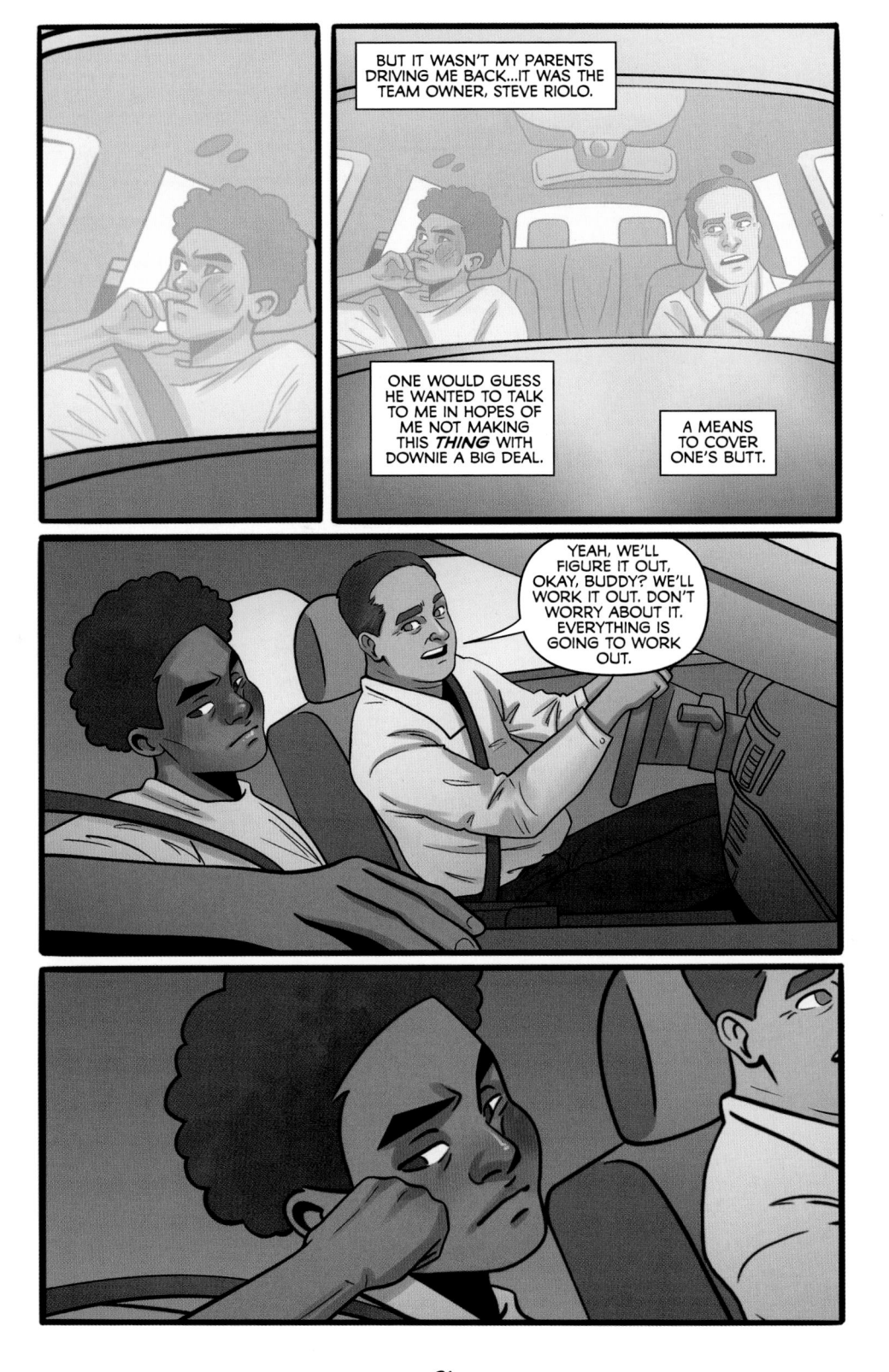

YOU PROBABLY DON'T WANT TO TALK ABOUT IT RIGHT NOW, BUT WE'RE GOING TO HAVE TO, SON.
...
HOW ARE YOU FEELING, AKIM?
...
...I just want to play...

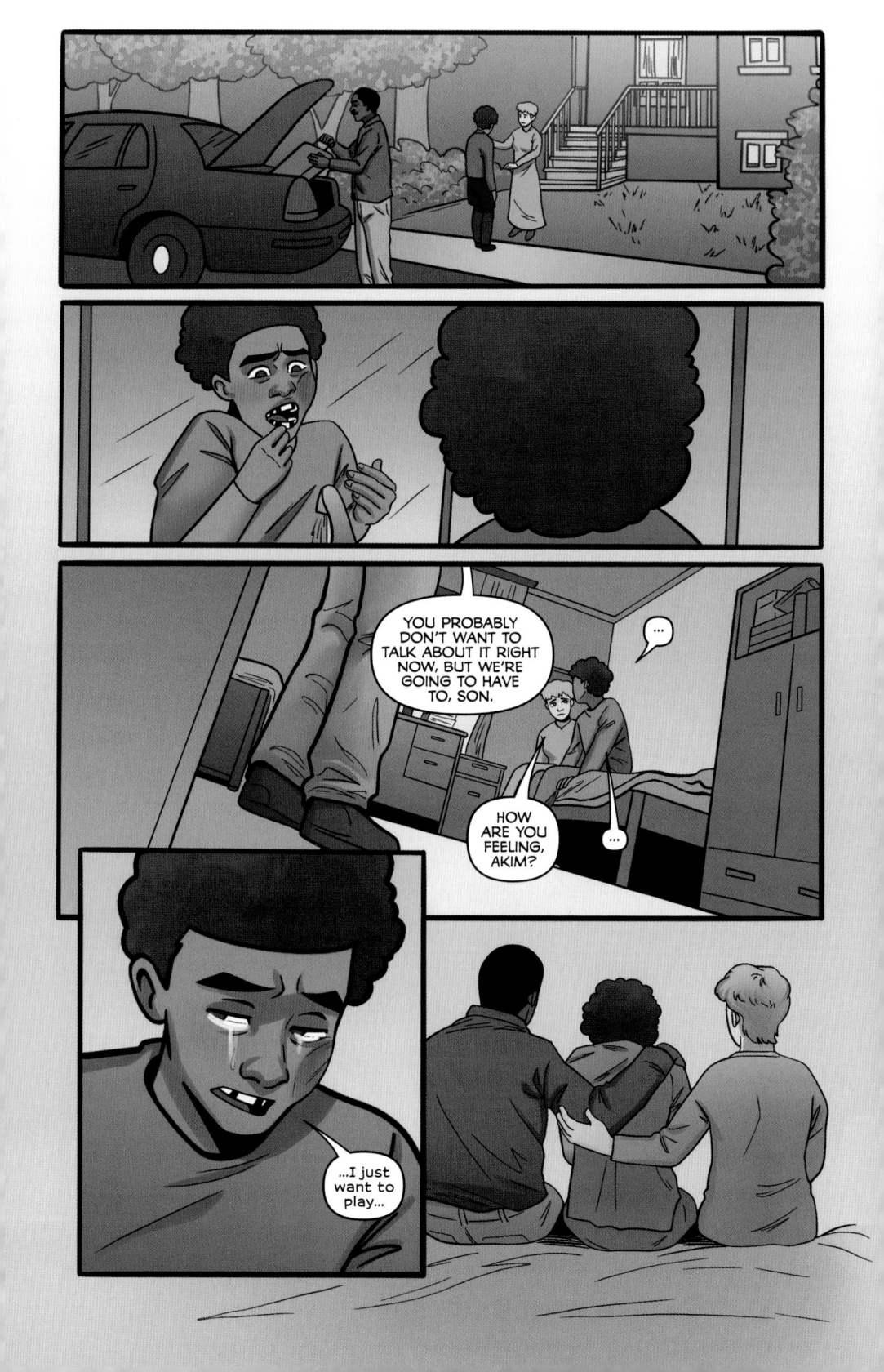

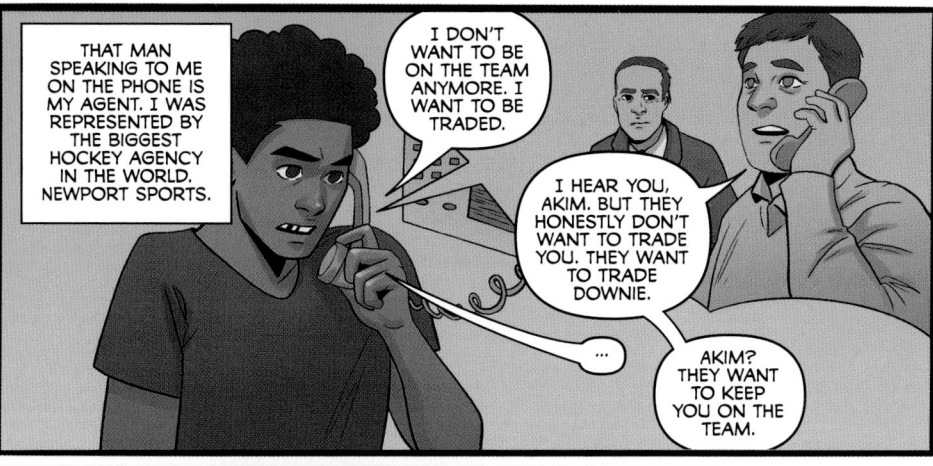

THAT MAN SPEAKING TO ME ON THE PHONE IS MY AGENT. I WAS REPRESENTED BY THE BIGGEST HOCKEY AGENCY IN THE WORLD. NEWPORT SPORTS.

I DON'T WANT TO BE ON THE TEAM ANYMORE. I WANT TO BE TRADED.

I HEAR YOU, AKIM. BUT THEY HONESTLY DON'T WANT TO TRADE YOU. THEY WANT TO TRADE DOWNIE.

...

AKIM? THEY WANT TO KEEP YOU ON THE TEAM.

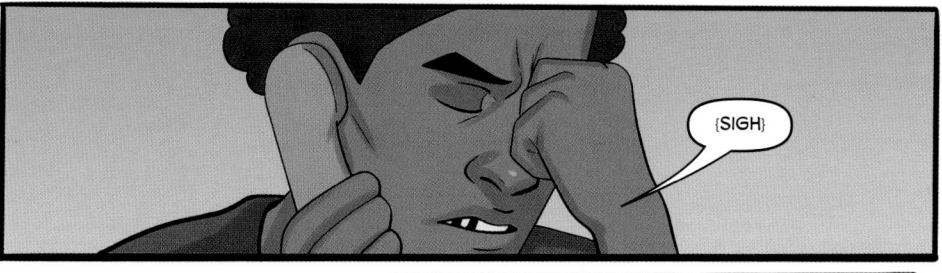

{SIGH}

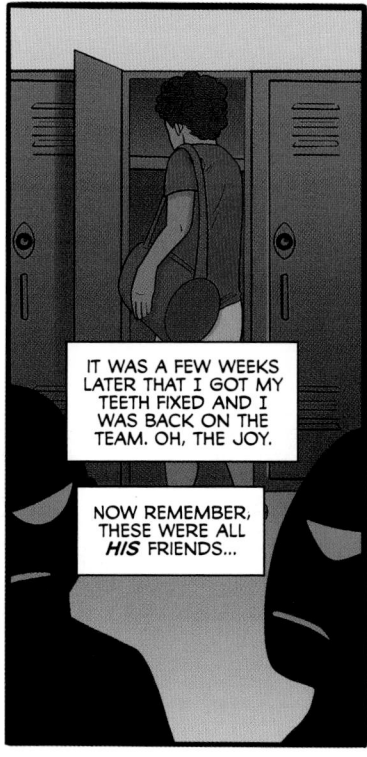

IT WAS A FEW WEEKS LATER THAT I GOT MY TEETH FIXED AND I WAS BACK ON THE TEAM. OH, THE JOY.

NOW REMEMBER, THESE WERE ALL *HIS* FRIENDS...

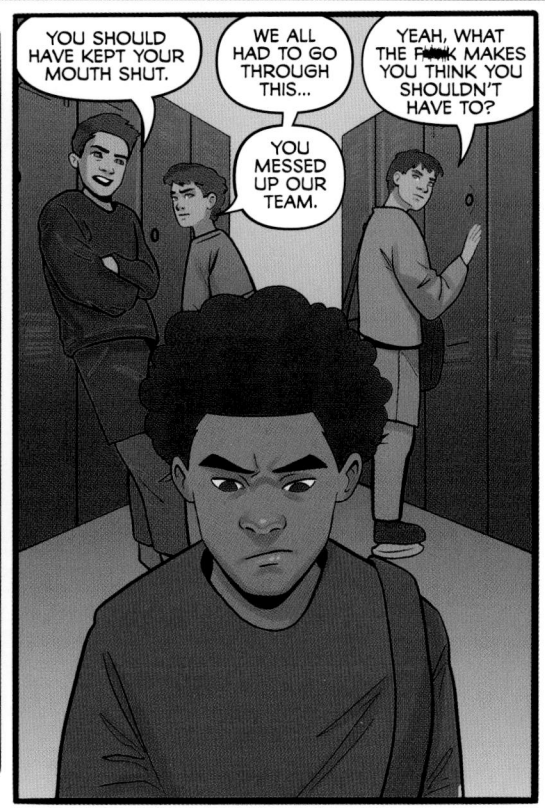

YOU SHOULD HAVE KEPT YOUR MOUTH SHUT.

WE ALL HAD TO GO THROUGH THIS...

YOU MESSED UP OUR TEAM.

YEAH, WHAT THE F**K MAKES YOU THINK YOU SHOULDN'T HAVE TO?

DESPITE THE HARDSHIPS I WAS DEALING WITH, SOMETHING TOTALLY UNEXPECTED WOULD FILL ME WITH JOY...
MY BROTHER, EDWARD-FREAKIN' EDWARD-CAME TO SEE ME PLAY!
WHOA, THIS DUDE IS REALLY MAKING THIS HAPPEN...
THERE HE WAS, A PART OF ABOUT 15,000 HOCKEY FANS, ACTUALLY SUPPORTING ME AFTER ALL THESE YEARS.
THAT'S MY BROTHER!
BUT OF COURSE THAT WOULD BE THE GAME WHERE A GUY TRIED TO JUMP OVER ME AND DIDN'T MAKE IT, THUS LANDING ON MY ACHILLES TENDON AND CUTTING IT IN HALF.
DAMN, MAN. YOU ARE TOUGH.
HAHA! UGH, THIS FREAKING SUCKS!
YOU WERE GREAT OUT THERE, THOUGH. I MEAN, BEFORE ALL *THAT* HAPPENED.
OF COURSE. I'M YOUR BIG BRO. I'M PROUD OF YOU.
I APPRECIATE IT. THANK YOU FOR COMING. FOR REAL, THIS MEANS A LOT.

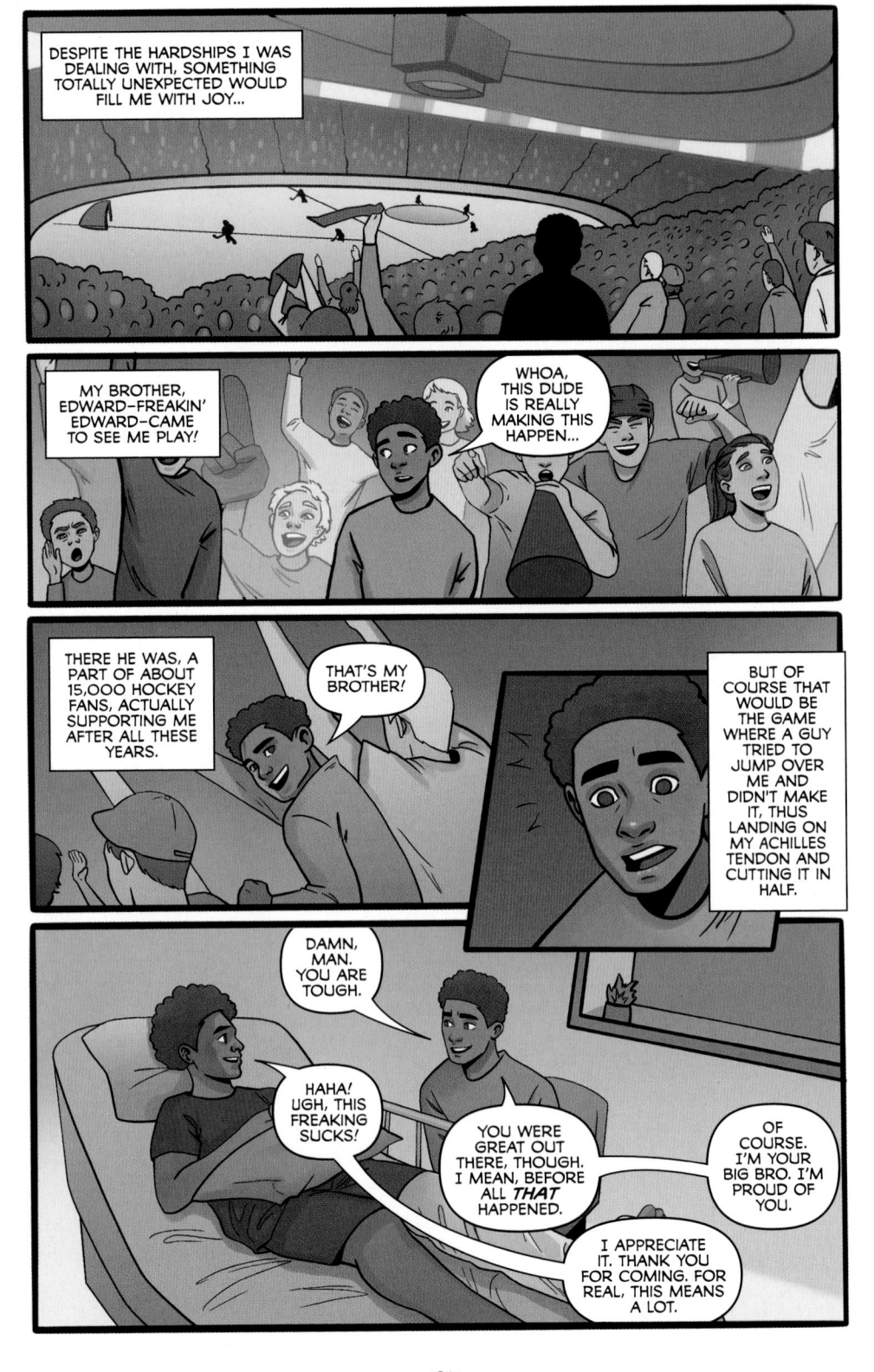

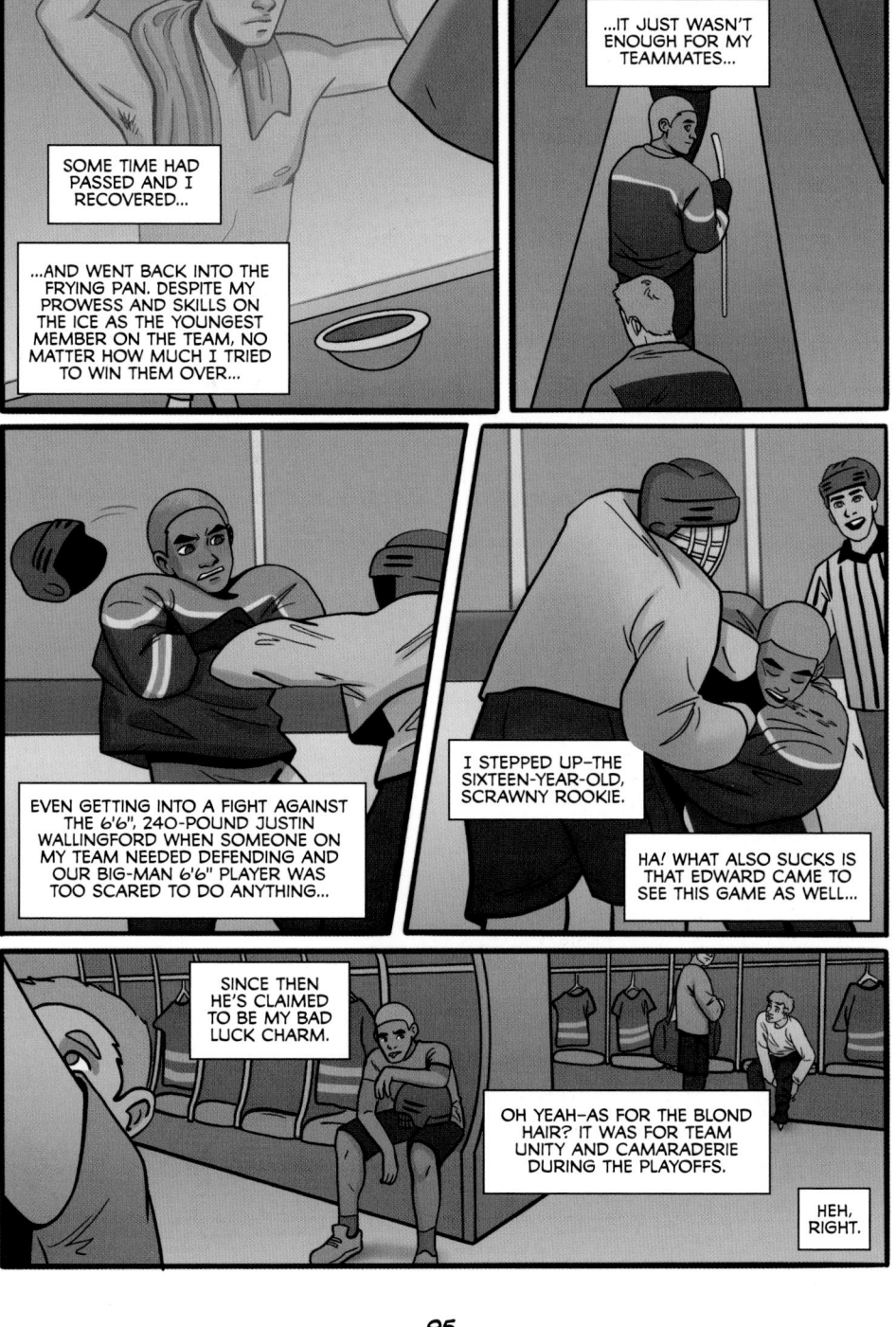

SOME TIME HAD PASSED AND I RECOVERED...

...AND WENT BACK INTO THE FRYING PAN. DESPITE MY PROWESS AND SKILLS ON THE ICE AS THE YOUNGEST MEMBER ON THE TEAM, NO MATTER HOW MUCH I TRIED TO WIN THEM OVER...

...IT JUST WASN'T ENOUGH FOR MY TEAMMATES...

EVEN GETTING INTO A FIGHT AGAINST THE 6'6", 240-POUND JUSTIN WALLINGFORD WHEN SOMEONE ON MY TEAM NEEDED DEFENDING AND OUR BIG-MAN 6'6" PLAYER WAS TOO SCARED TO DO ANYTHING...

I STEPPED UP—THE SIXTEEN-YEAR-OLD, SCRAWNY ROOKIE.

HA! WHAT ALSO SUCKS IS THAT EDWARD CAME TO SEE THIS GAME AS WELL...

SINCE THEN HE'S CLAIMED TO BE MY BAD LUCK CHARM.

OH YEAH—AS FOR THE BLOND HAIR? IT WAS FOR TEAM UNITY AND CAMARADERIE DURING THE PLAYOFFS.

HEH, RIGHT.

AS IF I WASN'T ALREADY DEALING WITH THIS CRAP AT PRACTICE...
I ALSO HAD TO DEAL WITH MY BACKSTABBING HOUSEMATE, MIKE!
SERIOUSLY, MAN. IT'S F[redacted]D UP! THE TEAM WAS FINE, WE WERE DOING FINE, AND HERE YOU GO, MESSING UP THE WHOLE DAMN TEAM WITH YOUR B[redacted]!
YOU KNOW WHAT? F[redacted]K YOU, MIKE! PULL THE CAR OVER RIGHT NOW! I'M GOING TO BEAT YOUR A[redacted]S!
GUYS, COME ON NOW. CHILL OUT.
GET OUT OF THE F[redacted]ING CAR, MIKE!
GET OUT!!
AKIM! CALM DOWN! IT'S NOT WORTH IT!
HEY, MAN. JUST DRIVE. I'M GONNA KICK IT WITH AKIM.
THAT'S MICKEY RENAUD. NUMBER 18.
THE ONE FRIEND AND SUPPORT I ACTUALLY *DID* HAVE ON THE TEAM...
YOU GOTTA KEEP YOUR HEAD UP, MAN. YOU KEEP ALLOWING THOSE GUYS TO STRESS YOU OUT.
EASIER SAID THAN DONE, BRO. YOU SERIOUSLY DON'T KNOW WHAT IT'S LIKE. AND I'M TIRED, MAN. I AM SO FREAKING TIRED. I HONESTLY JUST WANT TO BE TRADED AND GET THE HELL OFF THIS DAMN TEAM!
...
YOU'RE RIGHT. I DON'T KNOW WHAT IT'S LIKE. I CAN ONLY IMAGINE.
BUT YOU GOT ME, MAN. I'M HERE NOW. WHY DON'T YOU COME OVER? LET'S HANG OUT FOR A BIT.

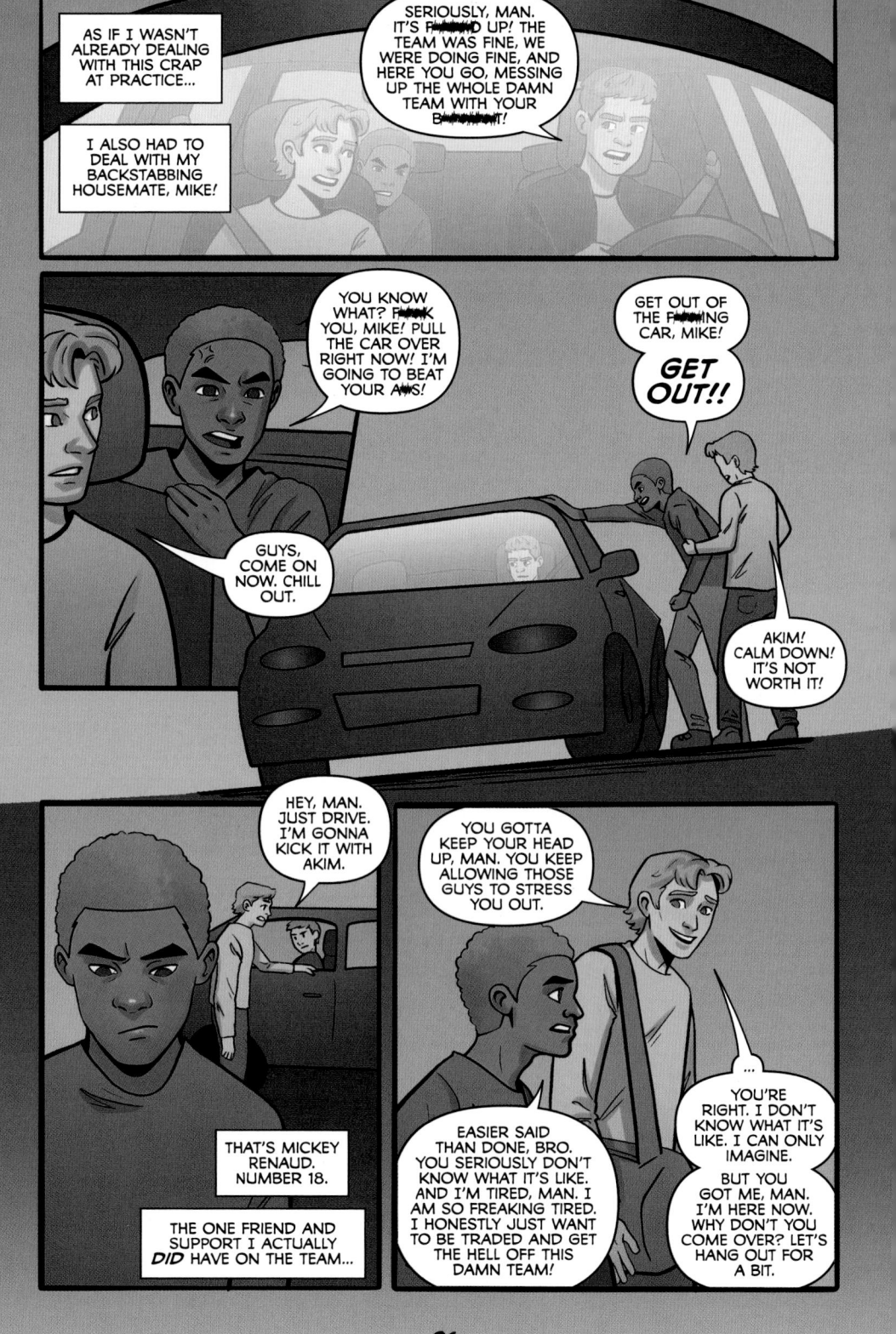

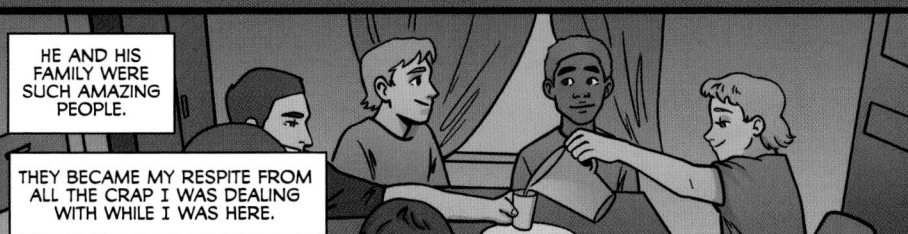

HE AND HIS FAMILY WERE SUCH AMAZING PEOPLE.

THEY BECAME MY RESPITE FROM ALL THE CRAP I WAS DEALING WITH WHILE I WAS HERE.

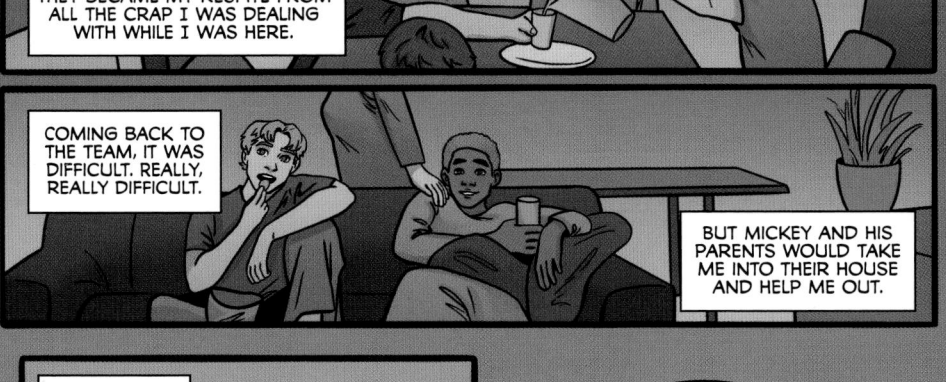

COMING BACK TO THE TEAM, IT WAS DIFFICULT. REALLY, REALLY DIFFICULT.

BUT MICKEY AND HIS PARENTS WOULD TAKE ME INTO THEIR HOUSE AND HELP ME OUT.

HE BECAME ONE OF MY BEST FRIENDS.

AND WHEN I WAS DOWN, HE'D ALWAYS TELL ME...

KEEP YOUR HEAD UP.

"KEEP YOUR HEAD UP."

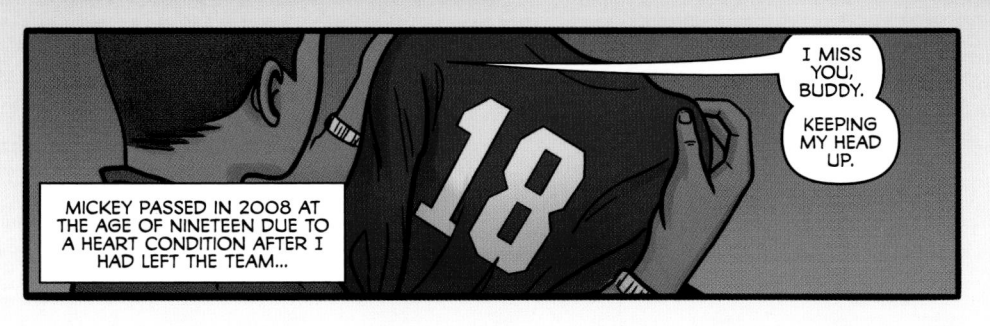

I MISS YOU, BUDDY.

KEEPING MY HEAD UP.

MICKEY PASSED IN 2008 AT THE AGE OF NINETEEN DUE TO A HEART CONDITION AFTER I HAD LEFT THE TEAM...

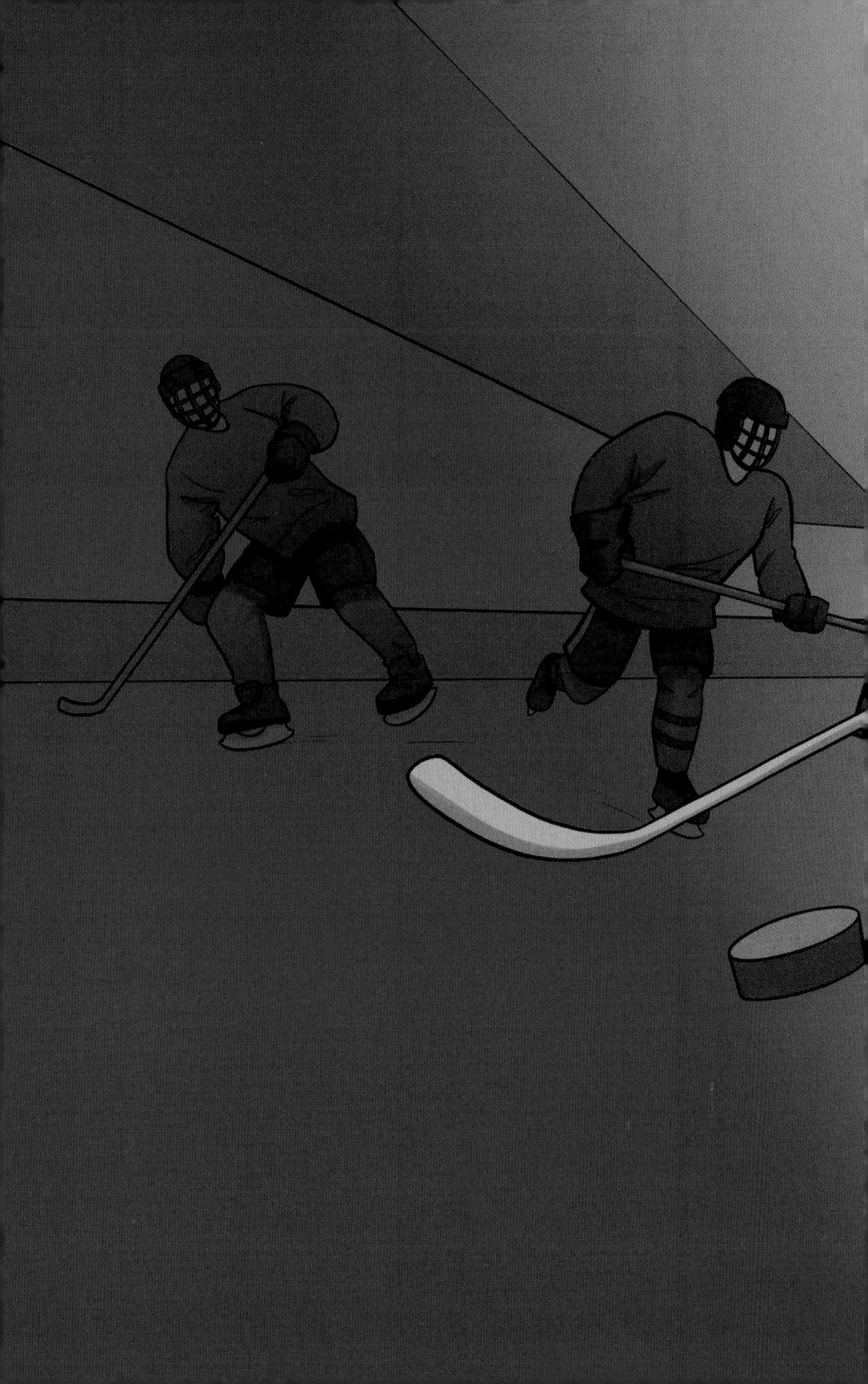

CHAPTER
SIX

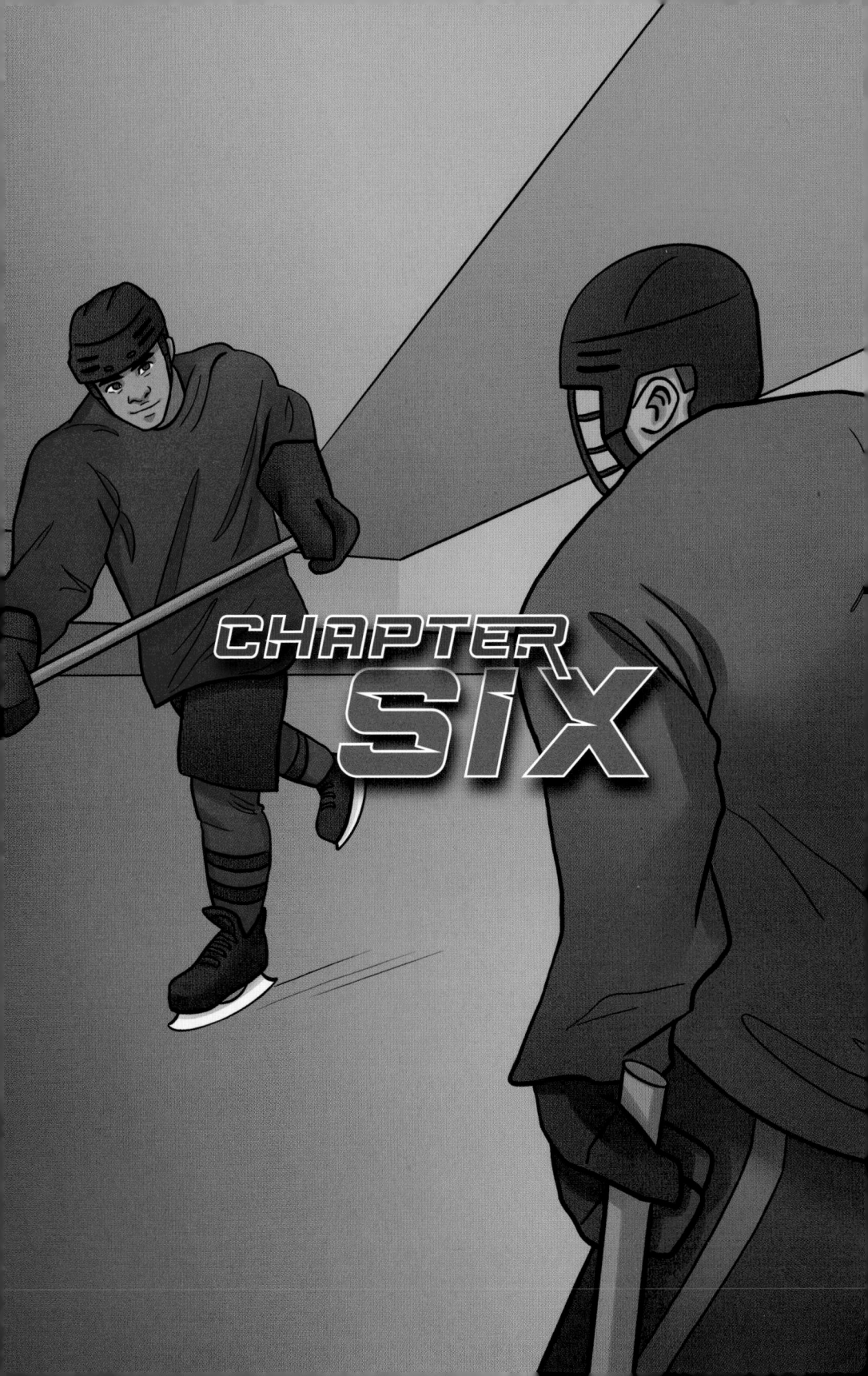

AFTER WINDSOR AND PLAYING WITH THE SPITFIRES, I WAS *FINALLY* TRADED TO THE SUDBURY WOLVES.
I CONSISTENTLY PLAYED WELL AND WAS PUTTING UP NUMBERS.
ALL IN TIME FOR THE ***TOP PROSPECT GAMES!***
WHERE FORTY OF THE TOP DRAFT-ELIGIBLE PROSPECTS IN THE WORLD AT THAT AGE GROUP PLAY A GAME AGAINST ONE ANOTHER.
I WON THE FASTEST SKATER AWARD!

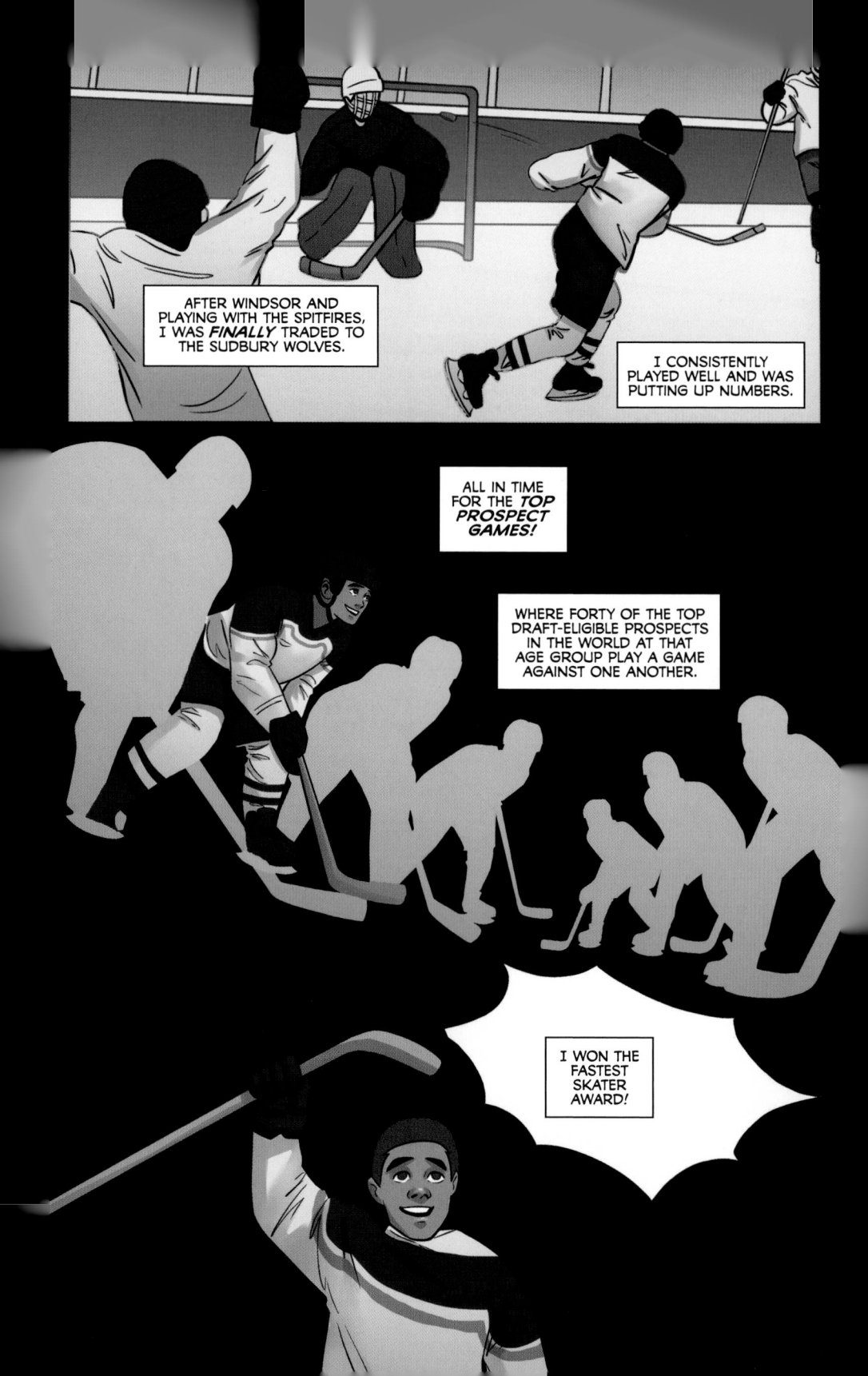

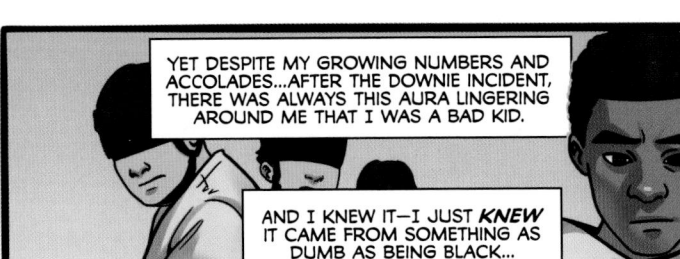

YET DESPITE MY GROWING NUMBERS AND ACCOLADES...AFTER THE DOWNIE INCIDENT, THERE WAS ALWAYS THIS AURA LINGERING AROUND ME THAT I WAS A BAD KID.

AND I KNEW IT—I JUST *KNEW* IT CAME FROM SOMETHING AS DUMB AS BEING BLACK...

MY APPEARANCE, MY 'FRO...JUST THE WAY I AM. I WAS DIFFERENT.

I DIDN'T LOOK LIKE A REGULAR HOCKEY PLAYER, ESPECIALLY AT THAT AGE IN THESE SMALL TOWNS.

ON TOP OF THAT, MY RANKINGS NEVER CORRELATED WITH HOW WELL I WAS PLAYING. IF YOU LOOKED AT MY NUMBERS AT THE TIME, I SHOULD HAVE BEEN TOP 20 IN THE WORLD. BUT INSTEAD I WOULD BE RANKED 30 TO 50.

IT ALL SEEMED TO GO BACK TO THE SITUATION WITH DOWNIE, WHERE SOMEHOW I WAS THE ONE PAINTED AS THE BAD GUY.

BLACK GUY, WHITE GUY IN HOCKEY. THE BLACK GUY *MUST* HAVE BEEN THE PROBLEM AND WAS NOW USING THE RACE CARD.

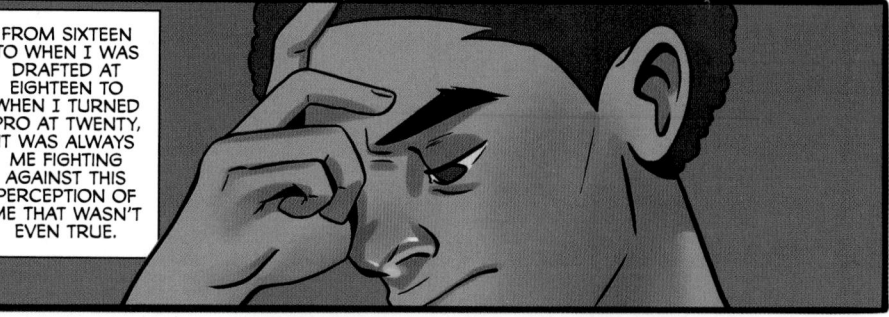

FROM SIXTEEN TO WHEN I WAS DRAFTED AT EIGHTEEN TO WHEN I TURNED PRO AT TWENTY, IT WAS ALWAYS ME FIGHTING AGAINST THIS PERCEPTION OF ME THAT WASN'T EVEN TRUE.

WHEN YOU ASK SOMEBODY, "WHERE DID YOU HEAR THAT FROM? WAS IT FROM A TEAMMATE? WHERE IS THIS COMING FROM?"

YOU'D GET, "WELL, I JUST HEARD..."

AND SPEAKING OF GOING PRO—THIS IS WHERE WE START TO FINALLY GET TO HITTING THE DREAM...

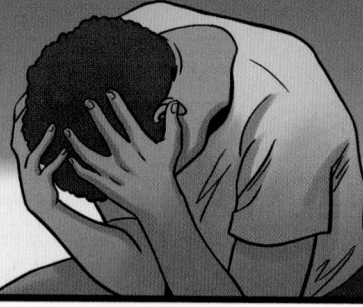

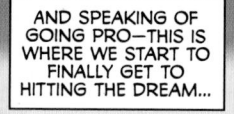

DRAFT DAY WAS APPROACHING, AND I WAS ON THE PHONE WITH MY AGENT...

NO, NO, NO. YOU'RE GOING TO BE IN THE TOP 15. I'VE BEEN TALKING TO TEAMS. YOU'RE GOOD, AKIM. TRUST ME. YOU'VE GOT NOTHING TO WORRY ABOUT.

I DON'T REALLY WANT TO GO.

WHAT? WHAT ARE YOU TALKING ABOUT? YOU *HAVE* TO GO.

{SIGH} OKAY... SURE.

I DON'T REALLY WANT TO GO IF I'M NOT GOING TO GET PICKED ON THE FIRST DAY. IT'S JUST A BUZZKILL. I'LL WATCH IT FROM HOME.

THE DRAFT WAS GOING TO TAKE PLACE IN COLUMBUS, OHIO. HAVING TO MAKE SUCH AN EXPENSIVE TREK WITH MY FAMILY...WHAT WOULD HAVE BEEN THE POINT?

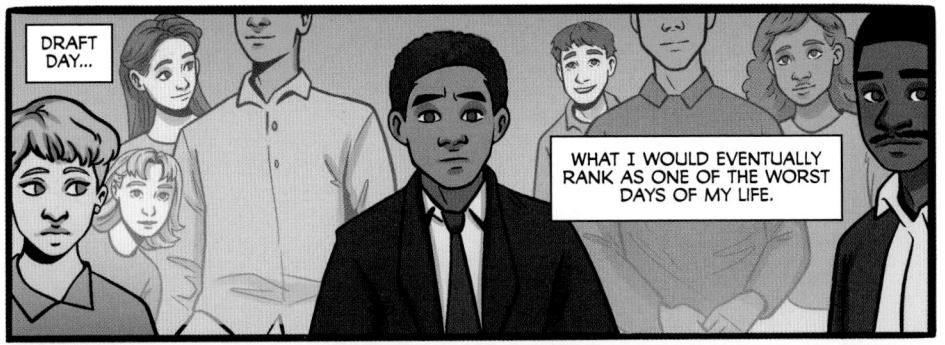

DRAFT DAY...

WHAT I WOULD EVENTUALLY RANK AS ONE OF THE WORST DAYS OF MY LIFE.

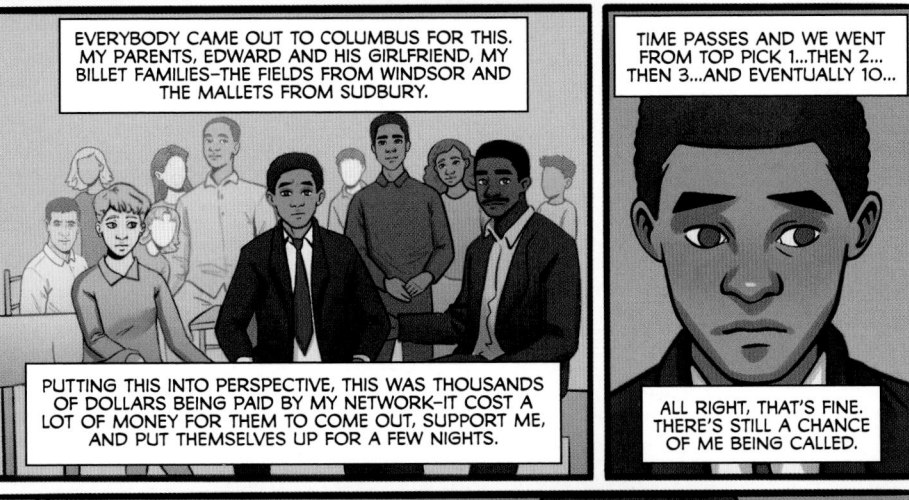

EVERYBODY CAME OUT TO COLUMBUS FOR THIS. MY PARENTS, EDWARD AND HIS GIRLFRIEND, MY BILLET FAMILIES—THE FIELDS FROM WINDSOR AND THE MALLETS FROM SUDBURY.

PUTTING THIS INTO PERSPECTIVE, THIS WAS THOUSANDS OF DOLLARS BEING PAID BY MY NETWORK—IT COST A LOT OF MONEY FOR THEM TO COME OUT, SUPPORT ME, AND PUT THEMSELVES UP FOR A FEW NIGHTS.

TIME PASSES AND WE WENT FROM TOP PICK 1...THEN 2... THEN 3...AND EVENTUALLY 10...

ALL RIGHT, THAT'S FINE. THERE'S STILL A CHANCE OF ME BEING CALLED.

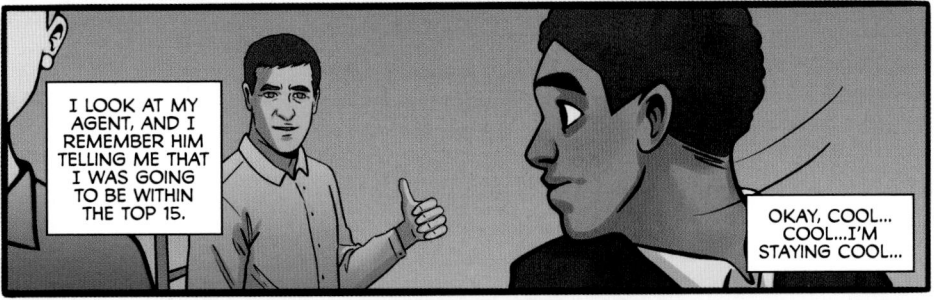

I LOOK AT MY AGENT, AND I REMEMBER HIM TELLING ME THAT I WAS GOING TO BE WITHIN THE TOP 15.

OKAY, COOL... COOL...I'M STAYING COOL...

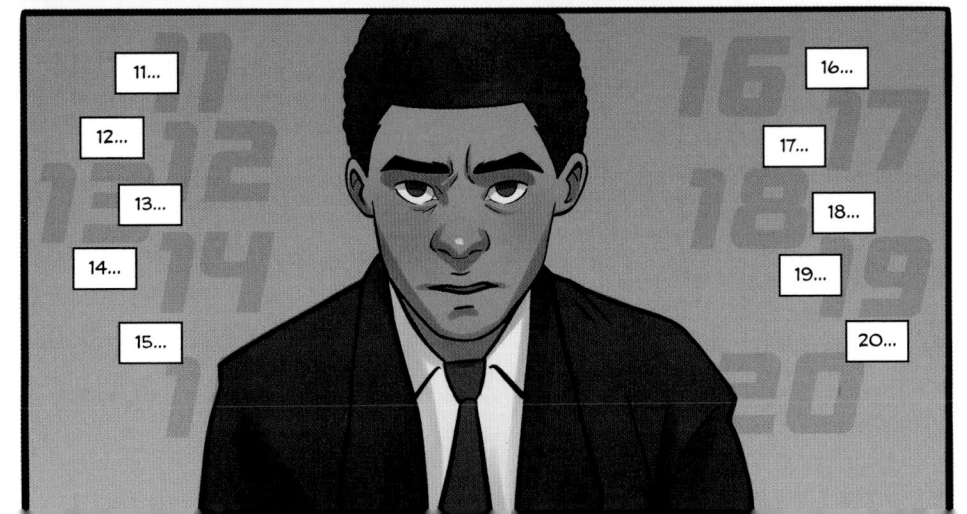

11...

12...

13...

14...

15...

16...

17...

18...

19...

20...

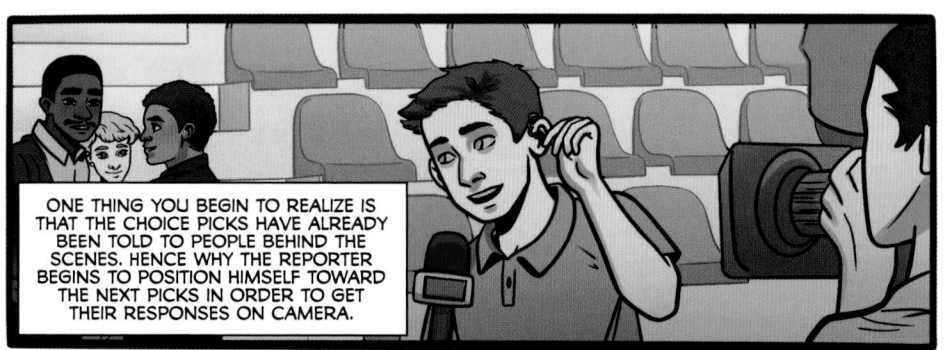

ONE THING YOU BEGIN TO REALIZE IS THAT THE CHOICE PICKS HAVE ALREADY BEEN TOLD TO PEOPLE BEHIND THE SCENES. HENCE WHY THE REPORTER BEGINS TO POSITION HIMSELF TOWARD THE NEXT PICKS IN ORDER TO GET THEIR RESPONSES ON CAMERA.

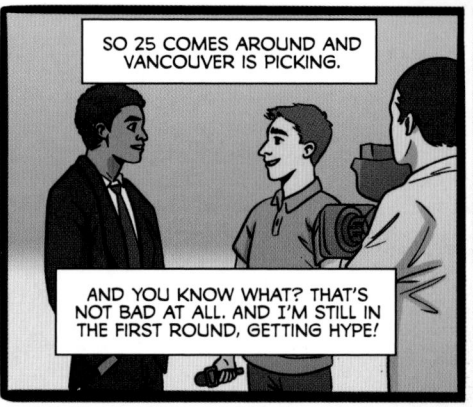

SO 25 COMES AROUND AND VANCOUVER IS PICKING.

AND YOU KNOW WHAT? THAT'S NOT BAD AT ALL. AND I'M STILL IN THE FIRST ROUND, GETTING HYPE!

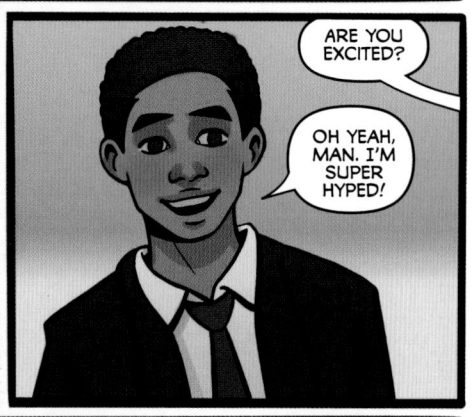

ARE YOU EXCITED?

OH YEAH, MAN. I'M SUPER HYPED!

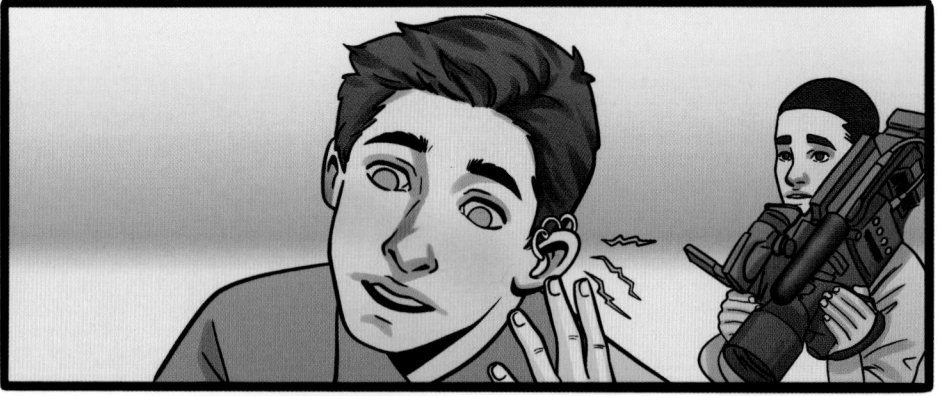

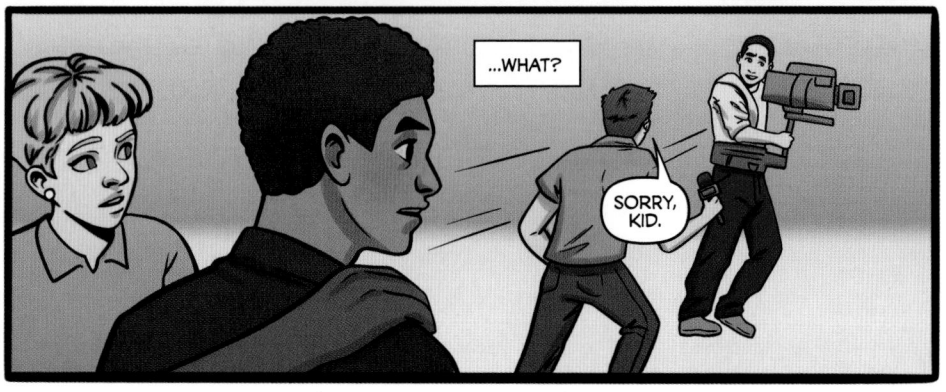

...WHAT?

SORRY, KID.

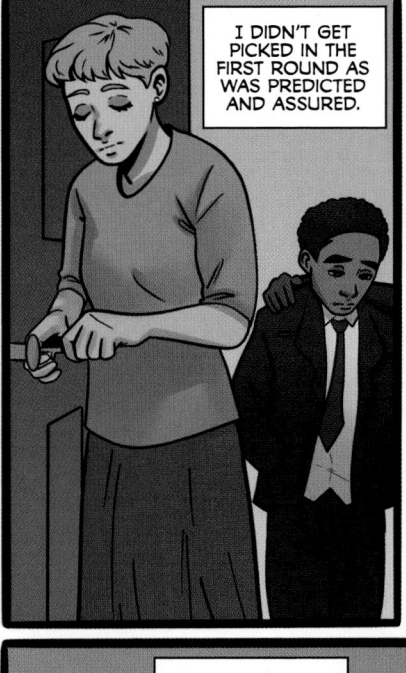

I DIDN'T GET PICKED IN THE FIRST ROUND AS WAS PREDICTED AND ASSURED.

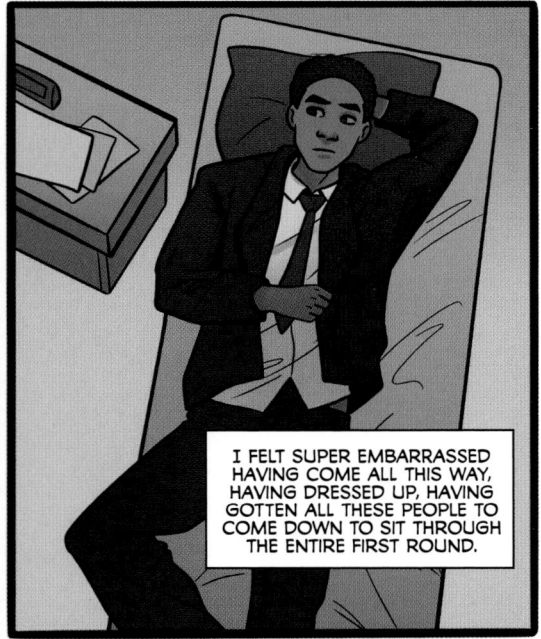

I FELT SUPER EMBARRASSED HAVING COME ALL THIS WAY, HAVING DRESSED UP, HAVING GOTTEN ALL THESE PEOPLE TO COME DOWN TO SIT THROUGH THE ENTIRE FIRST ROUND.

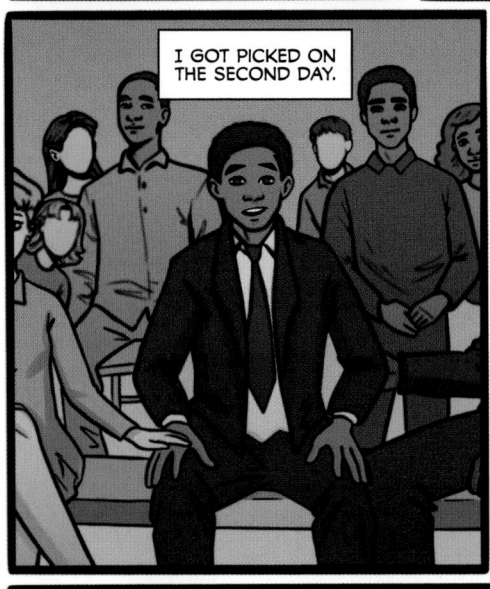

I GOT PICKED ON THE SECOND DAY.

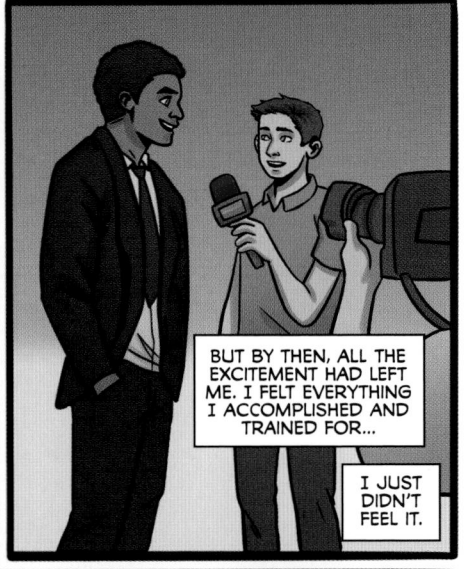

BUT BY THEN, ALL THE EXCITEMENT HAD LEFT ME. I FELT EVERYTHING I ACCOMPLISHED AND TRAINED FOR...

I JUST DIDN'T FEEL IT.

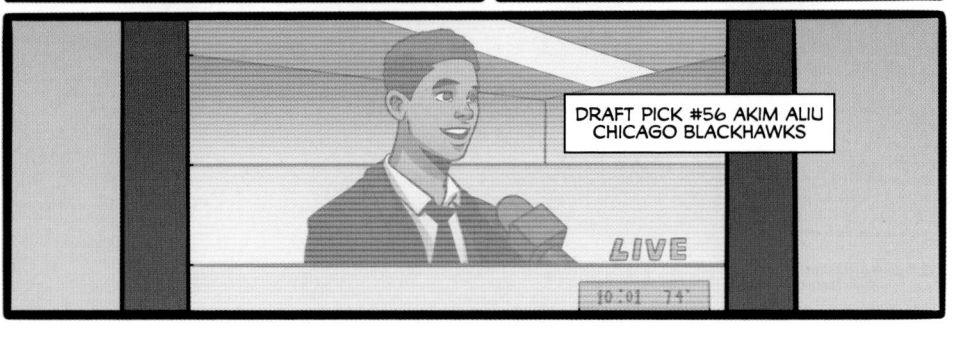

DRAFT PICK #56 AKIM ALIU CHICAGO BLACKHAWKS

TWO YEARS LATER, AFTER FINISHING UP MAJOR JUNIOR...
I WAS *FINALLY* PRO...
THE NHL.
AND GUESS WHAT? I FREAKING FELT IT.

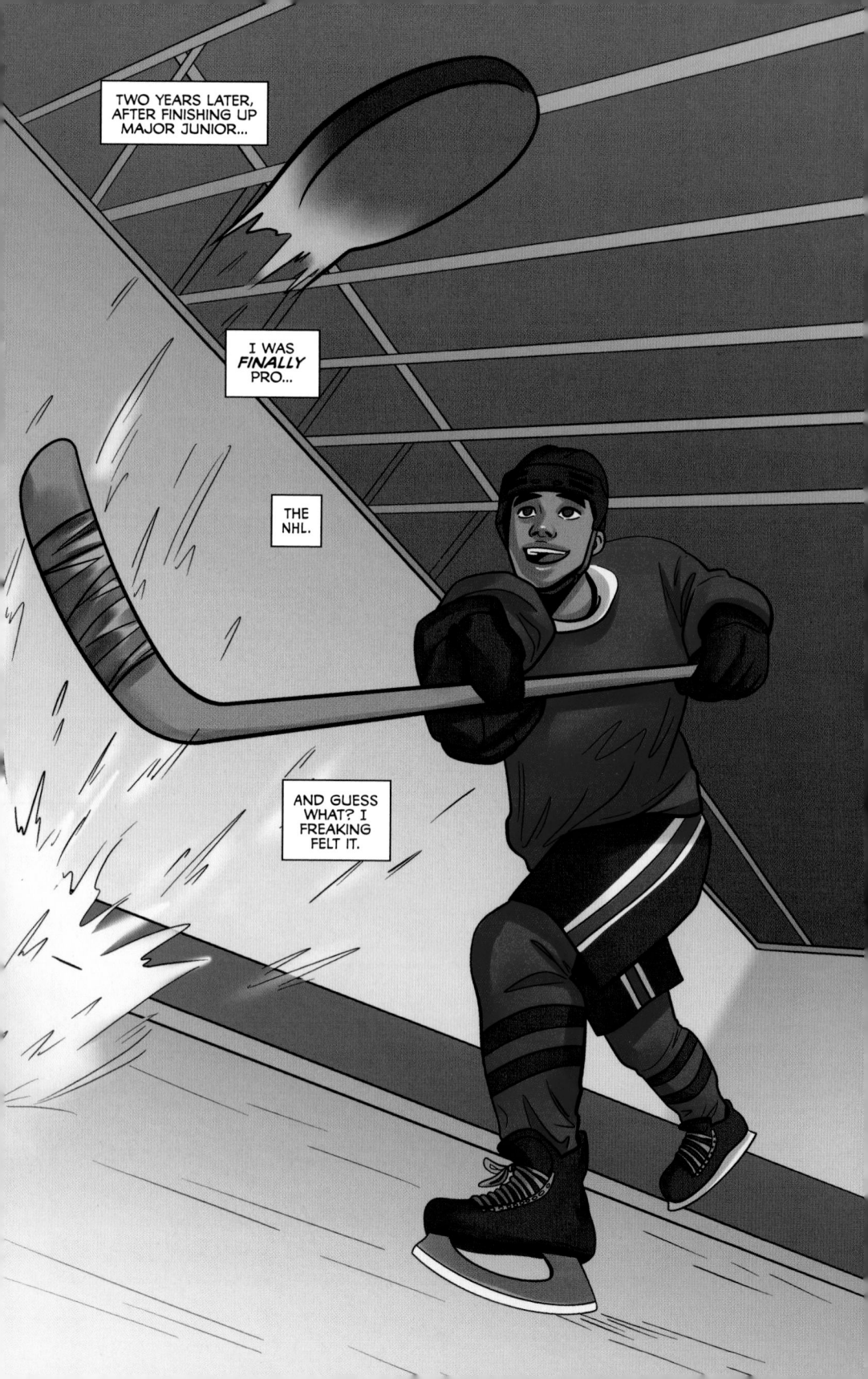

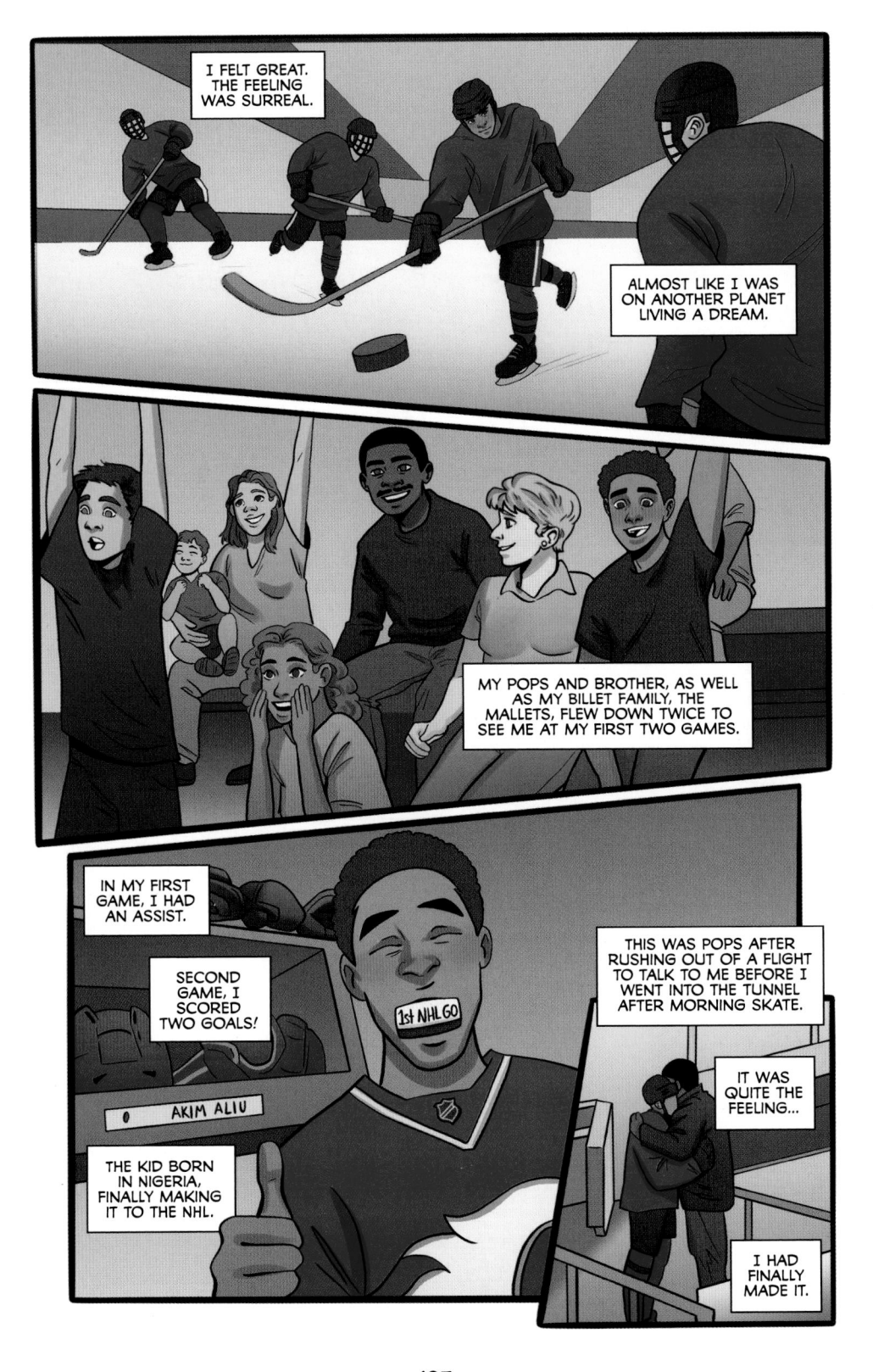

I FELT GREAT. THE FEELING WAS SURREAL.

ALMOST LIKE I WAS ON ANOTHER PLANET LIVING A DREAM.

MY POPS AND BROTHER, AS WELL AS MY BILLET FAMILY, THE MALLETS, FLEW DOWN TWICE TO SEE ME AT MY FIRST TWO GAMES.

IN MY FIRST GAME, I HAD AN ASSIST.

SECOND GAME, I SCORED TWO GOALS!

1st NHL GO

AKIM ALIU

THE KID BORN IN NIGERIA, FINALLY MAKING IT TO THE NHL.

THIS WAS POPS AFTER RUSHING OUT OF A FLIGHT TO TALK TO ME BEFORE I WENT INTO THE TUNNEL AFTER MORNING SKATE.

IT WAS QUITE THE FEELING...

I HAD FINALLY MADE IT.

BUT IT TOOK ME A FEW YEARS TO GET TO CALGARY. I STARTED OUT IN THE MINORS PLAYING FOR THE ROCKFORD ICEHOGS.

DURING PREPARATION FOR THE MORNING SKATES AND PRACTICE, I WAS IN CHARGE OF THE MUSIC.

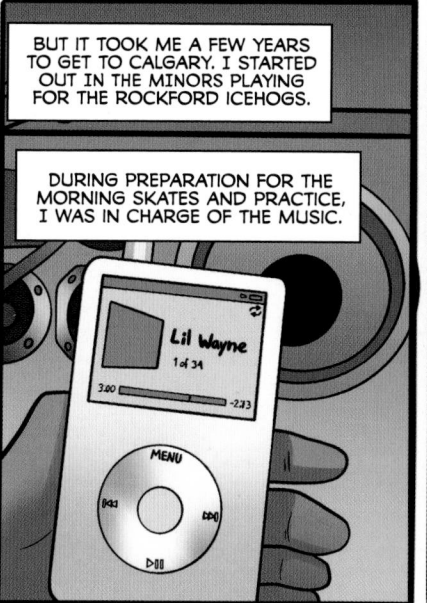

Lil Wayne
1 of 34

3:00 -2:13

MENU

I GOT THE 'ISH POPPING!

AND I WAS INTO AND PLAYED ALL TYPES OF MUSIC:

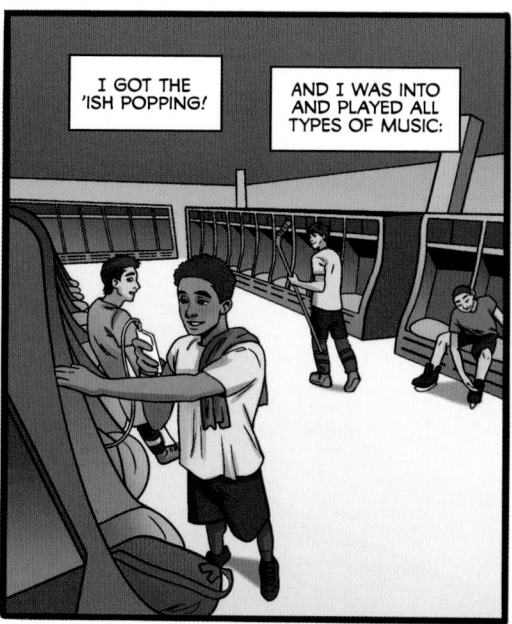

HIP-HOP, RAP, COUNTRY, DANCE...

I TRIED TO PLAY A LITTLE BIT OF EVERYTHING, AS EVERYONE HAD DIFFERENT TASTES.

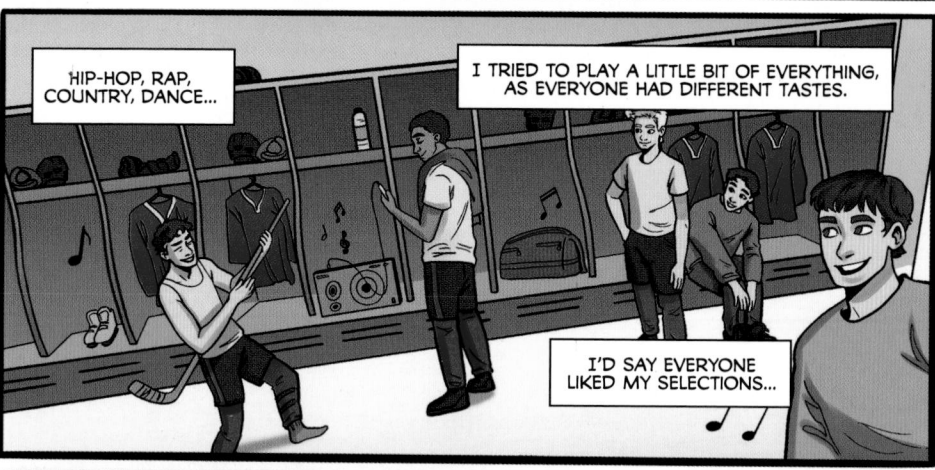

I'D SAY EVERYONE LIKED MY SELECTIONS...

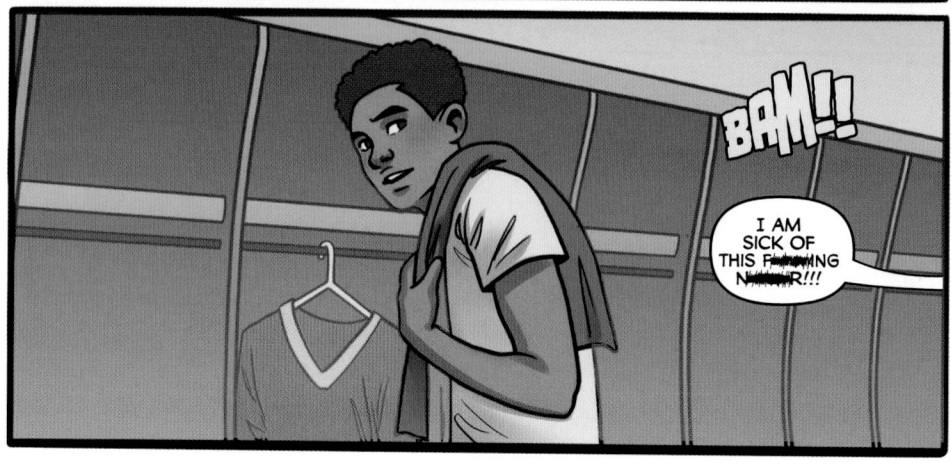

BAM!!

I AM SICK OF THIS F*****G N****R!!!

COACH BILL PETERS LOOKED DEAD AT ME WHEN HE ENTERED...
AND WHEN HE LOOKED ME IN THE EYE IN 2009 IN OUR LOCKER ROOM, AND SAID THAT SAME WORD I'D HEARD IN QUEBEC...
N[redacted]R THIS, N[redacted]R THAT!
...OVER AND OVER IN FRONT OF ME AND MY TEAMMATES JUST BECAUSE HE DIDN'T LIKE MY CHOICE OF MUSIC...
[redacted]
...IT WAS THAT SAME FAMILIAR FEELING.
WHOEVER IS PLAYING THIS S[redacted], I'M F[redacted]NG SICK OF IT!
HE KNEW EXACTLY WHO WAS PLAYING IT.
HOW MANY TIMES ARE WE GOING TO LET THIS N[redacted]R SCORE?!
THE WAY THEY USED THAT WORD, THEY COMPLETELY STRIPPED ME OF MY HUMANITY.
WHAT'S THIS N[redacted]R DOING IN MY HOUSE?
TO THEM, I WAS NOTHING.
COACH PETERS MADE THAT IMMENSELY CLEAR.

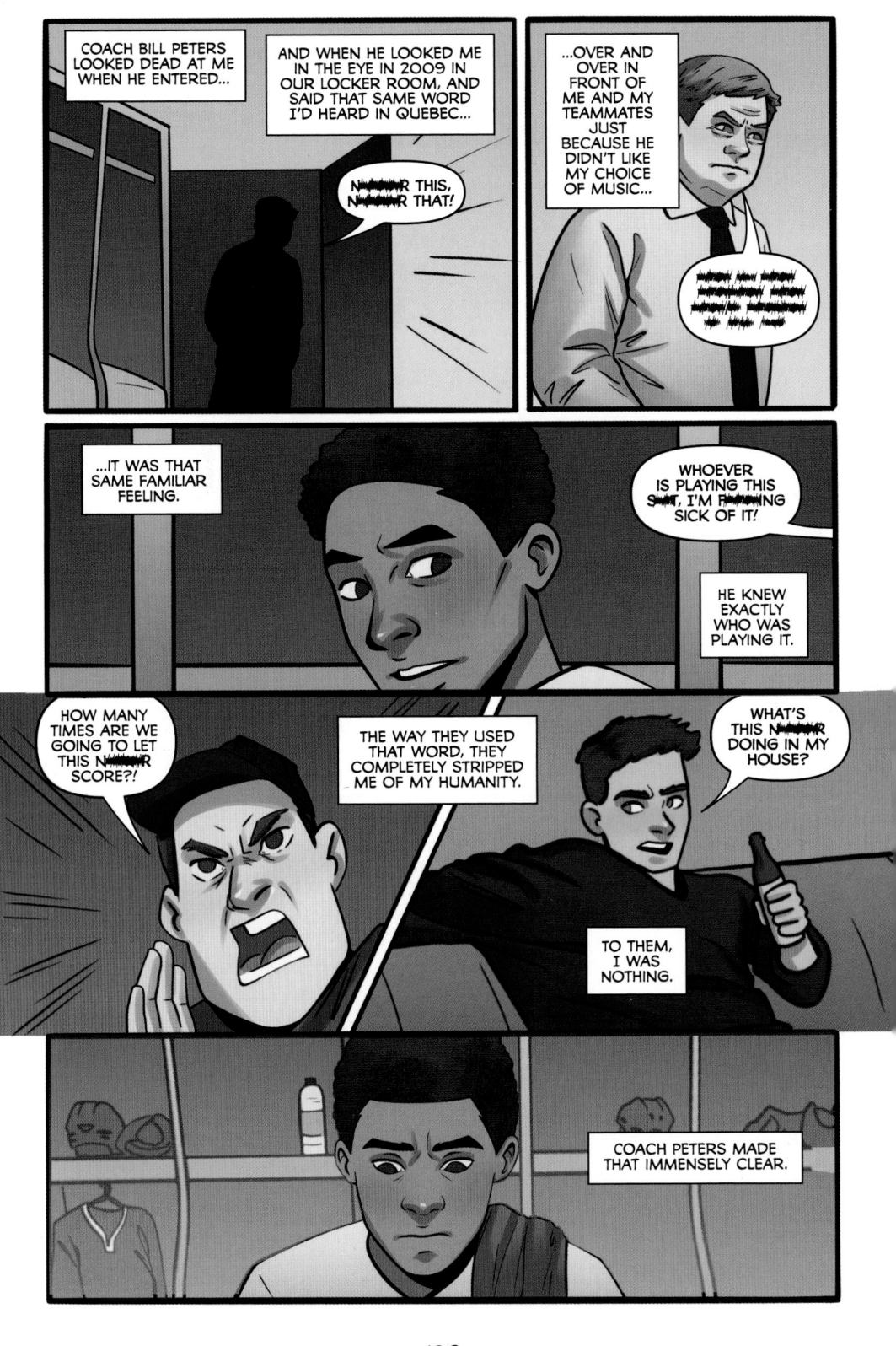

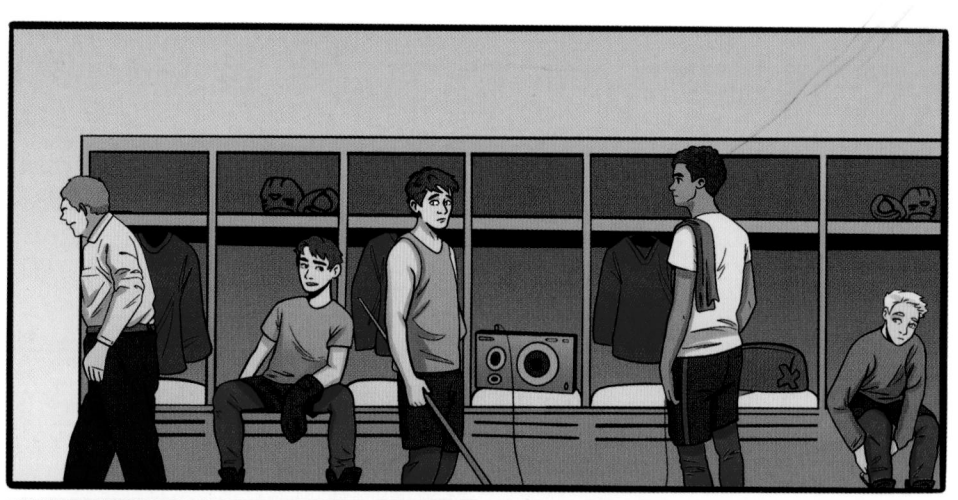

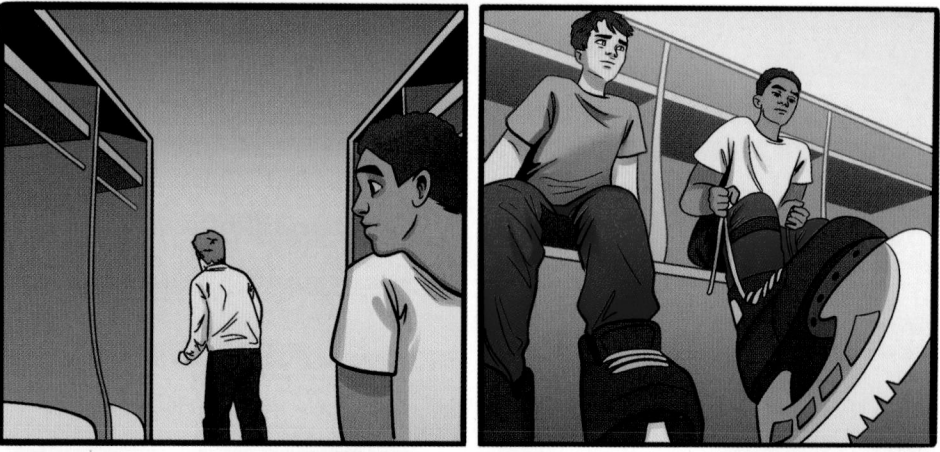

OUR TEAM CAPTAIN, JAKE DOWELL

ARE YOU ALL RIGHT?

YEAH, MAN. I'M GOOD. IT'S WHATEVER. DON'T WORRY ABOUT ME.

BUT HE *WAS* WORRIED ABOUT ME.

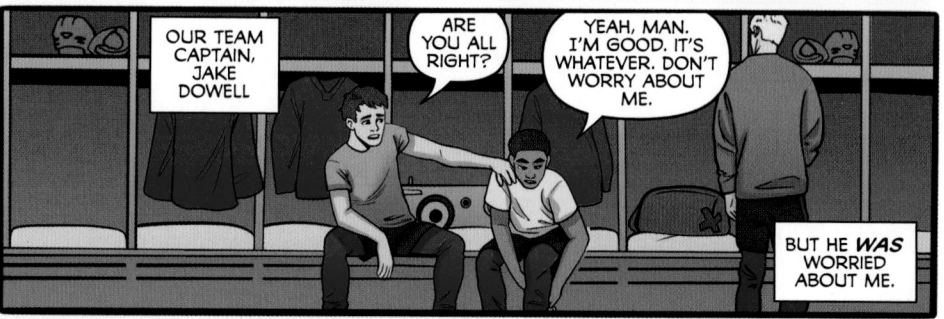

JAKE CONFRONTED PETERS AFTER WHAT HE DID TO ME, BUT THERE WAS ONLY SO MUCH JAKE COULD DO.

I RESPECT JAKE FOR EVEN TAKING MY SIDE AND MAKING A STAND. BUT HE KNEW THAT TO HAVE ANY FUTURE IN THE SPORT—TO MAKE MONEY AND SUPPORT HIS FAMILY...

...HE COULD ONLY PUSH PETERS SO FAR.

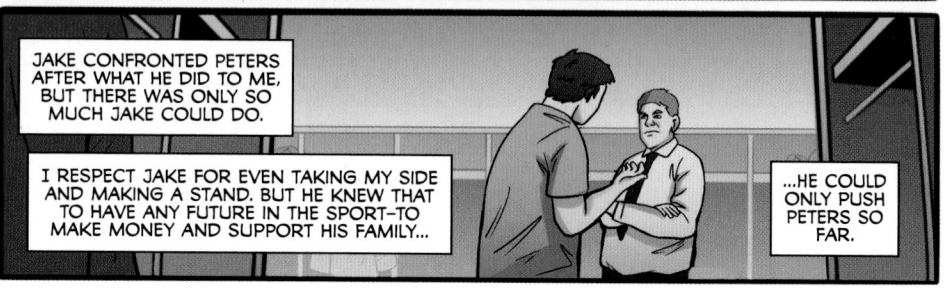

TIME HAD PASSED, AND I NEVER GOT AN APOLOGY OR ANYTHING RESEMBLING REMORSE.
PETERS JUST DOUBLED DOWN AND TREATED ME LIKE CRAP EVERY DAY.
AND IF HE WASN'T YELLING AT ME AT PRACTICE, HE WAS MAKING REMARKS ABOUT WHAT I WAS WEARING OR EVEN HOW MY HAIR WAS.
ONE DAY HE CAME UP TO ME DURING PRACTICE AND STARTED HIS TIRADE.
AT THIS POINT, I'D HAD ENOUGH...
YO, WHO THE HELL YOU TALKING TO LIKE THAT?! DON'T TALK TO ME LIKE THAT!
AT THIS POINT, I WAS ACTUALLY LEADING MY PRO TEAM IN SCORING AS A TWENTY-YEAR-OLD ROOKIE...
BEFORE I KNEW IT, HE SENT ME DOWN TO THE LOWER LEAGUE...

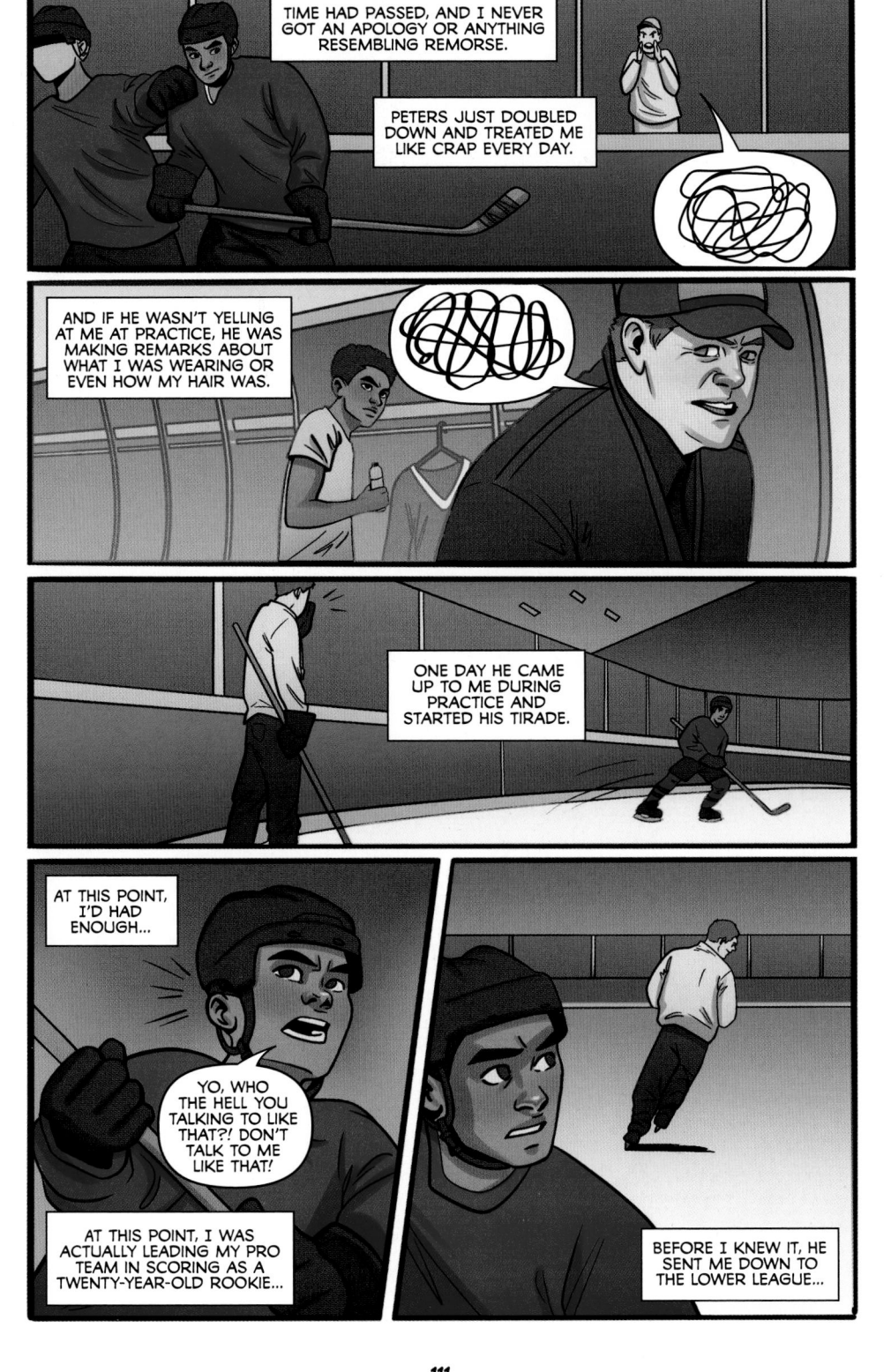

ENOUGH FOR HIM TO SEND ME AWAY.
HE WROTE A LETTER TO THE GM AND GOT ME SENT DOWN A LEVEL TO THE ECHL, ONE LEVEL BELOW AAA HOCKEY. I WAS ON PACE TO BE ONE OF THE TOP YOUNG SCORERS ON THE TEAM, BUT THAT DIDN'T *MATTER* ANYMORE...
...I EVENTUALLY GOT TRADED TO CALGARY, WHERE I MADE IT TO THE NHL.
...THAT WAS THE FULL POWER OF THE OPPRESSIVE HOCKEY MACHINE AT WORK.
THERE ARE HUNDREDS OF COACHES AT *ALL* LEVELS OF HOCKEY IN CANADA AND THE UNITED STATES JUST LIKE HIM. THEY OPERATE UNDER THE PRETENSE OF ABSOLUTE POWER.
THEY WILL ***PUMMEL*** YOU MERCILESSLY UNTIL YOU BREAK, OR UNTIL YOU GIVE IN, WHICHEVER COMES FIRST.
THAT, RIGHT THERE, IS WHAT I BELIEVE TO BE THE CRUX OF THE PROBLEM. THERE IS A POWER STRUCTURE IN PLACE TO TURN BRIGHT, LOVING KIDS INTO SOME-THING THEY WERE NOT BORN TO BE.
AT THIS POINT, IT HAD BEEN NINE YEARS AFTER THIS MOMENT BETWEEN PETERS AND ME...

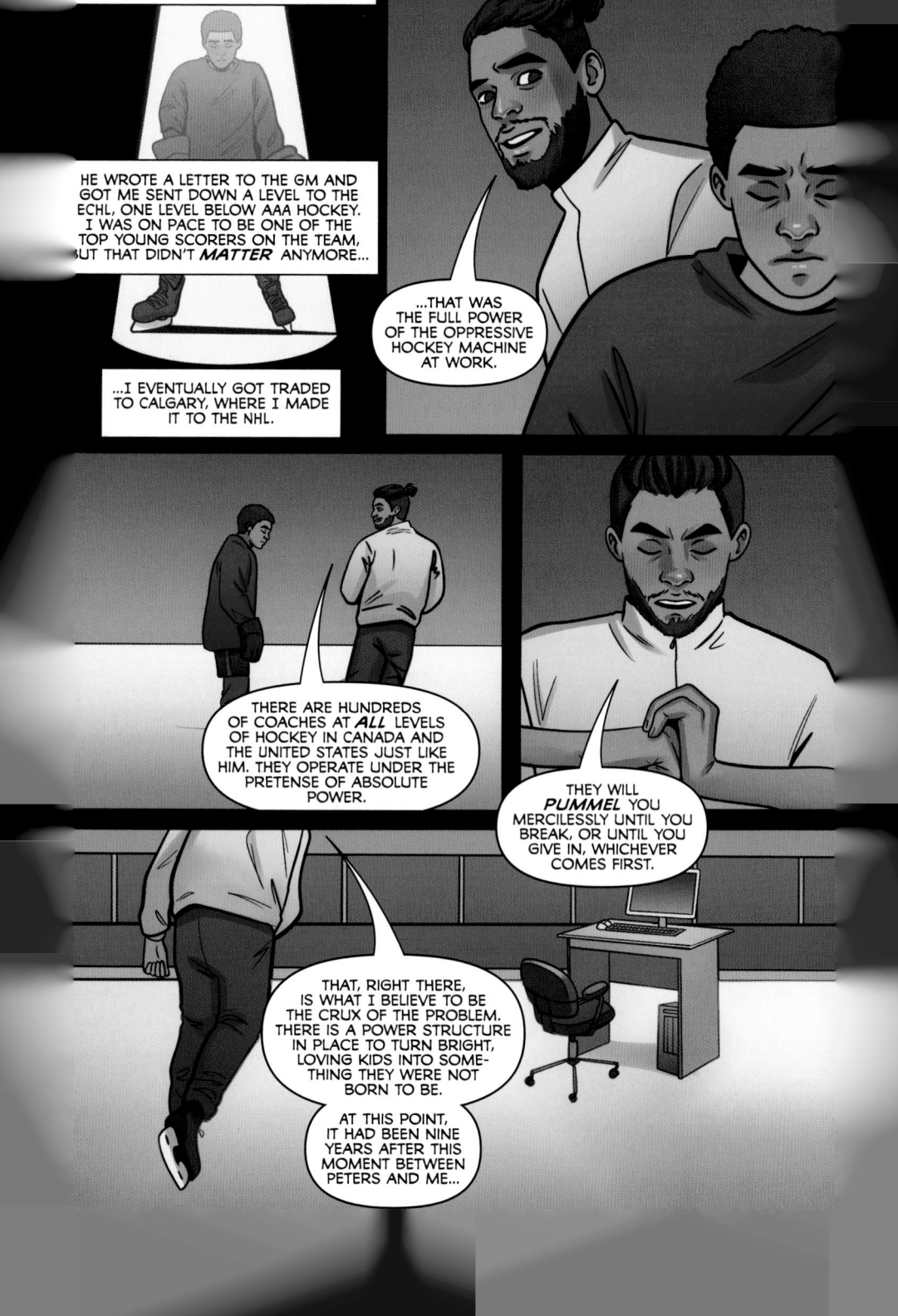

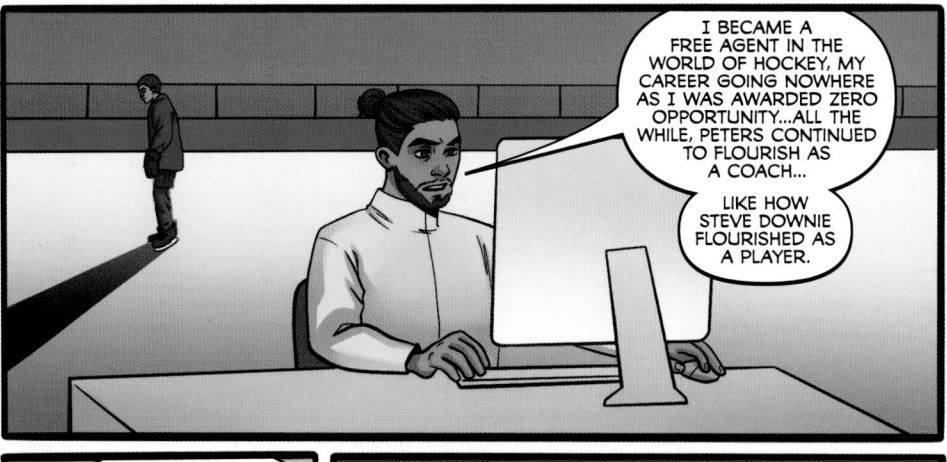

I BECAME A FREE AGENT IN THE WORLD OF HOCKEY, MY CAREER GOING NOWHERE AS I WAS AWARDED ZERO OPPORTUNITY...ALL THE WHILE, PETERS CONTINUED TO FLOURISH AS A COACH...

LIKE HOW STEVE DOWNIE FLOURISHED AS A PLAYER.

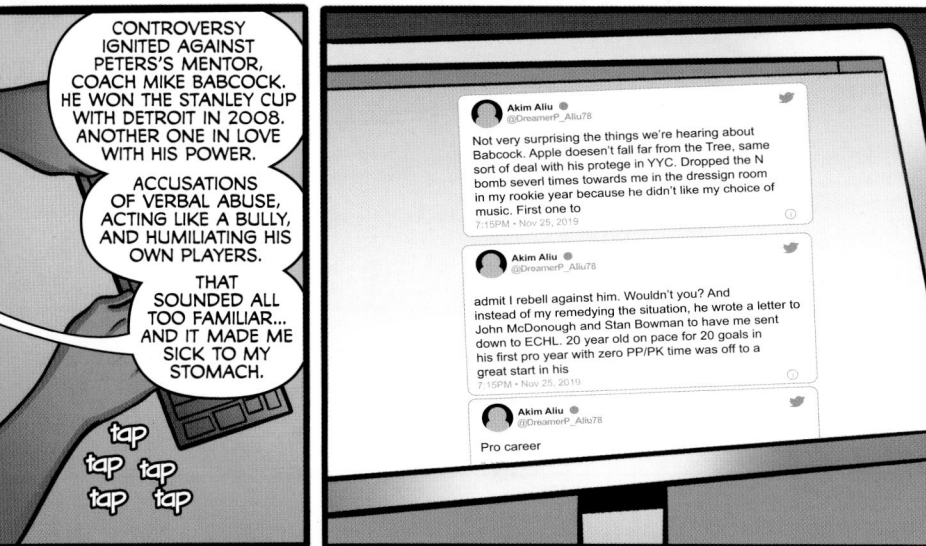

CONTROVERSY IGNITED AGAINST PETERS'S MENTOR, COACH MIKE BABCOCK. HE WON THE STANLEY CUP WITH DETROIT IN 2008. ANOTHER ONE IN LOVE WITH HIS POWER.

ACCUSATIONS OF VERBAL ABUSE, ACTING LIKE A BULLY, AND HUMILIATING HIS OWN PLAYERS.

THAT SOUNDED ALL TOO FAMILIAR... AND IT MADE ME SICK TO MY STOMACH.

tap
tap tap
tap tap

Akim Aliu @DreamerP_Aliu78

Not very surprising the things we're hearing about Babcock. Apple doesen't fall far from the Tree, same sort of deal with his protege in YYC. Dropped the N bomb severl times towards me in the dressign room in my rookie year because he didn't like my choice of music. First one to
7:15PM · Nov 25, 2019

Akim Aliu @DreamerP_Aliu78

admit I rebell against him. Wouldn't you? And instead of my remedying the situation, he wrote a letter to John McDonough and Stan Bowman to have me sent down to ECHL. 20 year old on pace for 20 goals in his first pro year with zero PP/PK time was off to a great start in his
7:15PM · Nov 25, 2019

Akim Aliu @DreamerP_Aliu78

Pro career

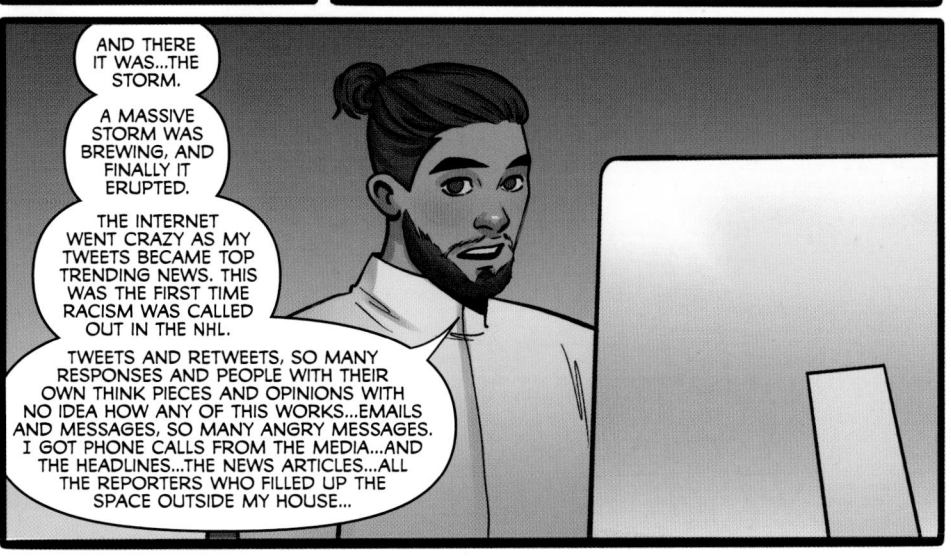

AND THERE IT WAS...THE STORM.

A MASSIVE STORM WAS BREWING, AND FINALLY IT ERUPTED.

THE INTERNET WENT CRAZY AS MY TWEETS BECAME TOP TRENDING NEWS. THIS WAS THE FIRST TIME RACISM WAS CALLED OUT IN THE NHL.

TWEETS AND RETWEETS, SO MANY RESPONSES AND PEOPLE WITH THEIR OWN THINK PIECES AND OPINIONS WITH NO IDEA HOW ANY OF THIS WORKS...EMAILS AND MESSAGES, SO MANY ANGRY MESSAGES. I GOT PHONE CALLS FROM THE MEDIA...AND THE HEADLINES...THE NEWS ARTICLES...ALL THE REPORTERS WHO FILLED UP THE SPACE OUTSIDE MY HOUSE...

113

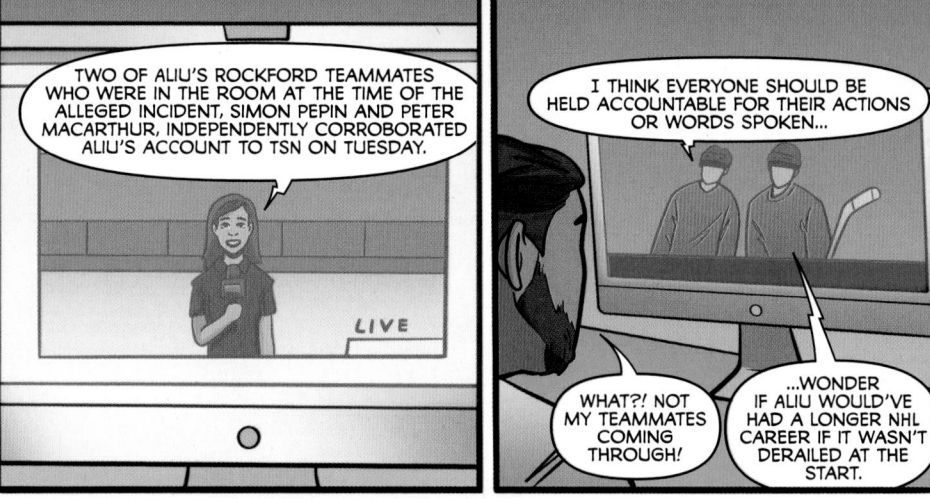

TWO OF ALIU'S ROCKFORD TEAMMATES WHO WERE IN THE ROOM AT THE TIME OF THE ALLEGED INCIDENT, SIMON PEPIN AND PETER MACARTHUR, INDEPENDENTLY CORROBORATED ALIU'S ACCOUNT TO TSN ON TUESDAY.

LIVE

I THINK EVERYONE SHOULD BE HELD ACCOUNTABLE FOR THEIR ACTIONS OR WORDS SPOKEN...

WHAT?! NOT MY TEAMMATES COMING THROUGH!

...WONDER IF ALIU WOULD'VE HAD A LONGER NHL CAREER IF IT WASN'T DERAILED AT THE START.

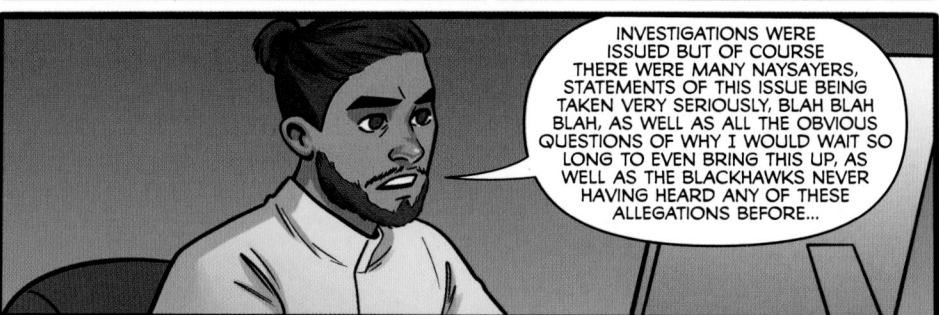

INVESTIGATIONS WERE ISSUED BUT OF COURSE THERE WERE MANY NAYSAYERS, STATEMENTS OF THIS ISSUE BEING TAKEN VERY SERIOUSLY, BLAH BLAH BLAH, AS WELL AS ALL THE OBVIOUS QUESTIONS OF WHY I WOULD WAIT SO LONG TO EVEN BRING THIS UP, AS WELL AS THE BLACKHAWKS NEVER HAVING HEARD ANY OF THESE ALLEGATIONS BEFORE...

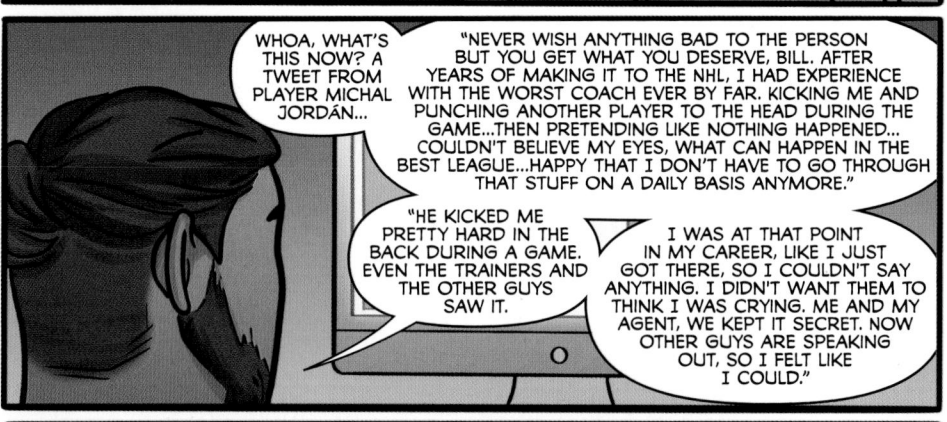

WHOA, WHAT'S THIS NOW? A TWEET FROM PLAYER MICHAL JORDÁN...

"NEVER WISH ANYTHING BAD TO THE PERSON BUT YOU GET WHAT YOU DESERVE, BILL. AFTER YEARS OF MAKING IT TO THE NHL, I HAD EXPERIENCE WITH THE WORST COACH EVER BY FAR. KICKING ME AND PUNCHING ANOTHER PLAYER TO THE HEAD DURING THE GAME...THEN PRETENDING LIKE NOTHING HAPPENED... COULDN'T BELIEVE MY EYES, WHAT CAN HAPPEN IN THE BEST LEAGUE...HAPPY THAT I DON'T HAVE TO GO THROUGH THAT STUFF ON A DAILY BASIS ANYMORE."

"HE KICKED ME PRETTY HARD IN THE BACK DURING A GAME. EVEN THE TRAINERS AND THE OTHER GUYS SAW IT.

I WAS AT THAT POINT IN MY CAREER, LIKE I JUST GOT THERE, SO I COULDN'T SAY ANYTHING. I DIDN'T WANT THEM TO THINK I WAS CRYING. ME AND MY AGENT, WE KEPT IT SECRET. NOW OTHER GUYS ARE SPEAKING OUT, SO I FELT LIKE I COULD."

HOCKEY COACH BILL PETERS RESIGNS FROM THE NHL

I WASN'T ALONE. SO MANY PEOPLE HAVE THEIR STORIES. TO SEE THERE WERE PEOPLE LIKE ME, LIKE MICHAL, ALL JUST WANTING TO PLAY YET HAVING TO DEAL WITH ALL THIS PETTY CRAP...
I THOUGHT IT WAS TIME FOR ME TO FINALLY SHARE MY STORY. THERE WAS NO WAY I WAS ALONE IN THIS. I COULDN'T HAVE BEEN. IT WAS TIME TO EXPOSE THE MONSTERS UNDER THE BED AND IN MY CLOSET...
RACISM IS EVERYWHERE IN THE WORLD. ***EVERYWHERE.*** SO IF YOU FALL DOWN BECAUSE OF THEM, YOU ARE GOING TO REGRET IT. YOU HEAR IT, YOU LET IT PASS...
YOU LET IT GO INTO ANOTHER THING AND FOCUS ON WHATEVER YOU ARE DOING...YOU KEEP YOUR MIND ON YOUR DREAM.
I'M SORRY, POPS, BUT I THINK IT'S TIME FOR ME TO ALTER THAT DREAM A BIT.
DON'T WORRY ABOUT US, SON. WE ARE PROUD OF YOU.
DO WHAT YOU NEED TO DO, AKIM. WE ARE HERE TO SUPPORT YOU.
GIVE THEM HELL.
HOCKEY IS NOT FOR EVERYONE
By Akim Aliu
You ever fought for your life? Like, *really* fought for your life? In 2005, in a tiny arena in Windsor, Ontario, I fought for my life.

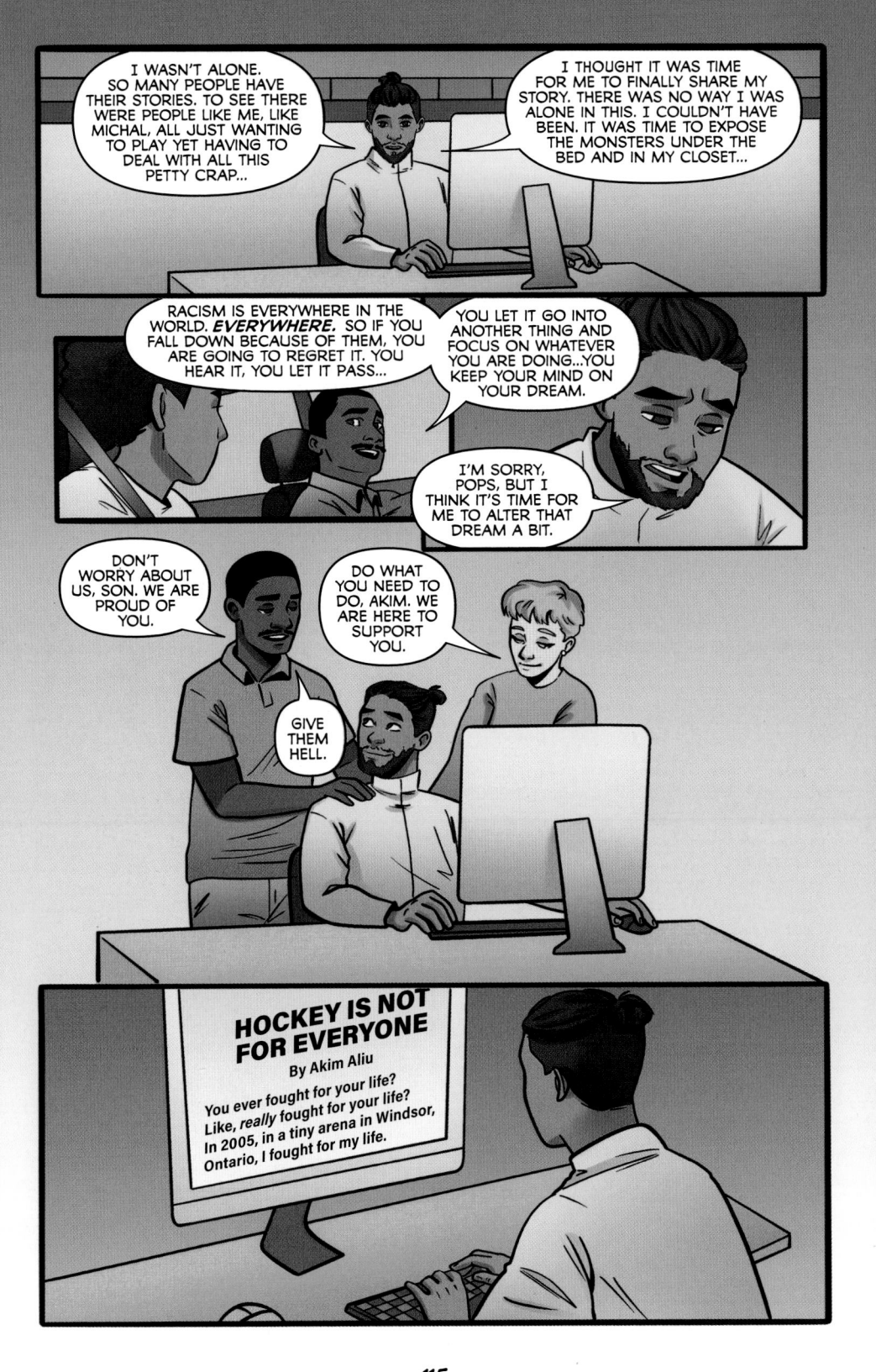

2019...

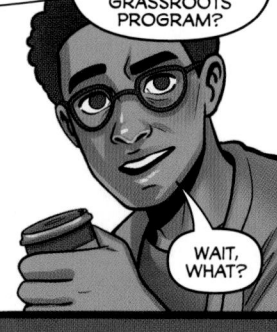

HEY, EDWARD. DO YOU HAVE ANY IDEAS ON HOW TO PUT TOGETHER A GRASSROOTS PROGRAM?

WAIT, WHAT?

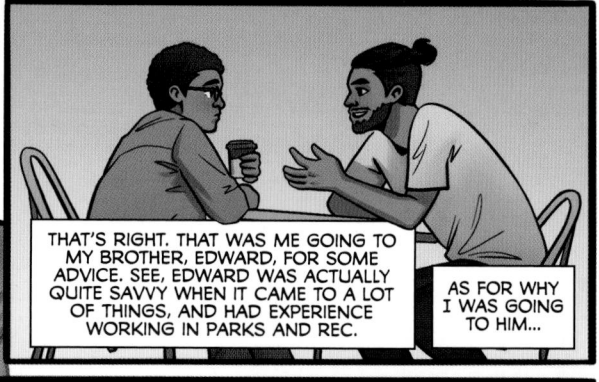

THAT'S RIGHT. THAT WAS ME GOING TO MY BROTHER, EDWARD, FOR SOME ADVICE. SEE, EDWARD WAS ACTUALLY QUITE SAVVY WHEN IT CAME TO A LOT OF THINGS, AND HAD EXPERIENCE WORKING IN PARKS AND REC.

AS FOR WHY I WAS GOING TO HIM...

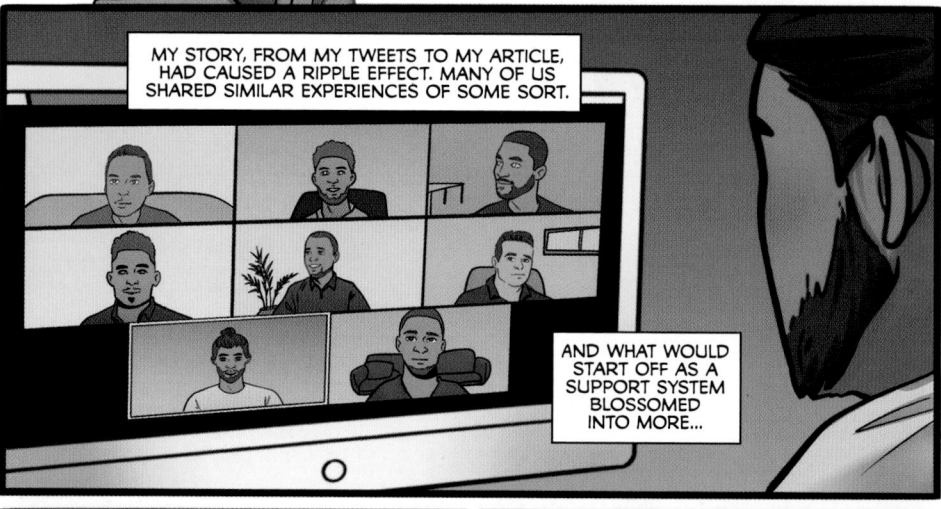

MY STORY, FROM MY TWEETS TO MY ARTICLE, HAD CAUSED A RIPPLE EFFECT. MANY OF US SHARED SIMILAR EXPERIENCES OF SOME SORT.

AND WHAT WOULD START OFF AS A SUPPORT SYSTEM BLOSSOMED INTO MORE...

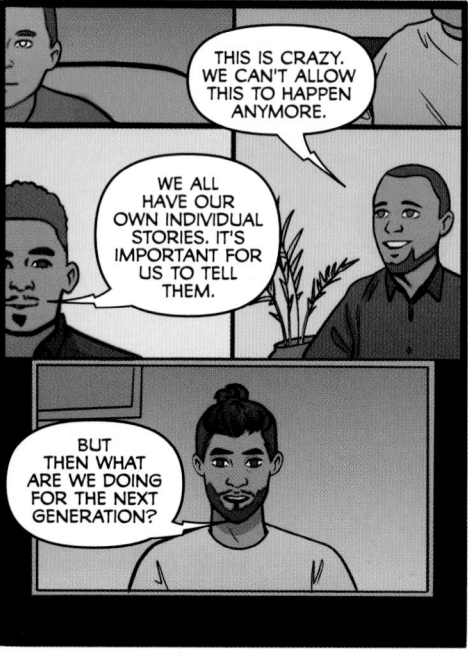

THIS IS CRAZY. WE CAN'T ALLOW THIS TO HAPPEN ANYMORE.

WE ALL HAVE OUR OWN INDIVIDUAL STORIES. IT'S IMPORTANT FOR US TO TELL THEM.

BUT THEN WHAT ARE WE DOING FOR THE NEXT GENERATION?

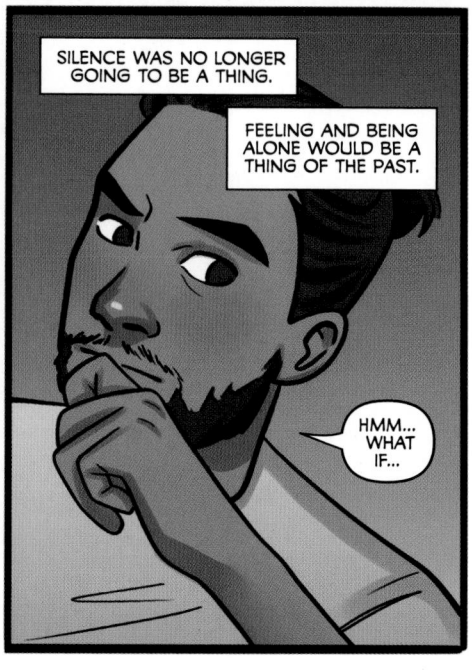

SILENCE WAS NO LONGER GOING TO BE A THING.

FEELING AND BEING ALONE WOULD BE A THING OF THE PAST.

HMM... WHAT IF...

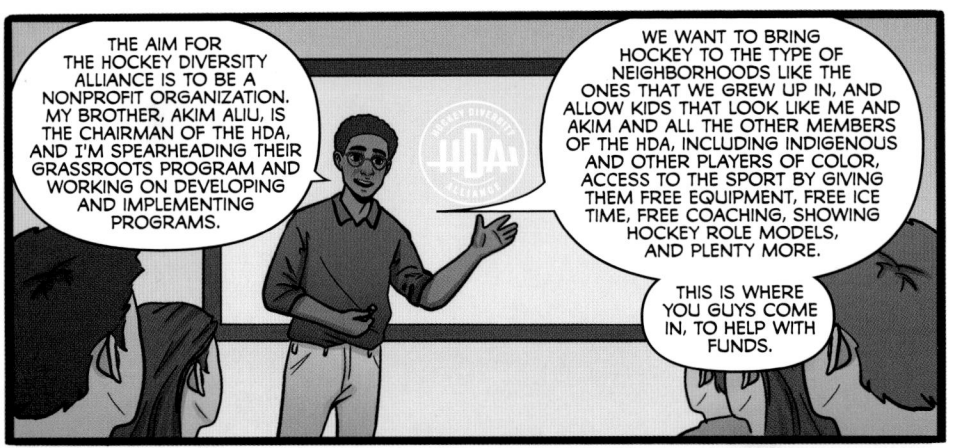

THE AIM FOR THE HOCKEY DIVERSITY ALLIANCE IS TO BE A NONPROFIT ORGANIZATION. MY BROTHER, AKIM ALIU, IS THE CHAIRMAN OF THE HDA, AND I'M SPEARHEADING THEIR GRASSROOTS PROGRAM AND WORKING ON DEVELOPING AND IMPLEMENTING PROGRAMS.

WE WANT TO BRING HOCKEY TO THE TYPE OF NEIGHBORHOODS LIKE THE ONES THAT WE GREW UP IN, AND ALLOW KIDS THAT LOOK LIKE ME AND AKIM AND ALL THE OTHER MEMBERS OF THE HDA, INCLUDING INDIGENOUS AND OTHER PLAYERS OF COLOR, ACCESS TO THE SPORT BY GIVING THEM FREE EQUIPMENT, FREE ICE TIME, FREE COACHING, SHOWING HOCKEY ROLE MODELS, AND PLENTY MORE.

THIS IS WHERE YOU GUYS COME IN, TO HELP WITH FUNDS.

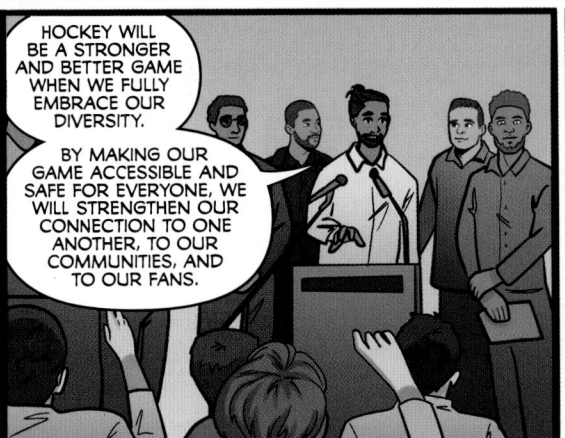

HOCKEY WILL BE A STRONGER AND BETTER GAME WHEN WE FULLY EMBRACE OUR DIVERSITY.

BY MAKING OUR GAME ACCESSIBLE AND SAFE FOR EVERYONE, WE WILL STRENGTHEN OUR CONNECTION TO ONE ANOTHER, TO OUR COMMUNITIES, AND TO OUR FANS.

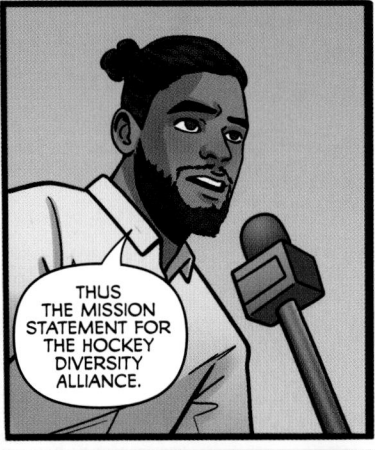

THUS THE MISSION STATEMENT FOR THE HOCKEY DIVERSITY ALLIANCE.

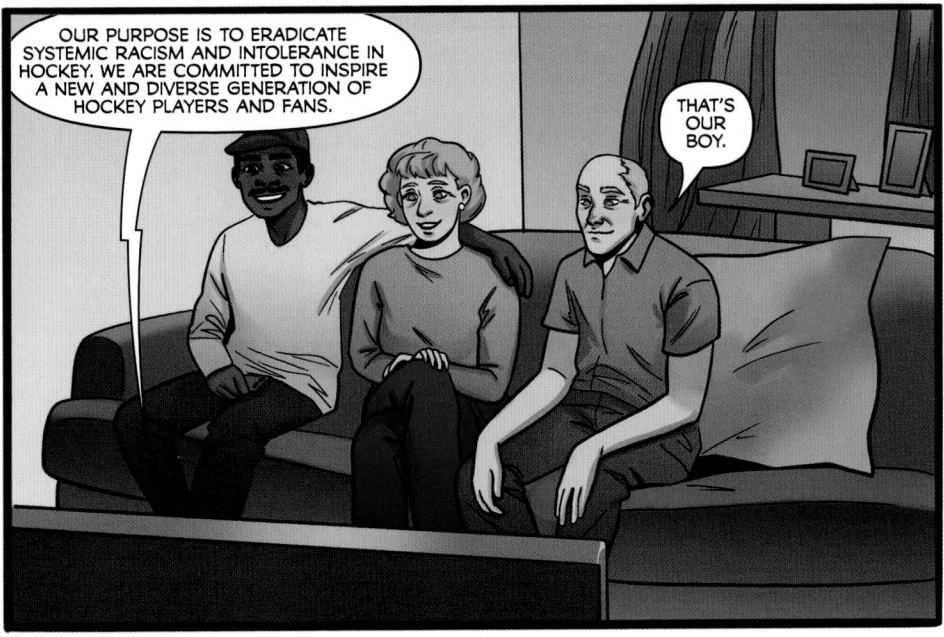

OUR PURPOSE IS TO ERADICATE SYSTEMIC RACISM AND INTOLERANCE IN HOCKEY. WE ARE COMMITTED TO INSPIRE A NEW AND DIVERSE GENERATION OF HOCKEY PLAYERS AND FANS.

THAT'S OUR BOY.

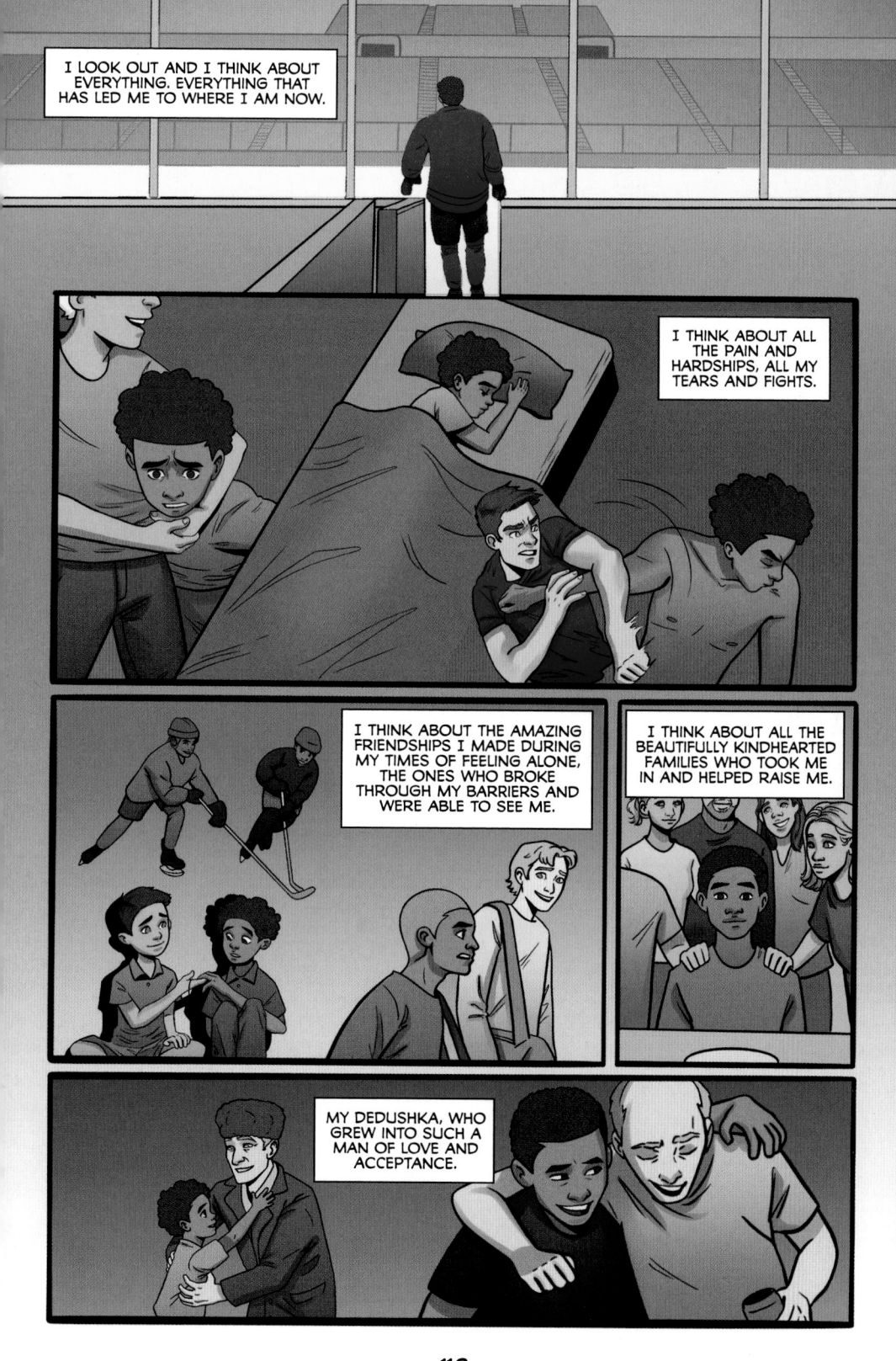

I LOOK OUT AND I THINK ABOUT EVERYTHING. EVERYTHING THAT HAS LED ME TO WHERE I AM NOW.

I THINK ABOUT ALL THE PAIN AND HARDSHIPS, ALL MY TEARS AND FIGHTS.

I THINK ABOUT THE AMAZING FRIENDSHIPS I MADE DURING MY TIMES OF FEELING ALONE, THE ONES WHO BROKE THROUGH MY BARRIERS AND WERE ABLE TO SEE ME.

I THINK ABOUT ALL THE BEAUTIFULLY KINDHEARTED FAMILIES WHO TOOK ME IN AND HELPED RAISE ME.

MY DEDUSHKA, WHO GREW INTO SUCH A MAN OF LOVE AND ACCEPTANCE.

I THINK ABOUT MY PARENTS, TAI AND LARISSA ALIU, AND MY BROTHER, EDWARD.
ALL THE SACRIFICES THEY MADE, ALL THE HITS MY FATHER RECEIVED, YET HE CONTINUED TO STAND AND MOVE FORWARD.
ALL THE SIDE-EYES AND MISGUIDED ANGER MY MOTHER ENDURED.
I THINK ABOUT ALL THE PIZZAS MY FATHER DELIVERED, ALL THE MOTEL ROOMS MY MOTHER FIXED UP AND CLEANED.
PIZZA
ALL THE MISSED VACATIONS AND PENNIES CRUNCHED.
I THINK OF ALL THE TEASING FROM MY BROTHER, AND ALL THE TIMES HE TOOK CARE OF ME WHEN MY FATHER WAS BUSY HUSTLING.
AND THE TIMES HE WAS SECRETLY CHEERING ME ON WHILE BEING SUCH A JERK TO MY FACE.
I THINK OF MY FAMILY AND EVERYTHING THEY HAVE DONE TO HELP ME AND I THANK THEM. I LOVE YOU. FOR NOTHING I HAVE ACCOMPLISHED WOULD HAVE BEEN POSSIBLE WITHOUT YOU.

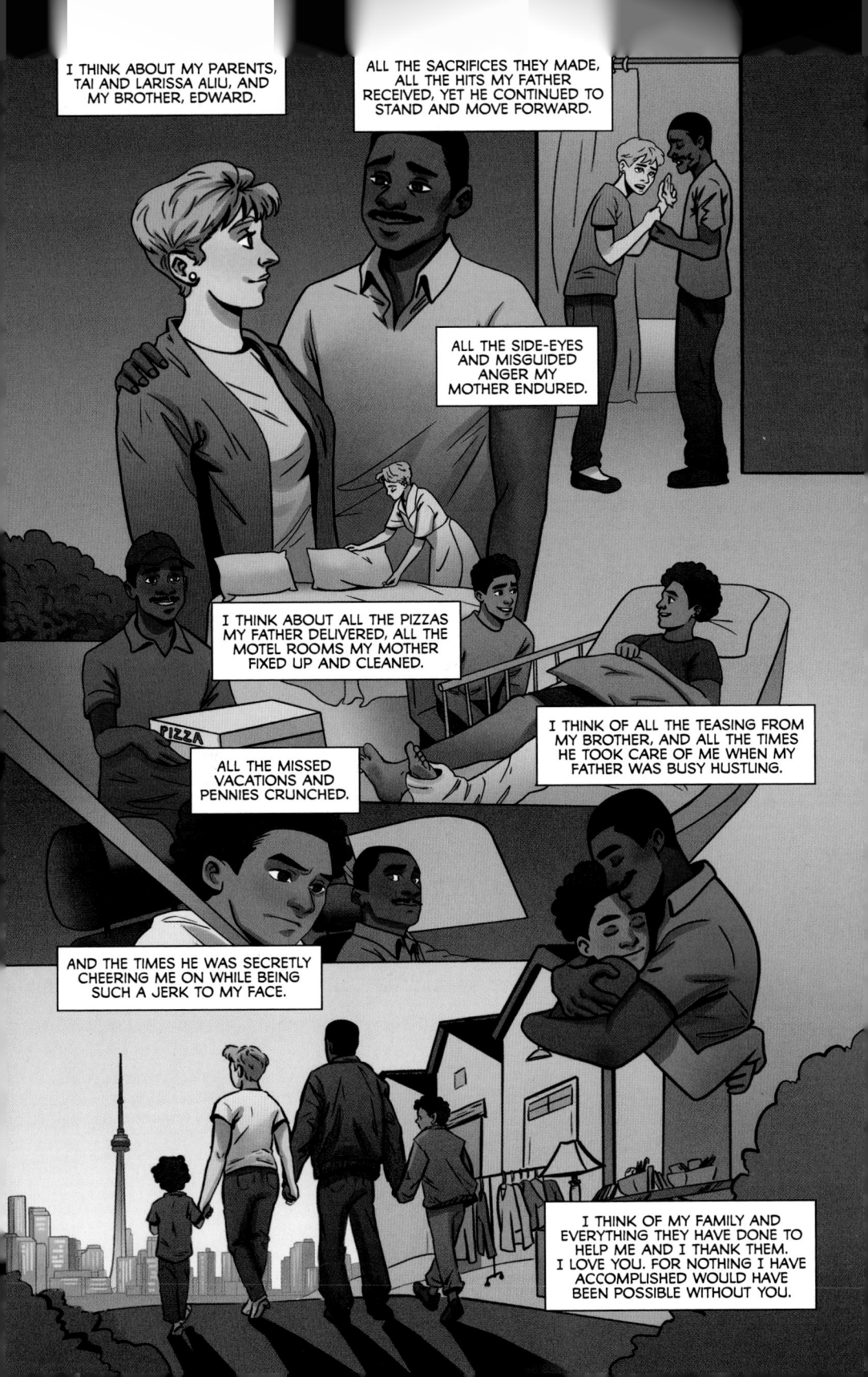

HERE'S TO ACCOMPLISHING THE DREAM.
END.

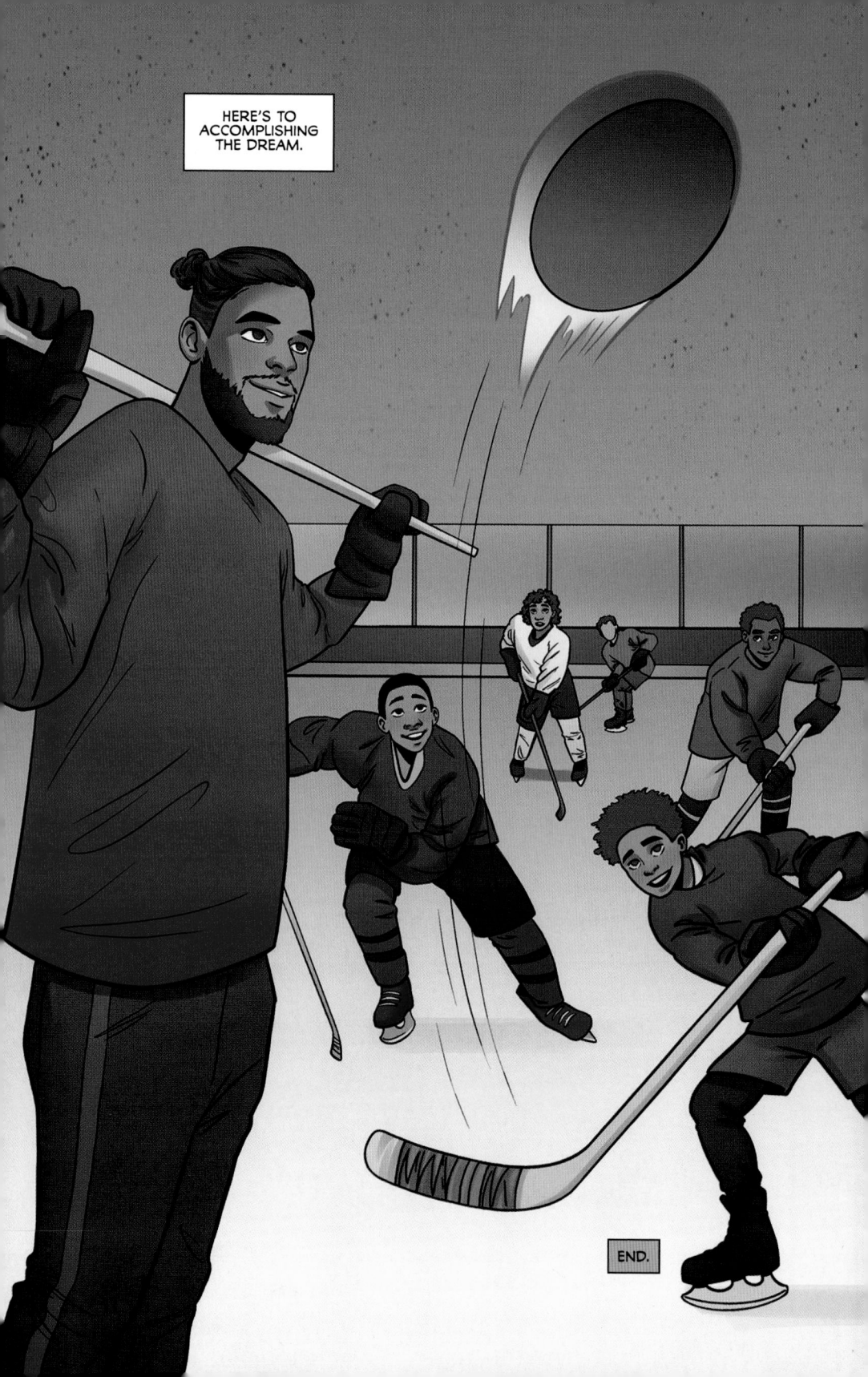

HOCKEY DIVERSITY ALLIANCE

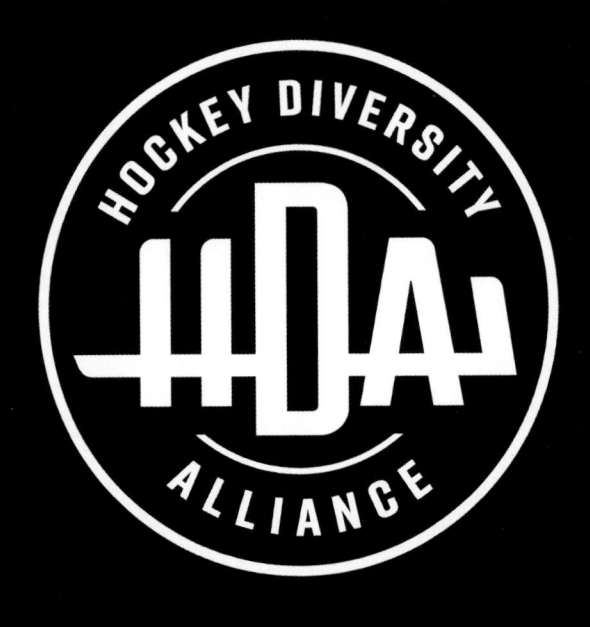

In 2020, Akim Aliu, along with six other active and former NHL players, announced the formation of the Hockey Diversity Alliance. The executive committee of the board included Trevor Daley, Matt Dumba, Wayne Simmonds, Chris Stewart, and Joel Ward, with Aliu and Evander Kane serving as co-heads. The board's mission statement is as follows:

We strive to create sustainable change on all levels of hockey. At the top, we will educate and encourage accountability from our leagues and leaders. At the grassroots level, we will work to ensure hockey is accessible to anyone who loves the game.

ALLY
STAFF
HDA

Credit: Hockey Diversity Alliance.

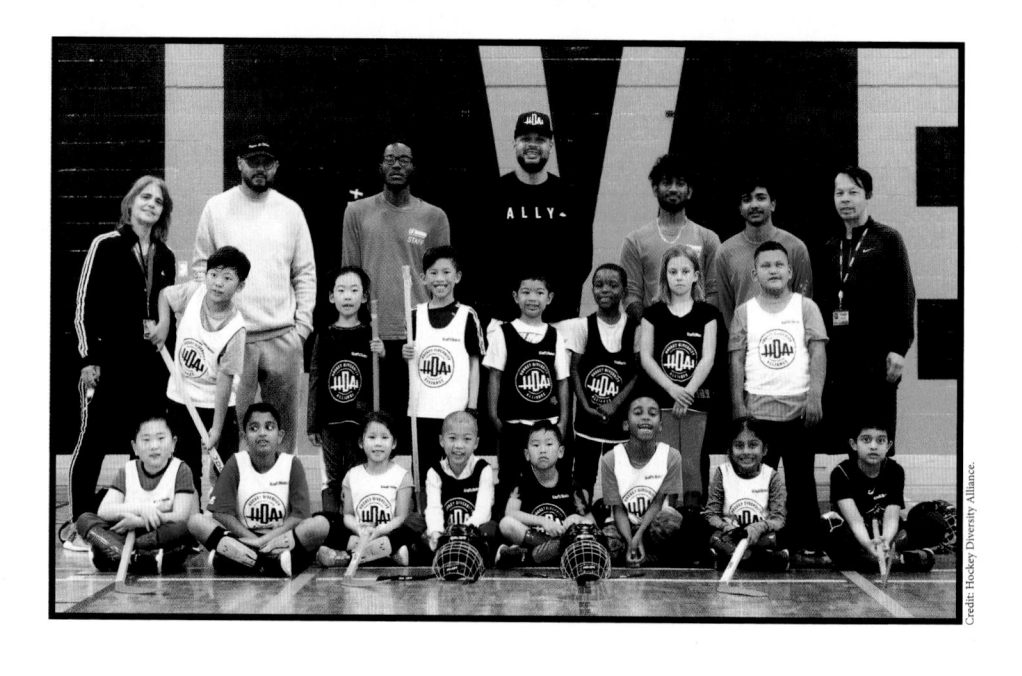

The HDA announced in June 2022 a new program designed to bring hockey to children from diverse communities underrepresented in the sport. "We know from experience that kids of color are often unable to play hockey because of access. Through HDA Ball Hockey Skills, we're removing barriers by bringing hockey to kids in their own neighborhoods so kids from every kind of background and every circumstance feel welcome in the sport we love," said Akim Aliu, chair of the HDA.

The HDA Ball Hockey Skills pilot program offered an introduction to hockey to children between six and fifteen years old who aren't registered in an organized league. The free program started in five communities in Toronto with a high proportion of BIPOC residents.

In 2020, Akim established his own organization: the Time to Dream Foundation. TTD aims to make youth sports, including the game of hockey, more diverse, inclusive, affordable and accessible to all, regardless of race, gender, and socioeconomic background. To make sure every dreamer has a chance to realize their goals.

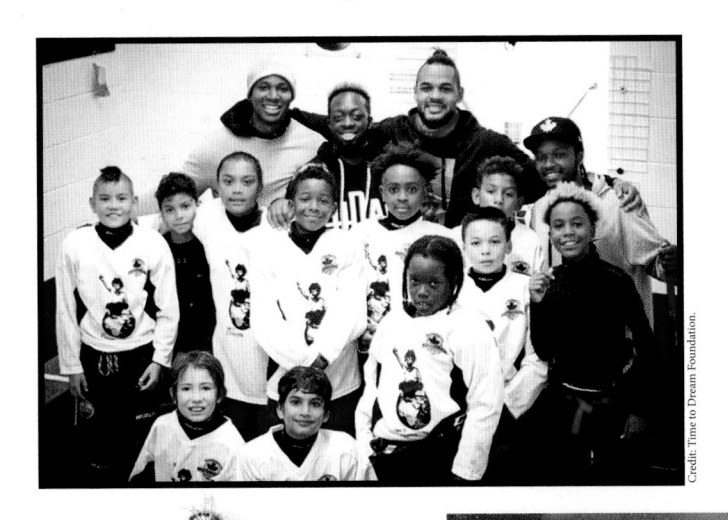

Credit: Time to Dream Foundation.

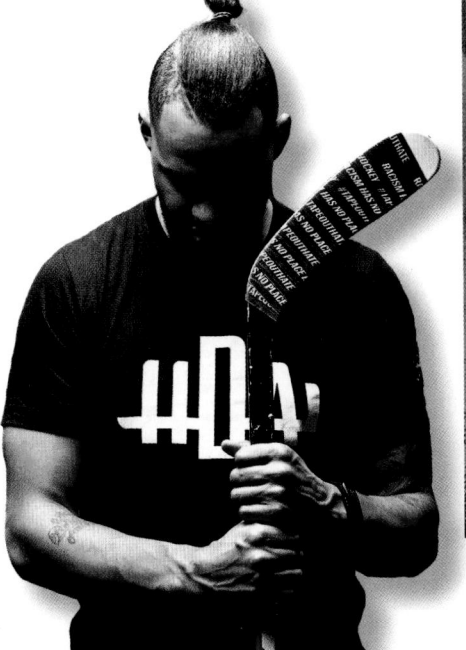

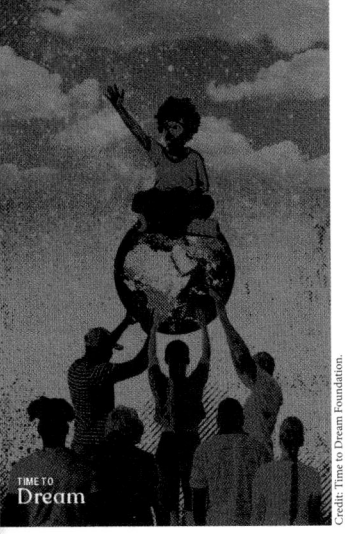

TIME TO
Dream

Credit: Time to Dream Foundation.

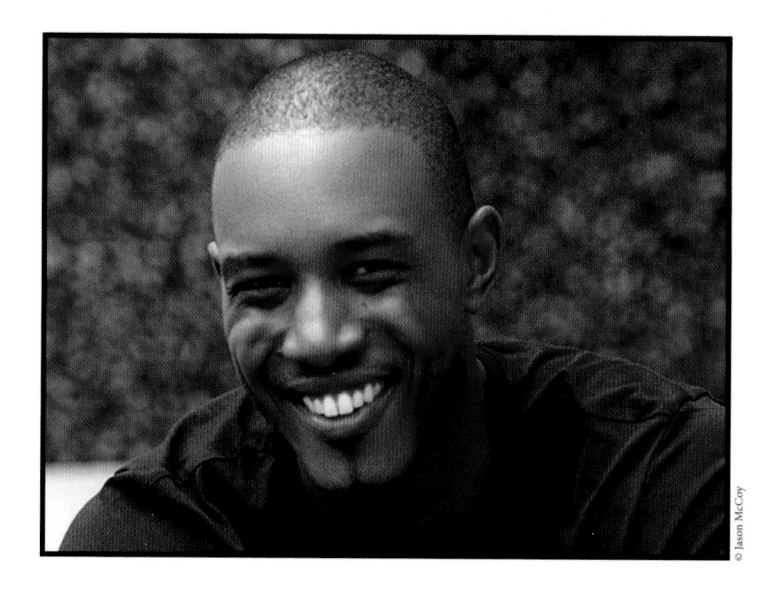

© Jason McCoy

Greg Anderson Elysée is a Brooklyn-born, Haitian American writer, educator, filmmaker, and model. He has been teaching various forms of filmmaking, including narrative and documentary, from elementary-level students to the elderly since 2012. A former journalist for TheOuthousers.com, he ran his own column, (Heard It Thru) The Griotvine, where he showcased independent creators of color and LGBTQ creators. He also wrote for the independent pop culture news website Bleeding Cool.

Greg's original comic series *Is'nana: The Were-Spider* is a seven-time Glyph Comics Award winner. His other work includes *The Gentleman: Darkness of the Void* and *Marassa*, both published by Evoluzione Publishing, *OneNation: Stronghold* published by 133art Publishing, and work in the Lion Forge graphic novel collection *Puerto Rico Strong*. He lives in Brooklyn.